Patrick Henry

MW00780994

Often referred to as "the voice of the Revolution," Patrick Henry played a vital role in helping to launch the revolt of the American colonies against British rule. After the Revolution, Henry played an active part in the debates over the founding of the United States. As a leading anti-federalist, he argued against the ratification of the Constitution because he feared the federal government would be too distant and powerful, but once it was adopted, he defended the Constitution and the federal government against the radical states' rights challenge of Thomas Jefferson and James Madison. In both his political triumphs and defeats, Henry was influential in establishing the nature of public discourse for a generation of new Americans.

In this concise biography, John A. Ragosta explores Henry's life and his contributions to shaping the character of the new nation, placing his ideas in the context of his times. Supported by primary documents and a supplementary companion website, *Patrick Henry: Proclaiming a Revolution* gives students of the American Revolution and early Republic an insightful and balanced understanding of this often misunderstood American founder.

John A. Ragosta is a Fellow at Virginia Foundation for the Humanities and a Visiting Assistant Professor of History at Randolph College. He is the author of *Religious Freedom: Jefferson's Legacy, America's Creed* (2013) and *Wellspring of Liberty: How Virginia's Religious Dissenters Helped Win the American Revolution and Secured Religious Liberty* (2010).

ROUTLEDGE HISTORICAL AMERICANS

SERIES EDITOR: PAUL FINKELMAN

Routledge Historical Americans is a series of short, vibrant biographies that illuminate the lives of Americans who have had an impact on the world. Each book includes a short overview of the person's life and puts that person into historical context through essential primary documents, written both by the subjects and about them. A series website supports the books, containing extra images and documents, links to further research, and, where possible, multi-media sources on the subjects. Perfect for including in any course on American History, the books in the Routledge Historical Americans series show the impact everyday people can have on the course of history.

Woody Guthrie: Writing America's Songs
Ronald D. Cohen

Frederick Douglass: Reformer and Statesman
L. Diane Barnes

Thurgood Marshall: Race, Rights, and the Struggle for a More Perfect Union
Charles L. Zelden

Harry S. Truman: The Coming of the Cold War
Nicole L. Anslover

John Winthrop: Founding the City upon a Hill
Michael Parker

John F. Kennedy: The Spirit of Cold War Liberalism
Jason K. Duncan

Bill Clinton: Building a Bridge to the New Millennium
David H. Bennett

Ronald Reagan: Champion of Conservative America
James H. Broussard

Laura Ingalls Wilder: American Writer on the Prairie
Sallie Ketcham

Benjamin Franklin: American Founder, Atlantic Citizen
Nathan R. Kozuskanich

Brigham Young: Sovereign in America
David Vaughn Mason

Mary Lincoln: Southern Girl, Northern Woman
Stacy Pratt McDermott

Oliver Wendell Holmes, Jr.: Civil War Soldier, Supreme Court Justice
Susan-Mary Grant

Belle La Follette: Progressive Era Reformer
Nancy C. Unger

*Harriet Tubman: Slavery, the Civil War, and Civil Rights
in the Nineteenth Century*
Kristen T. Oertel

Muhammad Ali: A Man of Many Voices
Barbara L. Tischler

Andrew Jackson: Principle and Prejudice
John M. Belohlavek

Sojourner Truth: Prophet of Social Justice
Isabelle Kinnard Richman

Ida B. Wells: Social Reformer and Activist
Kristina DuRocher

Patrick Henry: Proclaiming a Revolution
John A. Ragosta

PATRICK HENRY
PROCLAIMING A REVOLUTION

JOHN A. RAGOSTA

Routledge
Taylor & Francis Group

NEW YORK AND LONDON

www.routledge.com/cw/HistoricalAmericans

First published 2017
by Routledge
711 Third Avenue, New York, NY 10017

and by Routledge
2 Park Square, Milton Park, Abingdon, Oxon, OX14 4RN

Routledge is an imprint of the Taylor & Francis Group, an informa business

Library of Congress Cataloging-in-Publication Data
Names: Ragosta, John A., author.
Title: Patrick Henry : proclaiming a revolution / John A. Ragosta.
Description: New York, NY : Routledge, [2016] | Series: Routledge historical
    Americans | Includes bibliographical references and index.
Identifiers: LCCN 2016006793| ISBN 9781138023017 (hardback) |
    ISBN 9781138023024 (pbk.) | ISBN 9781315776729 (e-book)
Subjects: LCSH: Henry, Patrick, 1736–1799. | Legislators—United
    States—Biography. | United States. Continental Congress—Biography. |
    Virginia—Politics and government—1775–1783. | United States—Politics
    and government—1775–1783. | Henry, Patrick, 1736–1799—Sources.
Classification: LCC E302.6.H5 R65 2016 | DDC 973.3092—dc23
LC record available at http://lccn.loc.gov/2016006793

ISBN: 978-1-138-02301-7 (hbk)
ISBN: 978-1-138-02302-4 (pbk)
ISBN: 978-1-315-77672-9 (ebk)

Typeset in Minion Pro and Scala Sans
by Apex CoVantage, LLC

For Greg, who also overcame many challenges

CONTENTS

Acknowledgments

Of course, a book is not crafted in isolation, and I owe a great debt of gratitude to a number of people for their assistance (although I readily accept all
responsibility for any errors). I am grateful that Paul Finkelman asked me to
undertake the project over a thoroughly enjoyable lunch at Seymour's near
Clinton, New York and then provided insightful comments and suggestions
on the manuscript. I also appreciate the assistance of my Routledge editors, Margo Irvin and Dan Finaldi, who face a formidable task in bringing
authors' works to print.

In trying to understand Henry, I have benefitted greatly from visits at
Red Hill, Hanover Courthouse and Tavern, Scotchtown, Colonial Williamsburg, and St. John's Church. I appreciate the excellent work that the people
at each of these sites do to preserve history and present it to the public in
a useful format. Important new work of a different nature is now being
performed in the Papers of Patrick Henry project at Documents Compass
at the Virginia Foundation for the Humanities (VFH), and I appreciate the
assistance that I have received from Sue Perdue and Will Kurtz, although
I wish that their work had progressed much further before I undertook
this task.

I am especially grateful to the opportunity that I have had to research and
write through the wonderful support of Robert Vaughan, Jeanne Siler, Ann
Spencer, and all of the staff at, and benefactors of, VFH. Much of the work
on this volume was done while I was honored with the Edna and Norman
Freehling Fellowship in South Atlantic Studies at VFH. The insights and
encouragement of Peter Onuf are also to be noted; as he has reminded me,
he will "always" be my advisor. The opportunities to discuss Henry and his
time with Mark Couvillon, Johann Neem, David Konig, Carolyn Eastman,

Greg O'Malley, George van Cleve, and others were always highly valued. And I apologize for the many others who have, directly and indirectly, provided assistance but who are not mentioned specifically here. Then there is, too, the great and continuing support that my work receives through the home in which I live and work and the loving encouragement of Liz.

PREFACE

Writing a biography is different from writing other histories. Several problems face those who accept the task. First, one has to try to understand deeply what motivated an individual, likely someone long dead; their thoughts, actions, tastes, and disposition must be lived-in. This is a daunting task; we struggle to understand fully ourselves, much less the actions and motivations of someone whom we likely have never met. Second, there is a tendency toward "capture," becoming so entranced with the subject with whom you have spent years of study that all objectivity is lost, and the person studied looms larger and larger. After all, who would spend those years with an unimportant subject? I worked to overcome both of these challenges in preparing this biography. I hope that readers will find that I did so successfully.

Patrick Henry presents a particularly interesting subject for a biography. He is, perhaps, the least remembered of the important Founding Fathers. Most Americans recall only that he made several great speeches, but many of his most famous speeches are only poorly recorded (and some historians dismiss as fiction the versions that have been passed down to us). Much of his life story is tradition.

Politically, while he played a critical role in the Revolution, Henry never held national office under the Constitution, greatly limiting the availability of evidence of his political contributions. He declined numerous offices – Supreme Court justice, secretary of state, senator, ambassador to France or Spain – any one of which would have inevitably increased his prominence in the early republic, providing useful grist for historians. In fact, he was the greatest of anti-federalists, opposing the new Constitution which would become a national icon because he feared that it created a government that was too powerful and distant. As a result, many of the modern radical right have adopted Patrick Henry as a prophet for their efforts to oppose expansive federal authority (never mind the serious problem of applying the wisdom of any of the Founding Fathers to a modern, integrated, dependent world which they could not have imagined). Yet he would die a Federalist, having reentered politics at the express entreaty of George Washington to oppose the efforts of Thomas Jefferson and James Madison to use a radical states' rights doctrine to challenge the authority of the federal government under that Constitution, to "nullify" federal actions. He is ill-at-ease in the position that some would now place him. At best, his political views are complicated and ill-understood.

And Henry has not been treated well by history. Henry's decision to oppose the budding Democratic-Republican party's assaults on the federal government earned him the insult of being called an "apostate" to the states' rights movement that he had helped to found. Jefferson, in particular, vilified Patrick Henry, calling him ignorant, uneducated, greedy, and malicious. Jefferson's personal animosity was generated in large part by Henry's role in helping to launch a legislative investigation of Jefferson's wartime governorship after the invading British seemed to be successfully over-running Virginia. Add to that Henry's final political campaign in opposition to Jefferson's policies (for Jefferson, another betrayal), not to mention a good bit of jealousy of Henry's abilities. Whatever the cause, the historic consequences for Henry were substantial. Jefferson, who outlived Henry by 27 years, spent decades viciously attacking Henry's abilities and legacy, and much of Jefferson's vitriol is repeated by historians.

Henry did not always help. Unlike many of the Founders (Washington, Jefferson, Benjamin Franklin, and John Adams among them), Henry was not consumed with how he would be remembered by history. As a result, there are far fewer records from his life than a historian would wish. Many records he intentionally destroyed.

What is available, though, still paints a rich picture of not only a great orator, but a seasoned politician, an accomplished lawyer, a loving father, and a patriot. I should note that I found my training as a lawyer particularly useful in trying to understand Patrick Henry: He was a consummate lawyer, more so than many of his contemporaries who also practiced law.

In drafting this story, I tried to be particularly sensitive to exposing readers to some of the problems faced by historians. Often the existence of conflicting evidence is noted. Sometimes questions cannot be resolved. The motivation of various sources must be carefully considered. None of these challenges makes the result the whim of the author, nor do they make the practice of history worthless, but they do demonstrate the care with which the task must be approached and the tentative nature of many conclusions. In many cases, readers will have to judge for themselves. The goal of this work is to provide the material and the context to allow them to do so.

PART I

PATRICK HENRY

INTRODUCTION

In early September 1774, delegates from 12 British North American colonies gathered at the First Continental Congress in Philadelphia. They came to decide what should be done about the "Intolerable Acts" that Britain had imposed to punish Massachusetts after the Boston Tea Party on December 16, 1773.[1]

The British Parliament had been deeply disturbed by the destruction of private property by a Boston mob and Boston's apparent lack of interest in finding and punishing the rioters. Tensions between the colonies and mother country had simmered hot and cold for almost ten years after colonial protests against the 1765 Stamp Act as "taxation without representation," and Parliament thought that it had been tolerant, perhaps too tolerant. Now, with tea soaking in Boston harbor, it chose to act decisively in an effort to stop this lawlessness.

In a series of laws known as the Coercive Acts in Britain and the Intolerable Acts in America, Parliament closed the port of Boston to all trade, a heavy blow for a city that lived on its commerce. Parliament also fundamentally changed the Massachusetts government. All members of the Council (the upper branch of Massachusetts' legislature), previously elected, would now be royal appointees, and all sheriffs (who chose juries in court cases) would be appointed by the royal governor. British troops patrolled Boston streets, and British warships patrolled the harbor. Unless it paid for the tea that had been destroyed, Boston was threatened with hunger and economic collapse, and Massachusetts feared that its dearest liberties were lost. Massachusetts desperately needed the help of the other colonies.

Yet, it was not at all clear that the other colonies would support Massachusetts. Many colonists believed that hot-heads in Massachusetts had acted illegally in rioting and destroying the tea, and few colonial leaders condoned such attacks on private property. Even if Parliament was wrong to impose taxes on the importation of tea into America, the tea dumped into Boston's harbor belonged to the East India Company. Further complicating matters for Boston, colonists from outside of New England generally did not have a natural sympathy for, or even an intimate familiarity with, Massachusetts. Commerce and communications in the colonies ran like spokes on a wheel with London (the metropole) at the center. As a result, delegates from southern and middle colonies usually had closer ties with Britain – economic, commercial, political, and family relations – than they did with Boston. Should they risk also being punished by Britain if they supported illegal activity in Boston? Was an open dispute with Britain justified by a very small tax on tea imports and Boston's violent and illegal reaction to the tax?

Other colonies had protested the Tea Act and had refused to allow taxed tea to land in their ports. In Philadelphia, a "Committee for Tarring and Feathering" easily persuaded British sea captains that they should not even try to unload taxed tea. Only in Boston had the protests resulted in massive violent mobs and open destruction of private property. Moderates reminded colonial leaders that peaceful demonstrations had worked in the past; Britain had withdrawn the Stamp Tax in 1765, and in 1770 the Townshend Duties on paper, paint, and lead had been removed after colonial protests and commercial boycotts, leaving only a small tax on tea. Was Massachusetts leading the colonies in a dangerous and unjustified direction? These were questions that faced the delegates at the First Continental Congress.

The Congress was populated with many of the most famous and gifted men in the colonies – Sam Adams (probably the best known of the Boston hot-heads), his cousin John, George Washington (respected for his bravery in the French & Indian War), Peyton Randolph (Speaker of Virginia's House of Burgesses); but in the age before easy transportation and mass communication, most of the delegates were strangers to each other. Many of the delegates had the natural caution of lawyers and businessmen. As these proud men, each a leader in his own colony, gathered in Carpenter's Hall in Philadelphia, they introduced themselves to one another and tried to take the measure of their new colleagues. After settling on a place to meet and electing a speaker and secretary, the delegates seemed to be at a bit of a loss on how best to proceed.

Into the uncertainty, a tall, thin Virginian rose to address the gathering. He was dressed in a plain suit like a "Presbyterian clergyman," according to one observer. Many delegates had heard of Patrick Henry because of his famous resolutions against the Stamp Act in 1765 (and the treasonous speech that accompanied them). He had also participated on the Committee of Correspondence that helped to maintain communication between the colonies during their struggles with Great Britain. But probably no one outside of the Virginia delegation had ever seen him or heard his mesmer-izing voice.[2]

Yet, the minute he launched into his speech, the group's attention was focused on the man who became known as the "trumpet of the American Revolution" (with George Washington being "the sword" and Thomas Jefferson "the pen"). "Henry from Virginia insisted that by the oppression of Parliament all Government was dissolved, and that we were reduced to a State of Nature," wrote a delegate from New York. "Fleets and armies and the present state of things show that government is dissolved," Henry warned the delegates. It was immediately clear that Henry planned to throw his full support behind the suffering patriots of Massachusetts and, to rally that support, this most Virginian of men declared to rapt delegates that "The distinctions between Virginians, Pennsylvanians, New Yorkers, and New Englanders, are no more. I am not a Virginian, but an American." When Thomas Jefferson came to Congress a year later, he was told that Henry "had captivated all, by his bold and splendid eloquence."[3]

One can hardly blame the delegates for being moved. Henry's emphatic declaration, coming from a leader of the largest American colony, set an important tone of unity and cooperation for the rest of the meeting of the First Continental Congress. Members could not help but notice that Henry embraced the word "American." For years prior to the Continental Congress, the term was used primarily by Englishmen almost as an insult, as a way to distinguish "colonials" who were somehow not fully English. Yet, as the Revolution approached, the name "American" was increasingly used proudly on the western shores of the Atlantic. Henry's declaration in Philadelphia was part of that important change, part of forming a new people.[4]

Edmund Randolph, soon a leader in the patriot movement in his own right, explained that "It was Patrick Henry . . . awakening the genius of his country, and binding a band of patriots together to hurl defiance at the tyranny of so formidable a nation as Great Britain." Jefferson, who would in later life develop a deep-seated hatred, some would say jealousy, of Henry, conceded that Henry's influence in these early days of the American Revolution was essential. "[I]t is not now easy to say what we should have done without Patrick Henry," said Jefferson. "He was far before all in maintaining the spirit of the Revolution . . . he was our leader in the measures of the Revolution in Virginia, and in that respect more is due to him than to any other person." Henry "certainly gave the first impulse to the ball of the revolution." Henry's "I am . . . an American" speech helped to unite the colonies and drive the Revolution forward.[5]

All of this is true. Yet, as is often the case with history, there was also a different story being acted out by Patrick Henry in Philadelphia. The context of his speech is critical. As the delegates gathered in Philadelphia, largely unknown to each other and unsure of how to proceed, one of the first and most important questions faced was how to vote in the Congress: Should each colony have one vote or should larger colonies have more votes? This was an especially important issue for Virginia, the largest colony in both population and land. Should Virginia have the same vote as Delaware (which had far less than one-tenth of Virginia's population)? Thus, when Henry rose to break the silence in Philadelphia, he was not simply making a moving speech about the ties that bound all North American colonists together, about British oppression destroying the old political system, and how shared interests were greater than local interests, he was also politicking for his own colony, trying to increase its voting power in the Congress.[i]

Does this mean Henry did not mean to state an important principle about American identity? That he should not be remembered for leading the call for revolution?

No. But it does suggest that this speech, like his other speeches, was not simply eloquent and persuasive. Henry was an intelligent politician and lawyer, and his speeches, whether in a political assembly or in a courtroom, drove at a particular purpose.

In popular memory, Henry's legacy has been his stirring oratory, or at least what we think he said – very few of his speeches were written down at the time they were given (see Appendix). Yet, while those speeches were enormously important, Henry's real legacy goes beyond speech-making. Henry was one of the most dynamic and respected leaders in the crucial years leading up to the beginning of the American Revolution. He was Virginia's first governor after independence, serving successfully during very trying war years. Henry later became the most vocal and well-known opponent of ratification of the U.S. Constitution, believing that it created a government that was too powerful and too distant and that would undermine the authority of the states, a recipe for tyranny he believed. His objections played an important role in development of the Bill of Rights. As he approached death, he was called upon by George Washington to help the nation through another crisis, and Henry re-entered the political fray to insist that any changes to

---

i Henry's effort to have population decide the voting strength of each state failed in Philadelphia when smaller states objected. Unanimity among the colonies was so essential if opposition to Britain was to be successful that the larger states agreed to one state, one vote. This issue would haunt the young nation into the constitutional convention in Philadelphia in 1787 and beyond. Henry also suggested at the time that slaves be excluded from any population count to set voting, even though Virginia had the largest number of enslaved people. Henry, *Patrick Henry*: I: 221–222 (quoting John Adams diary). This question – whether slaves should be included in calculating the voting power of states – would also become one of the most hotly contested issues in the constitutional convention. Henry was ahead of his time in recognizing that a state should not be given additional voting power for maintaining a large enslaved population.

the government be made legally and that radical attacks on federal authority based on states' rights threatened to split the union and should be rejected. His legacy includes both his speeches and his important political contributions.

It is striking that of the leading Founding Fathers, Henry is arguably the least remembered. One problem for historians is that his written record of letters, reports, memoranda, and other papers pales next to that of the Revolution's sword, George Washington, and its pen, Thomas Jefferson. Henry, far less concerned than Washington, Jefferson, John Adams, or other early leaders about how future generations would remember his role, simply did not spend a lot of time focused on preserving his legacy, leading one frustrated historian to declare that he had "a miserable sense of history." In fact, it has been suggested that the memory of Henry's famous speeches has ill-served his legacy, with Americans remembering him only for a few important phrases (like "give me liberty or give me death") rather than his other contributions, and many historians dismiss even that legacy as a later fabrication.[6]

There may be some truth in that, but there are other reasons why Henry does not loom as large in our national memory as his importance justifies. Foremost among these is the fact that Henry opposed the new Constitution. Not only did he oppose adoption of the framework of government that has achieved a status in American history as strong as Scripture, but he refused to serve in the new national government that the Constitution created, declining offers of a position on the Supreme Court, as secretary of state, as senator, as ambassador, or a likely election to the vice-presidency. His absence from federal office in the early republic certainly dramatically diminishes his historical memory.

Henry's memory also suffers very seriously because many of his political opponents rose to power and lived long after Henry's death in 1799. The problem is made worse by the fact that Henry – having been one of the leading anti-federalists during the battle over ratification of the Constitution – entered his final political campaign as a Federalist, concerned with the danger of disunion posed by the extreme states' rights position reflected in the Kentucky and Virginia Resolutions drafted by Jefferson and James Madison respectively. In retaliation, Jefferson and his acolytes declared that Henry was an "apostate" shortly before his death. With the Jefferson-Madisonian Democratic-Republican party gaining near total dominance of American politics after 1800, many individuals who otherwise would have honored Henry's accomplishments and principles found little reason to support his memory. Jefferson in an effort to try to justify his own actions, found it necessary to tell history that Henry was uneducated, inconsistent, narrow-minded, "avaritious & rotten hearted," and a traitor to the cause of states' rights that Henry had originally championed. While Henry was far more successful as an attorney than Jefferson, the latter also attacked Henry's legal abilities, insisting that his legal training was "not worth a copper" (a penny). There is a good argument that Jefferson's outrage hid his own envy of a self-made, successful, and popular man, but the negative opinion of Jefferson and his supporters had an enormous impact. The history that has been transmitted to us is deeply influenced by less than flattering, and less than fair, remembrances of Henry.[7]

More recently, there has been some increased interest in Patrick Henry's role in the Revolution and early republic, but this has not necessarily improved the historic understanding of his life and contributions. Today, conservatives often use Henry's opposition to a distant and powerful government in their own attacks on the federal government, allowing them to claim the legacy of one of America's greatest Founders. This, too, can obscure the real historic figure. After all, to cite Henry's fears of a powerful and distant government for support for states' rights today is to read into Henry much that he did not, could not have said or believed. Henry did not witness a devastating Civil War that resulted from states' refusal to protect people with the rights of citizens; he could not have anticipated the rapid growth in technology and commerce linking the nation from sea-to-sea and beyond; he could not have imagined an increasingly fragile world in which uncontrolled freedom of individuals to do as they please, even on their own lands, risks the environment for millions yet unborn; he could not have foreseen the international challenges that the nation would face in the twentieth and twenty-first centuries. Equally important, even in his own times, he advocated limits on the states' rights doctrine. At best, he stands ill at ease in the dress placed on him by some twenty-first century conservatives.

How such an important historical figure can be so wrongly belittled and equally wrongly lionized can be perplexing. Understanding Patrick Henry and his contribution to our history then is not only a question of understanding his youth, career, and principles, but also an exercise in understanding the American nation that he helped to birth and how history is written and remembered. One must cut through both the myth that makes him almost a demi-god and the equally strained outrage of his enemies.

* * * * *

Patrick Henry was one of the first of the patriots to push the new nation toward the Revolution. Even Jefferson conceded that Henry provided essential leadership by inspiring and "maintaining the spirit of the Revolution." He spoke words so powerful and beautiful that "He appeared to me to speak as Homer wrote" – an extraordinary compliment coming from Jefferson, and he was often compared to Cicero or Demosthenes, the greatest of orators in classical Rome and Greece. Those who might have waivered were strengthened by his speeches; many of those who fought did so with the slogan that he made famous – "liberty or death" – on their minds, many with the slogan emblazoned on their shirts. He was steadfast.[8]

As Virginia's first elected governor (and the only person ever elected six times to that post), he helped to organize and lead resistance. When not serving as governor, he was among Virginia's most effective legislators. He worked closely with political allies and opponents, learning the important art of compromise. After the war, he led unsuccessful efforts to reassert government's role in supporting religion.

When the problems of the nation shifted from revolution to organizing a national government, Henry stood against George Washington, James Madison, Benjamin Franklin, James Wilson, and a host of others to oppose a new government that he thought too powerful and too unresponsive to the people. His opposition helped to propel the adoption of the Bill of Rights (although Henry always felt that more restraints on the federal government were needed). Nonetheless, with the Constitution in place, Henry became a sincere advocate of working within that system of government. When he thought that political parties threatened the union based on their own interests, he died defending that same government, his nation, and the Revolution's legacy.

He is properly remembered for proclaiming a Revolution, but he did much more.

NOTES

1. Georgia did not send delegates to the First Continental Congress. Living in the newest and weakest British mainland colony, Georgians were concerned about conflicts with the Creek Indians and did not want to do anything that might interfere with receiving aid from British Redcoats should an Indian war erupt.
2. Edmund C. Burnett, ed., *Letters of Members of the Continental Congress*, vol. I (1921, reprint, Gloucester, MA: Peter Smith, 1963): 10 n. 2 (attributed to Charles Thompson, secretary of Congress).
3. Ibid. I: 12 (James Duane). William Wirt Henry, *Patrick Henry: Life, Correspondence and Speeches*, vol. I (New York: Charles Scribner's Sons, 1891): 221–222 (quoting John Adams diary). William Wirt Henry, "Patrick Henry: A Vindication of his Character, as an Orator and as a Man," *The Historical Magazine* (November 1873): 272 *et seq.*
4. See T. H. Breen, "Ideology and Nationalism on the Eve of the American Revolution: Revisions Once More in Need of Revising," *The Journal of American History* 84: 1 (June 1997): 30–31.
5. Edmund Randolph, *Richmond Enquirer*, September 2, 1815, 4. Notes of Daniel Webster, in George Ticknor Curtis, *Life of Daniel Webster*, vol. 1 (New York: D. Appleton and Co., 1889): 584–585. William Wirt, *Sketches of the Life and Character of Patrick Henry*, revised ed. (Ithaca, NY: Andrus, Gauntlett, & Co., 1850): 38.
6. Richard R. Beeman, "The Democratic Faith of Patrick Henry," *The Virginia Magazine of History and Biography* 95: 3 (July 1987): 301.
7. Memorandum from Thomas Jefferson to William Wirt, August 4, 1805, "Jefferson's Recollections of Patrick Henry," *The Pennsylvania Magazine of History and Biography* 34: 4 (1910): 387.
8. Henry, *Patrick Henry*, II: 166, I: 83.

CHAPTER 1

EARLY YEARS

Patrick Henry was "born in obscurity, poor, and without the advantages of literature," wrote Edmund Randolph in 1815. Others, notably Thomas Jefferson, also belittled Henry's status and education after they had developed deep political differences.[1]

In fact, Patrick Henry was neither born poor nor was he uneducated. (Although, for a member of the wealthy and well-connected Randolph family, perhaps most people seemed to be born poor and in obscurity.) Efforts to belittle Henry's education and the social standing of his family, though, served various purposes. Some were intended to exaggerate his later success: He rose from nothing to great heights supporters argued. Some of these efforts were simply unjustified personal attacks.

The truth bespeaks a talented and sometimes mischievous young man born into a well-respected gentry family who struggled for a period of time to find a niche in which he could be successful. Once Henry found his calling as a lawyer, though, success came quickly and in abundance, and he was launched on an important political career.

* * * * *

Patrick Henry's father, John Henry, was educated at King's College in Aberdeen, Scotland, at a time when higher education was reserved for the wealthy or the very talented and enterprising. By 1727, John had moved to the colonies where he worked as an overseer and tutor on the Studley Plantation owned by an earlier Scottish immigrant, John Syme (pronounced "Sim"), a wealthy Virginia planter and a distant relative of Henry's. In 1731, Syme died, leaving behind a young son, also named John, and a wealthy widow, Sarah Winston Syme. By 1734, John Henry had married the beautiful Sarah, but even before his marriage, he had begun to acquire large tracts of land on his own. As the years went on, John Henry would become a respected member of the gentry, a colonel in the local militia, and chief magistrate of the county court. With his marriage, Henry also became responsible for managing Studley until John Syme, Jr., came of age and could manage his own inheritance.

It was there, at Studley Plantation in Hanover County (16 miles from the center of modern Richmond), that Patrick was born on May 29, 1736 (n.s.).[2] He was the second son of John and Sarah Winston Syme Henry, who would later bring Patrick and his older brother, William, seven sisters. In the years ahead, the thin, young Patrick Henry would grow to something above middling height (family tradition said as tall as six feet), with eyes the color of the sky "on a perfectly cloudless day" his daughter Sarah said (although others would later describe his eyes as grey). As a young man, his hair was auburn, brown tending toward red.[3]

Rather than being poor and uneducated, Patrick was raised on plantations supported by enslaved people. He received a broad and effective education, initially attending a local grammar school. After grammar school, while his family could not afford to send him away to college, he was trained by his college-educated father who would later open a classical school for local students. He also certainly learned much from his uncle and namesake, the Reverend Patrick Henry, Anglican minister in Hanover County, who had been convinced to emigrate to America by his brother John. A great grandson, familiar with family lore, said that Patrick learned from his uncle "to be true & just in all my dealings. To bear no malice nor hatred in my heart . . . Not to covet other mens [sic] goods; but to learn & labor truly to get my own living, & to do my duty in that state of life into which it shall please God to call me." (Henry often referred to himself as "Patrick Henry, Junior," out of respect for his uncle.) While other colonial leaders received a more formal education and many had the benefit of attending a college (in America or in Britain), private tutoring from a highly educated Scotsman provided Patrick Henry with a firm foundation. Clearly he learned much history and a good deal of classical literature, including training in Latin and some Greek.[4]

Seeking to emphasize Henry's natural talents, his first biographer would describe the young Henry as having an "aversion to study" that was "invincible." According to William Wirt, Henry's mind was "almost entirely benumbed by indolence." Another early biographer wrote that Henry had "a mortal enmity to books, supplemented by a passionate regard for fishing-rods and shot-guns"; he was "disorderly in dress, slouching, vagrant, unambitious; a roamer in woods, . . . giving no hint nor token, by word or act, of the possession of any intellectual gift that could raise him above mediocrity, or even lift him up to it."[5]

True, Henry certainly loved the woods. He was known as a child to be particularly fond of his uncle William "Langloo" Winston, a famous frontiersman, hunter, and fisherman who often would regale his nieces and nephews with stories of his exploits (and later played an important role in recruiting Virginia men for service during the French & Indian War). But the historian must be careful with statements about Henry's lack of education. Many of these stories are simply untrue. Samuel Meredith, who grew up close to Henry and later became a brother-in-law, reports that as a boy Henry "became well acquainted with mathematics . . . was well versed in both ancient and modern history," that he was knowledgeable in Latin and a bit of Greek. Meredith said that the boy was "fond of reading, but indulged much in innocent amusements." Henry's love of hunting and fishing, though, is poor evidence of a lax education.[6]

How to judge among differing claims about Henry's education? To some extent, the "proof is in the pudding." Henry's later success as a lawyer required a more than adequate education. Even Wirt had to concede that Henry developed studiousness over the years. While Jefferson insisted that Henry "read nothing, and had no books," a recent study found that, at his death, Henry had a well-stocked library (by eighteenth-century standards) which included a good selection of law books, history, and classics, including some in Greek and Latin. One can conclude that Henry was a capable and successful student who enjoyed books, especially history, although he probably enjoyed escaping from his studies to hunt and fish even more, not unheard of among growing boys in colonial Virginia (or in other times and places).[7]

Henry certainly became an avid fisherman and accomplished hunter as a boy and continued those pursuits as an adult. Some would later say that Henry owed his "invariable habit of close and attentive observation" of human character to his careful contemplation of all things in nature. Edward Fontaine, a great grandson, explained that "in the woods & in nature's wild *he meditated* more than he read." If so, his time in the woods was hardly wasted. This skill of observation would serve him well in later life when his intimate knowledge of people and human nature was critical to his success as a lawyer and revolutionary.[8]

The young Patrick also developed a life-long love of music, becoming quite accomplished with the fiddle and the flute (which he apparently learned to play while suffering an enforced period of bed-rest after a broken collar bone). As with much of the rest of his learning, Henry's music education was informal, but his fiddling proved useful in numerous social gatherings and was something which Henry enjoyed until his death. His children and grandchildren often remembered his singing and playing, as well as a habit of crafting short poems and songs for the family (all of which he would burn after reading).

Patrick's father and uncle were committed members of the Church of England, the official church of Virginia before the Revolution. (All citizens, regardless of religion, were taxed to pay ministers of the official church a salary, and a host of regulations sought to protect the Anglican Church from competition.) Henry's mother was a Presbyterian and well aware of the religious discrimination that favored Anglicans; her father, Isaac Winston, was once fined for permitting Presbyterians to worship on his property without a licensed meeting house. While young, Patrick regularly attended his uncle's church, Fork Church (still standing in Hanover County), but his mother would also often take him to hear the local Presbyterian minister, the famous Samuel Davies, at Polegreen Meeting House.

Davies, the first non-Anglican minister licensed by Virginia's General Court, was a "new light" minister during the First Great Awakening (an evangelical revival movement that swept the colonies from the 1730s through the 1760s). He emphasized the personal and emotional nature of a religious commitment and was renowned for his passionate preaching, far different from the very measured, formal preaching of most Anglican ministers in the first half of the eighteenth century. Many "new lights" were labeled demagogues by those who were more traditional and old fashioned, a charge that would also be leveled at Henry. The future orator undoubtedly listened attentively to Davies, learning a great deal about persuasive speech. Family tradition says that his mother would quiz the boy on their return from church about what the minister had preached, and the young Patrick could often repeat large portions of the sermon virtually verbatim. Later in life Henry reportedly said that he was "first taught what an orator should be" by listening to the Reverend Samuel Davies, "the greatest orator he ever heard."[9]

Henry's uncle Patrick, Hanover County's "official" minister, was opposed to the "enthusiastic" religion that accompanied the First Great Awakening, and Henry would maintain his life-long association with the Anglican Church before the Revolution and its offspring, the Episcopal Church, after. Still, exposure to people who dissented from the established church, including his mother and grandfather, must have given him a first-hand appreciation of the need for religious liberty. Later, during the American Revolution, he would be a strong advocate for religious freedom, at least so far as to disestablish one legally preferred church.

Beyond the influence of evangelical preaching on his oratory and issues of religious freedom, Patrick Henry was a deeply religious person throughout his life. His speeches often used religious examples or arguments, and he undoubtedly believed in the power of God to influence the affairs of men. In his most famous speech, urging Virginians to arm for a likely war with Britain, he assured his listeners that "There is a just God who presides over the destinies of nations, and who will raise up friends to fight our battles for us" (see Document 5). Among his reasons to oppose the French Revolution in the 1790s was the manner in which it had turned against traditional religion. As he approached death, Henry would sincerely urge religion upon his children. If one is to understand Henry well, his religiosity must be an important part of that understanding.

* * * * *

In spite of his education and religious upbringing, as Patrick Henry passed from a boy to a young man, his future was far from clear. While his family was hardly poor, his father was facing financial problems at the time, and years later Patrick would rescue his father financially. Certainly he could not expect simply to be given a large plantation for his support; his family did not have that kind of wealth, and in any case, he was a second son (and second sons usually received far less from their parents in eighteenth-century Virginia). His father, though, hoped to launch him on a sound career, and he was able to get Patrick a job as a clerk for a local merchant when the young man was 15. A year later, in 1752, John Henry established his sons, William and Patrick, in business as owners of their own small store. Unfortunately, their customers seemed to give them more IOUs than cash, and that effort failed, a victim both of difficult economic times and the young owners' lack of experience.

When 18, still without a steady job, Patrick fell in love with and married 16-year-old Sarah Shelton (often called Sally) in spite of some misgivings from the young couple's parents. The Shelton's lived at nearby Rural Plains Plantation in Hanover County, where Sarah and Patrick were wed. Her dowry, property given by her family to help support the young couple, included 300 acres of land in Hanover with a small house, called Pine Slash, and six enslaved African-Americans to work the land. Henry tried his hand at farming the land for several years but without great success; the soil at Pine Slash was already worn out, and the market for tobacco was weak. When the home at Pine Slash burned to the ground in 1757, Henry moved his family – now including Sarah, daughter Martha (called Patsey), and son John – into the overseer's cottage and sold several slaves to fund another try as a shop owner, opening his new store in 1758 in the midst of the French & Indian War.

Henry's second effort as a merchant failed much like the first. Stories passed-on over the years have suggested that Patrick simply did not have his heart in the effort. One story tells that while Henry was sitting on a bag of salt he became engaged in an animated conversation with a local friend; a customer entered the store and interrupted to ask if Henry had any salt to sell. Henry reportedly sent him on his way saying that he had sold the last of it. The story seems unlikely. The carefully kept records from the store suggest that, in spite of Patrick's best efforts, once again Virginia's economy and difficult times proved fatal to the young man's plan to launch a business to support his growing family.

Still, the stories of Henry's lack of attention to the store may hold a grain of truth: Undoubtedly Henry was more interested in the stories, concerns, and hopes of the neighbors who often visited his store than in making a profit selling a few yards of fabric or tinware. He was likely far too willing to extend credit to hard-pressed farmers. While the store would not formally close until 1760 (after Henry became a lawyer), it became evident to Patrick that storekeeping was not to be his future. Still, the failed effort may have paid deep dividends. He had the chance for several years to observe closely Virginia's middling and "lesser" sorts and their problems and to develop his well-known sociability. While Henry avoided heavy drinking and gambling, two of colonial Virginians' favorite pastimes, he had an uncanny ability to connect with the common folk of Virginia; this undoubtedly arose in part from his having spent so much time among them and hearing their concerns. This connection with the people would prove to be an important foundation for his future success.

It might also be noted that during this period many Virginia men were enlisting to support the colony and the British Empire in the French & Indian War. The young George Washington, of course, developed his reputation for courage and his military knowledge during the war, as did many others who were to serve as officers in the American Revolution. The Reverend Samuel Davies successfully urged many to enlist against the Indians and Catholic French. Henry, though, did not enlist, and his lack of military experience later affected his very short military career during the Revolution. While there is nothing of record on the matter, and Henry certainly provides no explanation, one suspects that, unlike many young men of his age, Henry was preoccupied with efforts to support his rapidly growing family.

By 1760, Henry and his family had moved into the Hanover Tavern, owned by Sarah's father. While trying to make a success of his store and still supervising the overseer who continued to farm at Pine Slash, Henry also helped his father-in-law at the tavern. (In later life, Jefferson unkindly referred to Henry as a "bar-keeper," a story repeated in countless histories.) Still trying to find his path, Henry's time at the Hanover Tavern gave him more than the opportunity to serve drinks. Always a careful observer, it gave him an opportunity to watch and listen to the lawyers who visited regularly during court sessions at the Hanover Courthouse just across the road. By 1760, 23-year-old Patrick Henry, having failed as a store owner and a farmer, and with two small children at home, decided to become an attorney.[10]

* * * * *

Pursuit of the law, then and now, requires significant preparation and dedication. In 1760, there were no law schools in America. Most lawyers "read" the law and worked as apprentices in a local law office, sometimes for years, until they were prepared to be examined by a committee of well-established lawyers who would decide whether or not to grant them a license. Henry, bright, motivated, and sure of himself, and perhaps in a hurry to make a better living for his family, did not follow the traditional route. Instead, he borrowed some law books from local attorneys and studied diligently for several months. (No one seems quite sure how long; sources vary from one to nine months.) Lacking formal training, not to mention the expensive formal clothes usually worn by lawyers in the eighteenth century, a somewhat ill-clothed and ill-prepared Patrick Henry rode to Williamsburg for his examination in April 1760. Once there, he managed to convince three examiners to give him a license to practice law.

Stories about how he achieved this feat vary. One story, retold by Henry in later life, is that the well-bred Virginia Attorney General, John Randolph, was initially reluctant to even quiz the rather dusty Henry who looked more the part of a country farmer than court attorney. After some pleading from the young man, Randolph proceeded to ask more and more complicated questions as the examination continued for several hours, finally ending in an argument between Henry and Randolph over a nuanced point of law and natural rights. Breaking off the examination, Randolph told Henry that "You defend your opinions well, sir," but he insisted that they turn to some of the books in his well-stocked law library to answer the question. Having found his answer, Randolph turned to Henry and said "Behold the face of natural reason; you have never seen these books, nor this principle of the law; yet you are right and I am wrong; and from the lesson which you have given me (you must excuse me for saying it) I will never trust to appearances again." Randolph signed Henry's license.[11]

Henry's licensing as a lawyer is another interesting episode in the difficulties of reconstructing history and of what became the very heated relationship between Henry and Thomas Jefferson. Having convinced himself that Henry was uneducated (not to mention uncouth), Jefferson later would insist that George Wythe, Jefferson's own legal mentor and later the first law professor in America, "absolutely refused" to sign a law license for Henry. He also scoffed that Henry had come for his examination after only six weeks of limited study, convinced that Henry had bamboozled the examiners with his impressive but empty speech. Yet, a record of Henry's law license recorded in Goochland County in April 1760 proves Jefferson wrong: Wythe did sign Henry's license. One must also wonder about Jefferson's insistence that Henry had only studied for a few weeks.[12]

As it turns out, Henry and Jefferson first met during the Christmas season of 1759 at a party at the home of Nathanial Dandridge in Hanover

County. Jefferson was passing through on his way to attend the College of William and Mary, and Henry was a member of the local middling gentry and a good friend of Dandridge. Some have suggest that Henry and Jefferson, both avid amateur musicians, played violin (fiddle to Henry) together at the party – some concert that might have been. If so, listening to the side or perhaps on her father's lap must have been a very young Dorothea Dandridge, destined to be Henry's second wife 18 years later. The suave, wealthy Jefferson undoubtedly liked the charming Henry – everyone did – but when Henry arrived in Williamsburg seeking his law license a few months later, without any of the formal training that was so important to Jefferson, one wonders if Henry took the opportunity to "pull-the-leg" of the all-too-studious and serious Jefferson, telling the flabbergasted William & Mary student that he had only studied for six weeks. Perhaps it was only Henry's bravado with a young friend, and Jefferson missed the twinkle in Henry's eye. (Henry told another associate that he spent only four weeks.) Other reports show Henry reading the complicated eighteenth-century legal books for six to nine months before proceeding to Williamsburg. In any case, it is certainly true that Henry's preparation was minimal even by the lax standards of his day. Still, what Henry read, he read deeply and with understanding; later in life he would talk of reading Montesquieu's famous *Spirit of the Law* for one-half an hour, and then having ideas to meditate on all day.[13]

Reportedly several of Henry's examiners signed his license somewhat reluctantly but with promises from the earnest young man that he would continue to pursue his studies. They saw potential in him. Time would show that they had made a wise decision.

To this point, many have characterized Henry's life as a failure or, at best, a frivolous childhood ill spent, but it is evident that Henry had learned much that would be important in his career as a lawyer and politician. In particular, Henry had developed an appreciation for the problems of the small farmers and workers who were his neighbors. Not only had he worked hard both at farming and shop-keeping, and nonetheless failed, but his experience as a tobacco planter and merchant taught him that many of the economic problems that Virginians faced were largely beyond their control, and only the wealthiest planters could avoid the economic pinch. He also learned that many problems faced by Virginians resulted from British control of the colonies: Virginia tobacco farmers obtained a pittance, but tobacco taxes were a bonanza for the British treasury. Prices to farmers were also kept low by British Navigation Acts which required imports and exports to travel on British ships and be sold through British merchants – often Scottish "factors" who came to dominate trade with Virginia. Planters would have done far better had they been able to ship their tobacco on Dutch or French ships or been able to sell their tobacco directly into the lucrative European market. A scarcity of hard currency (gold or silver) also made trade and collecting debts more difficult, and British policies were at the root of this problem as well as English taxes and merchants siphoned-off the hard currency that was available. Henry was also exposed to many of the colony's wealthy citizens and saw first-hand that some of the financial problems that people faced were of their own making, a love of extravagance that outpaced their means. All of these lessons would prove important to the future lawyer and politician. He may have been thinking of his own early career problems when he later said: "Adversity toughens manhood, and the characteristics of the good or the great man, is not that he has been exempted from the evils of life, but that he has surmounted them." In any case, through hard experience, by the time he took to the law, Henry had developed a suspicion of a distant government and burdensome taxation and regulation.[14]

It is also true that, being from the middling gentry, having suffered several failures, and lacking the formal education and other advantages enjoyed by many of the men whom he would meet at the bar, Henry perhaps had a heightened desire for success and the good opinion of his friends and neighbors. Who could blame him? (George Washington was also always a bit self-conscious about his own lack of a formal higher education.) Wealthy political opponents would unfairly claim that as a lawyer Henry was only motivated by large fees, but it was natural for Henry, with a growing family and having finally found a field in which he could excel, to seek financial success and popularity, and the latter would eventually be turned to political purposes. Whatever the cause, he sought and earned the devotion of many of his neighbors, and he was to be enormously successful as a lawyer.

By early 1760, Patrick Henry, lawyer, was launched on his career in Hanover County. Henry's legal practice grew rapidly. His carefully kept records show that in his first three years of practice, he had almost 1,200 cases and was earning a good living, and collecting most of what was due from his clients, a difficult problem in colonial Virginia. (His account book also disproves Jefferson's later claim that he did not keep records, draw pleadings, or manage cases himself.) By this point, Henry was also providing significant financial support to his father and father-in-law, both of whom had come upon financial difficulties. At home, after the young lovers had endured many years of hard work and tight budgets, Patrick was beginning to be able to support his wife and growing family in the manner that he had hoped. Still, while his prospects for success as a lawyer were excellent, Henry was known only in several counties in the central Piedmont of Virginia where he had family and personal connections. This was all to change when destiny seemed to intervene in the guise of the Parsons' Cause.[15]

* * * * *

The Parsons' Cause was a lawsuit that raised important questions about taxes, the Anglican Church in Virginia, and Britain's role in overseeing Virginia's laws. The Church of England, the state-established church in Virginia, was supported by a host of laws and taxes. All citizens were required to attend the church at least once a month (or a licensed dissenting meeting house, of which there were very few); people had to be married by an Anglican priest; in each church parish, a committee of church leaders (the vestry) imposed taxes for the poor and orphans, and everyone (whether Anglican or not) paid taxes for the salary of the local Church of England priest. Church taxes were the largest tax that most paid.[16]

Given the scarcity of hard currency in Virginia, for many years the church tax, like a number of other fees and taxes, was actually paid in tobacco; the vestry of each parish had to pay the minister 16,000 pounds of tobacco annually and provide a working glebe (a home and farm where the minister lived). The vestry would assess each household for its share of the 16,000 pounds of tobacco that was due and its share of the cost of the glebe and poor relief. Generally this system worked well enough; but in times of very large tobacco crops, the price of tobacco dropped, and the salary of Anglican priests effectively dropped with them. In times of poor crops, when tobacco prices rose, so did the salary of priests.

In 1755, facing a very weak tobacco crop and economic distress resulting from the start of the French & Indian War, the Virginia House of Burgesses (Virginia's legislature) passed a law that allowed people to pay taxes that were due in tobacco with money at 2 cents per pound of tobacco for ten months' time. So, if your assessment for the parish priest was 40 pounds of tobacco, you could pay 80 cents instead. (Two pence a pound had been the average price, but tobacco prices were moving considerably higher in 1755.) Some ministers grumbled, but given the short duration of the law it was implemented with few difficulties. Three years later, again facing a shortage of tobacco from crop failure, and with the French & Indian War still contributing to hardships, the Burgesses again passed a "two penny" act, this time to last for two years.

At this point, many Anglican priests complained. From their perspective, people did not mind paying them with tobacco when there was a bumper crop (and prices were low); but when prices rose, laws were passed so that the priests would not enjoy the higher prices. Appealing to the king's Privy Council in London, a committee that was responsible for colonial matters, Virginia's Anglican ministers obtained an order that the law was invalid and was invalid from the moment it was enacted. Based upon the order from the Privy Council, a number of lawsuits were filed seeking damages: the difference between the 2 cents per pound paid and the real price of tobacco at that time (about 6 cents per pound) for the full 16,000 pound salary set by law. These cases were proceeding with mixed results in various counties when the Reverend James Maury's case came before the Hanover Court.

A number of circumstances make this case particularly interesting: Maury, who happened to have been the tutor of a young Thomas Jefferson, filed his case in Hanover County because he was concerned that a jury in Louisa County where he was the minister would decide against him because all the citizens would be subject to higher taxes if he won his suit. (Of course, this effort to shift the locale probably had little effect since ALL Virginians were subject to taxes to pay their local clergy.) Maury's attorney was Peter Lyons who would later become a judge on the Virginia Court of Appeals. The vestry who had paid Maury based on the 2 cents law (and local taxpayers) were represented by a well-known local lawyer, John Lewis. Yet, after the Hanover County Court ruled that the "2 penny" act was void – they had little choice given the ruling from London – Lewis withdrew as counsel; he assumed that there was little else that he could do to assist his client. At the last minute, as the case came up for argument on the amount of damages on December 1, 1763, the church's vestry hired a relatively new local attorney, Patrick Henry, to argue the question. The argument was to be held at Hanover County Courthouse (Document 1), at which Henry's father, John Henry, was the chief magistrate. One might suspect that the vestry was influenced by that fact in hiring Henry, but the magistrates had already ruled against the vestry. The only question was the amount of damages to be set by the jury; it seems that Henry was a last resort.

The case for Maury was rather straightforward; his attorney presented evidence that tobacco prices were about 6 cents a pound while the Reverend Maury had been paid at a rate of only 2 cents and then rested his case. Patrick Henry rose to respond. By several accounts he seemed nervous and began rather haltingly; it seemed to observers that he did not know quite what to say. Perhaps John Henry sat embarrassed and anxious. Yet, as Patrick warmed to the subject, he seemed transformed. (Later, it was often said that Henry started his speeches and arguments quietly and slowly and seemed to be transformed by his own performances.) There was little that Henry could say about the price of tobacco, and there was no question that the "2 penny" act had been declared void. Henry, though, understood the local small farmers who made up the jury, and several of them were dissenters from the Church of England, particularly unhappy about having to pay taxes to support an Anglican priest. Ignoring the simple question of the price of tobacco, Henry turned to the broader issue: What right had Britain to declare a good Virginia law void? Legally, the answer to that question was also simple – Virginia was a colony and had to conform its laws to British rules – but Henry was less concerned about rules and more interested in justice.

Henry began by explaining the relationship between rulers and the ruled: Citizens owed their allegiance to the king, but the king owed his people wise administration of the laws. If the king broke his part of the bargain, the people had no obligation to obey. (This was a classic argument about contract theory of government, stated most clearly by the seventeenth-century English political-philosopher John Locke. Locke's theories were to play an important part in the coming Revolution, but Henry would not quote Locke to the farmers and tradesmen sitting on the jury.) If Britain could invalidate a just and important law like the Two Penny Act, what else might Britain do? Warming to the subject Henry declared that "a King, by annulling or disallowing Laws of this salutary nature, from being the father of his people, degenerates into a Tyrant, and forfeits all rights to his subjects' obedience." At this, Peter Lyons, council for Maury, was astonished; he blurted out that Henry had spoken "treason," a capital offense. Other observers, perhaps some of the Anglican priests who had come to watch what they thought would be an easy victory, murmured "treason," but Henry's father and the other magistrates were being swept away by Henry's oratory and did not dare to interrupt (see Document 3).

The clergy, now, came within Henry's gaze. As with the king, Henry reminded the jury that ministers also owed their flocks loyalty and that they should support just laws that were adopted by the representatives of the people. By suing to undermine a just law, the clergy "ought to be considered as enemies of the community." Unless:

> ... they (the jury) were disposed to rivet the chains of bondage on their own necks, he hoped they would not let slip the opportunity which now offered, of making such an example of him [Maury] as might, hereafter, be a warning to himself and his brethren, not to have the temerity, for the future, to dispute the validity of such laws, authenticated by the only authority, which, in his conception, could give force to laws for the government of this Colony, the authority of a legal representative of a Council, and of a kind and benevolent and patriot Governor.

Not only were the clergy trying to overturn a just law properly adopted by the people's representatives, but they were suing their own parishioners in the hopes of gaining a windfall resulting from the poor tobacco crop, profiting from the people's misfortune:

> Do they [the ministers] manifest their zeal in the cause of religion and humanity by practicing the mild and benevolent precepts of the Gospel of Jesus? Do they feed the hungry and clothe the naked? Oh, no, gentlemen! Instead of feeding the hungry and clothing the naked, these rapacious harpies would, were their powers equal to their will, snatch from the hearth of their honest parishioner his last hoe-cake, from the widow and her orphan child their last milch cow! The last bed, nay, the last blanket from the lying-in woman!

Henry spoke for an hour, but people sat entranced (see Document 3).

Here, as with most other Henry speeches, historians cannot be sure of the precise words spoken. Henry never used a written-out speech, and throughout his career, there was rarely a stenographer present. Still, in the case of the Parsons' Cause, recollections of the speech were recorded shortly after it was given, and observers said that they remembered it well. In this case, historians and students can have a high degree of confidence in the general story of what was said and in key, catching phrases, even if the specific words must be taken with a grain of salt.

There is little doubt that the impact of Henry's argument was electric. The people who had crowded into the Hanover Courthouse were silent as they listened to Henry's assault both on the king and the clergy, pillars of eighteenth-century society. A friend and client of the young lawyer was concerned that he might have crossed the line into treason; "He exceeded the most seditious and inflammatory harangues of the tribunes of old Rome." The magistrates, not least Henry's father, sat mouths agape; the clergy who had come expecting to enjoy an easy victory were aghast.[17]

When Henry was done, the jury filed out to the jury room and, within five minutes, returned with a verdict in favor of Maury, as the law required, but they found damages of only 1 cent. The crowd burst into a roar of support for Henry and carried him out of the courthouse on their shoulders. The relatively young attorney had propelled himself to some fame and endeared himself to the small farmers and tradesmen of the Virginia Piedmont and frontier.[18]

The Reverend Maury told a correspondent that Henry met him in the courthouse yard after the suit and apologized, saying "his sole view in engaging in the cause, and in saying what he had, was to render himself popular" (Document 3). This is an interesting story, and exactly the type of story that was repeated by Henry's opponents. It is certainly possible that Henry politely apologized to Maury for any offense given (many lawyers might do the same) and said that he had appealed to the experience and common sense of the local farmers for a "popular" decision. Maury might have heard this as an admission. Henry was also well aware that his attacks on the clergy were aggressive and had almost certainly carefully planned them in advance. Reportedly he had asked his uncle, the Reverend Patrick Henry, not to attend for fear that he might have "pulled-his-punches" with his uncle sitting in the audience. And it is also true that Henry likely sought, both intentionally and unintentionally, the popular adulation that he received. Yet, it is highly unlikely that Henry felt there was anything wrong with his argument in the case, as Maury implies. (As with much about Patrick Henry, it can sometimes be difficult to separate fact from myth. Other sources report that the Reverend Patrick Henry did attend court that day and, in the courthouse yard after the argument, admonished his nephew: "You shall repent of this Patrick!" His biographer, Meade, refers to Henry's asking his uncle to leave as the "usual version.")[19]

The Parsons' Cause would have lasting implications. Many believe that it helped launch the American Revolution – with people in Virginia beginning to question the authority of Britain to control and over-turn local legislature. For Henry, his success as a practicing attorney was now assured, and his legal fees began to permit a much better lifestyle. He bought land in Louisa County, west of Hanover, on Roundabout Creek and moved his family there in 1764. Soon, his reputation would bring him not just more legal fees, but political opportunity in Louisa.

Legal success meant not simply more cases, but more important cases with much greater public visibility. Very shortly after the Parsons' Cause, Henry was hired by Nathaniel West Dandridge – the host at the 1759 party where Henry first met Jefferson and Henry's future father-in-law – to challenge the results of the Hanover County election to the House of Burgesses. Dandridge claimed that James Littlepage had won the election by illegally "treating" the citizens ("treating," providing food and alcohol to potential voters, was technically illegal in colonial Virginia but it was a common practice). In late November 1764, a rather scruffy looking Henry, dressed in "very coarse apparel" according to John Tyler, appeared in the committee room of the House of Burgesses in Williamsburg in order to argue the case. While initially offended by his dress, the members of the Burgesses' Committee of Privileges and Elections, including colonial leaders Peyton Randolph, Richard Bland, and Richard Henry Lee, were quickly impressed by Henry's arguments concerning the importance of a free and fair election. While Dandridge lost his challenge to the election – leaders likely did not want to open a hornet's nest of challenges to elections (including possibly their own) based on treating – Henry's performance pleased his client and, equally important, impressed the Burgesses among whom Henry would soon be a member.[20]

As 1765 approached, the successful young attorney from Hanover was rising in public stature. Thomas Johnson, a member of the Louisa vestry that Henry had represented in the Parsons' Cause, was particularly impressed with Henry as a forceful advocate for the interests of the small farmer and frontiersman. When Johnson's brother, William, resigned his seat in the House of Burgesses, Johnson supported Henry for the position in a special election in the spring of 1765 (some say William resigned in order to bring Henry into the House), and Henry easily won election as one of the two burgesses for Louisa County.

A new career as a politician and statesman lay ahead for Patrick Henry.

Notes

1. Randolph, *Richmond Enquirer*, September 2, 1815, 4.
2. In 1736, Henry's parents would have said that his birthday was May 18, but when the inaccurate Julian Calendar was replaced with the more accurate Gregorian Calendar in 1752, 11 days were added to dates to reflect the "new style" (n.s.) dating. See Edward L. Cohen, "Adoption and Reform of the Gregorian Calendar," *Math Horizons*, 7: 3 (February 2000): 5–11.
3. Henry, *Patrick Henry*, II: 245.
4. Edward Fontaine, *Patrick Henry: Corrections of Biographical Mistakes, and Popular Errors in Regard to His Character*, ed. by Mark Couvillon, 2nd ed. (Patrick Henry Memorial Foundation, 2011): 4 (emphasis deleted).
5. Wirt, *Sketches*, 14. Moses Coit Tyler, *Patrick Henry* (Boston: Houghton, Mifflin and Co., 1888): 5.
6. Henry, *Patrick Henry*, I: 8–9.
7. Kevin J. Hayes, *The Mind of a Patriot: Patrick Henry and the World of Ideas* (Charlottesville: University of Virginia Press, 2008). Curtis, *Life of Webster*, I: 585.
8. Henry, *Patrick Henry*, I: 9. Fontaine, *Corrections*, 6.
9. Henry Howe, *Historical Collections of Virginia* (Charleston, SC: Babcock & Co., 1845): 221. Henry, *Patrick Henry*, I: 15.
10. "Jefferson's Recollections," *Pennsylvania Magazine*, 393.
11. Wirt, *Sketches*, 22.
12. Ibid., 21–22. Goochland County Order Book No. 8 (1757–1761), April 1760, 284–285. Charles Campbell's famous *History of the Colony and Ancient Dominion of Virginia*, repeating Jefferson's canard, said of Henry's law license that "Mr. Wythe refused to sign it." Campbell, *History* (Philadelphia: J. B. Lippincott & Co., 1860), 525.
13. Robert Douthat Meade, *Patrick Henry: Patriot in the Making*, vol. 1 (Philadelphia: J. B. Lippincott Co., 1957): 55. Samuel Meredith, who knew Henry from childhood, reported to William Wirt that Henry studied law "not more than six or eight months." George Morgan, *The True Patrick Henry* (Philadelphia: J. B. Lippincott Co., 1907): 433. William Wirt received other reports, from seemingly knowledgeable sources, ranging from one to nine months. Meade, *Patrick Henry*, I: 370 n. 17.
14. Henry, *Patrick Henry*, I: 20.
15. Ibid., I: 25–27.
16. See, generally, John A. Ragosta, *Wellspring of Liberty: How Virginia's Religious Dissenters Helped to Win the American Revolution & Secured Religious Liberty* (New York: Oxford University Press, 2010): Chapter 1.
17. Henry, *Patrick Henry*, I: 44.
18. This and related Two Penny Act cases were again appealed to the Privy Council in England by John Camm, an Anglican minister and later president of William & Mary, but in 1767, the

cases were dismissed as improperly brought. As often happens in mixed legal-political disputes, by that point, with tension in the colonies mounting, the Privy Council simply wanted the matter to go away. Ibid., I: 45.

19. Mark Couvillon, *The Demosthenes of his Age: Accounts of Patrick Henry's Oratory by his Contemporaries* (Red Hill, VA: Patrick Henry Memorial Foundation, 2013): 2–3, quoting Thomas Trevillian to Nathaniel Pope, Nathaniel Pope Papers, 5, Manuscript Division, Library of Congress. Meade, *Patrick Henry*, I: 128; see also Henry, *Patrick Henry*, I: 36.

20. Wirt, *Sketches*, 37.

CHAPTER **2**

REVOLUTION

Patrick Henry was elected to the Virginia House of Burgesses at a particularly interesting moment in history.

Colonists from England, France, The Netherlands, and Spain (not to mention Germany, Ireland, Scotland, Sweden, and other European locales) had been settling in what would become the United States for well over 150 years, generally pushing aside Native Americans and often competing for land claimed by other European nations. Tensions between the various national and Native groups had sporadically erupted into open warfare. By the mid-1750s, French soldiers and fur traders moving down the Great Lakes and Ohio River valley from Canada found themselves confronting British subjects moving over the mountains from Pennsylvania and Virginia. In 1754, a young George Washington was sent on a mission to warn the French out of the area, but instead he helped to spark the French & Indian War (known as the Seven Years' War in Europe), a war for empire. By the war's end, Britain had won decisive victories not only in America but around the world. The Treaty of Paris of 1763 that settled the war left Britain nominally in control of Canada, Florida, and all of the lands east of the Mississippi River (except New Orleans), although Native Americans would continue to contest British and later American sovereignty for many years.

This victory, though, came at an enormous economic cost, and the British Ministry – the cabinet of officials responsible for recommending and implementing laws passed by Parliament – wanted to adjust its relationship with Britain's American colonies. Led by George Grenville, Lord of the Treasury and effectively Prime Minister, Britain wanted to incorporate the colonies more closely into its economic and political system; this would require increased control over colonial political offices, law enforcement, and the frontier. As a result, 10,000 British Redcoats were left in America to defend the Empire and maintain a close watch on the frontiers, in part seeking to keep American settlers from crossing the Allegheny Mountains, infringing upon Native American lands, and starting another war.

At the same time, the war increased Britain's national debt by two-thirds, drove up taxes in Britain, and led to new costs to maintain troops now stationed on the frontiers. These costs led the British Parliament to look for tax revenue in America. These concerns with both costs and control were reflected in Britain's 1764 decision to adjust its import duties on molasses (used in the making of rum) and increase enforcement of its custom laws. The Sugar Act (officially the American Revenue Act) actually reduced the import duty on molasses, but smuggling had become so prevalent that few people actually paid the old (higher) duty. Grenville intended to make sure that Americans paid the new import duty by strengthening the presence of the British Navy in American waters and clamping-down on smuggling. In 1764, Grenville's government also announced that a Stamp Tax would be imposed in America by 1765, with all legal papers, diplomas, newspaper, even playing cards, requiring a tax stamp to be sold or used in America.

These efforts to assert British control in America were met with strong objections. American colonists were thrilled with the outcome of the war, and they were truly proud to be British citizens, part of the world's greatest empire. New Englanders, descendants of the Puritans, were especially pleased that their old enemy, Catholic France, had been driven from Canada. Still, they felt that they had paid their share in the war in both blood and local taxes and were deeply disturbed by the idea of being taxed by Britain. Englishmen had long believed that taxes could only legally be imposed by their elected representatives, and colonists had no representatives in the British Parliament – thus the slogan "no taxation without representation." The fact that the taxes were small did not convince Americans to accept the laws; a principle was at stake. Accepting a small tax imposed in Britain might lead to larger taxes and eventually a total loss of local control, tyranny. The argument of Grenville and his supporters that Americans were "virtually represented" by members of Parliament from Britain who had the Americans' best interests at heart – and would not impose more than a reasonable level of taxes – was viewed as ridiculous and patronizing. Several of the colonies, including Virginia, filed formal protests with Parliament and the King in 1764, but the protests were having little effect in England. By the spring of 1765, ships were arriving in America with news that Grenville's new Stamp Tax had been formally adopted by Parliament and would go into effect November 1, 1765.[1]

Patrick Henry, with his new found popularity after the Parsons' Cause, stepped into a turbulent political world focused on the relationship between

Britain and its colonies. With his silver tongue and deep concern for his neighbors and fellow citizens, Henry would have an important influence on the course of events.

* * * * *

After being elected to the House of Burgesses from Louisa County, Henry traveled to Williamsburg for the May 1765 legislative session (see Document 1). Some of the members of the House likely remembered Henry from his persuasive, if unsuccessful, argument for Colonel Dandridge in 1764 concerning the disputed election in Hanover County. Still, he certainly would have been seen as a junior, unsophisticated, if not backward member. It did not improve his image that he came to Williamsburg without some of the fancy clothing expected of gentlemen in higher society.

The plainly dressed Henry, a bit short of his twenty-ninth birthday, took his seat on about May 20, and in less than a week he managed to anger many of the leaders of the colony. While Henry was intimately familiar with the economic distress faced by small planters on the frontier, many of the colony's wealthiest members were also facing a financial crisis, although it was a crisis largely the result of their own expensive tastes. The elite depended upon the sale of tobacco for income and, like small farmers, faced problems with the Navigation Acts and hard-dealing by British merchants. It seemed that every year the wealthy saw their debts increase as their tobacco crops never quite covered the cost of the luxuries that they imported from England. Since giving up English luxuries never seemed a real alternative for most of them, they could only hope for improved tobacco crops and prices to extract them from the pinch they were in.

What Henry could not have known at the time is that John Robinson, Speaker of the House of Burgesses, Treasurer of the colony, and one of the wealthiest men in America, had tried to help many of the plantation owners by lending them money. While this might seem charitable, Robinson did not lend his own money: he lent the planters money collected through taxes.[2] He presumably thought the funds would be paid back before anyone found out, and no one would be the wiser. As the loans had gotten larger and larger over the years, and tobacco prices never quite seemed to reach a level to permit loans to be repaid, the entire scheme was on the verge of collapse. The consequences could be disastrous, not only for Robinson, but for dozens of planters who would be called on to repay the loans immediately if the scheme was discovered.

To remedy the problem, Robinson had developed a new plan: If a colonial loan office could be created, it could borrow money from Britain at a reasonable interest rate and loan funds to the planters so that they could pay-off the loans to Robinson. In theory, the planters would then pay the

Virginia loan office back as prices and crops improved. The proposal for this loan scheme came before the House of Burgesses on May 24, 1765 and seemed likely to pass with little problem (as many of the Burgesses owed Robinson funds and others could see a benefit for the colony in a loan office that would make money more readily available).

Henry, though, was having none of this. He did not know about Robinson's illegal loans, but he was opposed to the loan office scheme. Why should the colony loan money to rich planters who had gotten into debt by overspending? From his days running a store, Henry was familiar with the problem of debt; some folks just could not pay for things they needed. He had no sympathy, though, for wealthy people who had run up debt. Rising to speak in the House of Burgesses, the new member from Louisa emphatically objected to the colonial loan office scheme, asking the House "is it proposed then to reclaim the Spendthrift from his dissipation and extravagance, by filling his pockets with money?" Did it make sense for the government to loan money to men who had bought luxuries and run-up huge debts? Would this make them more financially responsible? (As with many of Henry's speeches, this was not recorded at the time, but Jefferson, a student watching from the back of the room, said he "could never forget" the incident, and the tone of Henry's question was clear.) In one sentence, the new member from Louisa County managed to anger the leaders of the House (many older and wealthy men who knew what was at stake). Yet, in spite of the pointed question, Henry failed in his effort to block the proposal. It passed the House only to be rejected by the Council. (The Council, made up of even wealthier men, may have seen the loan office as a means to support some of their rivals.)[3]

Still, the incident is important. Henry, within days of arriving in Williamsburg, made clear that he was not afraid to speak his mind, was dedicated to the interests of the small planters and middle class, and was not afraid to challenge even the leaders of the House. This was to become even more evident five days later.[4]

On May 29, 1765, Henry's twenty-ninth birthday, the House of Burgesses again took up the issue of the Stamp Tax. Most of the leaders felt there was little else to be done. Virginia and many of her sister colonies had protested in 1764 by filing petitions with Parliament and the King. Those petitions had remained unanswered, and Parliament had finalized the law with the tax to go into effect that autumn. There seemed to be no alternative but submission. Even colonial agent Benjamin Franklin, lobbying in London on the colonies' behalf, thought there was little else to do. With little hope for any serious action in the remaining days of the legislative session, many of Virginia's burgesses had already left for home; apparently only 39 of 114 members were present. At best, opposition to British taxes seemed rudderless.

Once again, Henry was having none of it. Incensed by the notion that Parliament could tax Virginians without their consent, Henry met privately with like-minded House members in Williamsburg, and that group of young members, led by Henry, drew up seven resolutions. While the first four resolves did little more than restate the 1764 petitions from the House of Burgesses, the three additional resolves became progressively stronger and more emphatic: The fifth said the House of Burgesses had the "only and sole" power to lay taxes – that is, Parliament had no such authority; the sixth said that the people did not have to "yield obedience" to any tax that was not adopted by their own representatives; the seventh insisted that anyone who supported Parliament's right to tax the colonies "shall be deemed an enemy to his majesty's [King George's] colony" (see Document 4). These resolutions expressed open defiance of Parliament's authority and were seen by many as treasonous. While the exact progression of events is not perfectly known, it appears that Henry himself drafted the first five resolutions and the latter two were likely drawn-up in consultation with George Johnston, John Fleming, and several other young members of the House of Burgesses. On May 29, Henry rose in the House of Burgesses to introduce this renewed and strengthened protest in what had promised to be a sleepy, ill-attended session.[5]

Those members that remained were spellbound by Henry's speech; Jefferson, still a student at William & Mary watching from the back of the room, would later remember that moment clearly, saying that Henry "appeared to me to speak as Homer wrote" (extraordinary praise from someone who held the Greek poet Homer in such high regard as Jefferson). Henry explained that taxation without representation was tyranny. Warning that tyrants had faced assassination in the past, Henry declared "Caesar had . . . his Brutus, Charles the First his Cromwell, and George the Third. . . ." This produced cries of "treason" from Speaker Robinson and some other of the older members: Henry seemed to be calling for the assassination of King George III (Document 4).[6]

There continues to be controversy as to what happened next. Some reports by eye-witnesses that were written down years later say that Henry quickly added "may profit by their example. If this be treason, make the most of it." Yet, a Frenchman traveling in the colonies (perhaps a French spy in these years of tension between Britain and France) observed the speech and reported that Henry apologized to the Speaker for the outburst, and many historians have seized on this report to suggest that Henry was not quite the firebrand that his supporters later made him out to be (although no other report mentions an apology). It is equally likely, though, that any apology that was made was a ruse, one of the oldest tricks in the book for a trial lawyer like Henry: An attorney introduces evidence to a jury that it was not supposed to hear and, when someone objects, the attorney apologizes; the fact remains that the jury (in this case the House of Burgesses) has heard the inflammatory evidence (see Appendix).

Whether or not he apologized, Henry skated perilously close to treason to make a point. (He had done the same in the Parsons' Cause.) Tending to confirm the traditional story, Edmund Pendleton told James Madison some years later that "I remember to have heard a Gentleman commend Mr. Henry's dexterity in playing on the line of treason, without passing it."[7]

What is clear is that Henry's warning to the King and Parliament produced an outburst. The fifth resolution passed by only one vote, and given the closeness of that vote, the sixth and the seventh resolutions were apparently not introduced to the full House, although they may have already been reviewed by the Committee of the Whole House considering the matter.[i] Certainly the public was aware that stronger resolutions had been considered; the French traveler, for example, was aware of the seventh (unadopted) resolution. Lieutenant Governor Francis Fauquier, reporting to the British Board of Trade, tried to minimize the significance of the resolutions: "I have heard that very indecent language was used by a Mr. Henry a young lawyer" and that the radicals "had two more resolutions in their pocket, but finding the difficulty they had in carrying the 5th which was by a single voice, and knowing them to be more virulent and inflammatory; they did not produce them." For some of Virginia's conservative leaders, though, even the fifth resolution was too much. Peyton Randolph, soon to be the Speaker of the House, stormed out of the room blustering "by god, I would have given 100. Guineas for a single vote" to defeat the fifth resolution. There is even some question about which one of the resolutions elicited Randolph's ire. Jefferson suggests that it was the resolution usually referred to as the sixth, insisting that the people did not have to obey a tax passed by Parliament, that led to the eruption. Other historians suggest that it may have been the seventh, declaring that anyone supporting the right of Parliament to impose a tax in Virginia was an enemy to the colony. Most still embrace the conventional view that the insistence in the "fifth" resolution drafted by Henry that the Burgesses were the "sole" body permitted to tax, a clear, even if indirect challenge to Parliament, was the source of Randolph's outburst.[8]

There is some unavoidable confusion here. What is clear is that Henry's speech and resolutions put the House in an uproar. The next day, after Henry had left Williamsburg for his plantation and some of his more

---

i A Committee of the Whole House was a procedural trick which allowed all of the members to debate a matter without recording what was said or by whom, since committees did not keep such records at the time. Once the Committee of the Whole House had debated a matter, it could then be introduced into the House for formal consideration.

moderate supporters became concerned about what might be seen as a violent attack on the King and Parliament, the fifth resolution was deleted from the records of the House of Burgesses. (Supporters of the royal government had sought to have all of the resolutions struck, but that effort failed.) The fifth resolve was excised so completely that historians cannot now be sure of exactly what it said and most refer to the language in Henry's own handwriting that was found among his papers when he died. The four resolutions that were left on the books did little more than repeat the concerns expressed by the House in 1764. "Officially," it seemed as if nothing had been accomplished. In effect, that is what Lieutenant Governor Fauquier reported to the Board of Trade in London, adding that had the House been better attended none of the resolutions may have passed.

So why all the fuss?

Henry and his upstart supporters were not to be so easily defeated. While only four tepid resolutions were left on the official records in Virginia by May 30, it soon became apparent that before the vote Henry and the others had copied down all seven resolutions and sent them to correspondents in other colonies. The first published report came in the *Newport Mercury* in Rhode Island which printed six Virginia resolves on June 24, as if they had all passed, noting that they had been received from a person in Philadelphia. The *Mercury* copy excluded the third resolve but included trimmed-down versions of all of the more forceful resolves. On July 1, the *Boston Gazette* reprinted the story from Newport. On July 4, the *Maryland Gazette* printed all seven resolves. The story of the Virginia Resolves spread through the colonies like wildfire, and none of the newspapers reported that only the first four mild resolves had actually passed and stayed on the books. Such was the state of news reporting in the late colonial period (stories could not be confirmed with a telephone call or e-mail). While it is possible that Henry and his supporters were intentionally trying to deceive readers in other colonies, it is equally likely that they sent the resolves off in the expectation (perhaps vain hope) that all would pass, possibly after the resolves were approved in the Committee of the Whole.

While other colonies, like Virginia, had objected to the Stamp Tax, as in Virginia, senior politicians thought that there was not much else that could be done once Parliament passed the final law. Now, drawn forward by the Virginia Resolves, people throughout the mainland colonies took renewed courage. Governor Francis Bernard in Massachusetts reported that "publishing the Virginia resolutions proved an alarm-bell to the disaffected." Several colonies adopted their own resolves mimicking the stronger language which they thought, mistakenly, had been passed in Virginia. As political momentum in opposition to the Stamp Act built, a call went out for a Stamp Act Congress at which representatives of the colonies would decide on a common course to resist British attempts to tax the colonies. (Ironically, when the Stamp Act Congress met in New York in October of 1765, there was no representative from Virginia as the colonial governor, Francis Fauquier, would not call a session of the Burgesses together to appoint representatives.) Inflamed by the Virginia Resolves, riots broke out in Massachusetts and several other colonies. Proposals to boycott British goods until the Stamp Act was removed gained renewed energy.[9]

And Henry's name began to spread well beyond the Virginia Piedmont among both admirers and opponents. In addition to the report filed by Fauquier with the Board of Trade, the Anglican Church Commissary in Virginia, William Robinson (a cousin of Speaker Robinson), wrote to the Bishop of London criticizing Henry's actions in the Parsons' Cause and his Stamp Act speech. Henry "blazed out in a violent speech against the authority of Parliament and the King, comparing his Majesty to a Tarquin, a Caesar, and a Charles the First and not sparing insinuations that he wished another Cromwell would rise," Commissary Robinson complained. Even critics recognized that Henry had played the critical role in reigniting the dispute.[10]

The Stamp Act, of course, was withdrawn after renewed, sometimes violent protests throughout the mainland colonies. British merchants realized that they had much to lose if the colonies continued to boycott British manufactured goods because of the tax, and they lobbied Parliament effectively. At the same time, while withdrawing the Stamp Act, the British Parliament attempted to reassert its authority by adopting the Declaratory Act stating that it had authority over the colonies "in all cases whatsoever." The meaning of that power would again be tested in 1767 with the introduction of the Townshend Duties, import taxes on paper, lead, paint, and tea; but for now, Virginians were celebrating their success, and the new legislator, Patrick Henry, returned to his farm and legal practice with a growing following.

* * * * *

Over the course of the next ten years, as the colonies slowly moved toward open rebellion, Patrick Henry was to become an increasingly visible and important political leader in Virginia. In 1770, the Virginia legislature appointed him to an inter-colonial commission on Indian trade with Quebec, New York, New Jersey, Maryland, Pennsylvania, and Delaware (although the royal government blocked the commission from meeting). In other colonies Henry was known as "zealous in the Cause of American Liberty . . . the first Mover of the Virginia Resolves in 1765." When Virginia decided to renew its boycott of British goods in response to the Townshend Duties, Henry was there. In 1773, realizing the need for colonial cooperation, he helped to lead the call for a Committee of Correspondence between the American colonies so that they could coordinate effectively about concerns with British imperial policies. By 1774, he was to play a critical role as a Virginia delegate to the First Continental Congress.[11]

Before turning to those matters and the coming of the American Revolution, however, it is fair to pause and consider how Henry worked diligently throughout this period to grow his legal practice and raise his growing family. Henry also faced important challenges during this time concerning religious freedom and slavery, raising political and ethical issues that would confront him for the rest of his life.

From 1763 to 1771, Henry and Sarah had four more children, increasing their clan to six offspring. No longer a struggling farmer or failed merchant, Henry was becoming one of the most successful lawyers in Virginia and was in the process of buying thousands of acres of farmland to support his family and, ultimately, to provide each child with a material legacy. In 1771, already owning over 3000 acres spread across the Piedmont, Henry bought the Scotchtown plantation of 960 acres with one of the oldest and largest homes in Virginia – although far from the fanciest. Built in 1719, the massive home with high ceilings and doors and large rooms sat in Hanover County north of the small town of Richmond and just off the main road to Charlottesville in the west (see Document 1). The location was close enough to Williamsburg to permit active participation in the colonial (and, later, state) government, while still offering a large piece of land good for farming. Here, Henry's oldest children grew to adulthood and the younger grew-up as privileged gentry.

Of course, life's difficulties also visited Henry during these years; in 1769, two of Henry's sisters died, and in February 1773, Henry buried his beloved father, John Henry. Before selling Scotchtown in 1777, Henry was to have some of his greatest personal triumphs, but the home would also be the scene of heartbreaking personal tragedy. Sarah, Henry's beloved wife whom he had married in his youth, was increasingly ill in the Scotchtown years, probably suffering from severe post-partum depression after the birth of the last four children. Eventually she would lose her reason, apparently in her madness expressing a strong dislike for Henry and their children, and she had to be restrained and cared for in a basement room in Scotchtown, sometimes in a straight-jacket. It must have been a terrible and stressful time for Henry and the children, but the state of mental health treatment in the colony provided no better alternative. Sarah would never recover. She died at Scotchtown in February 1775, only months before Henry's most memorable "Liberty or Death" speech. While Henry's records provide very little information about Sarah or the tragedy, the strain must have weighed heavily on the husband and father. When he sold Scotchtown in 1777, Henry told friends that he needed "to move away from all objects reminding him of" Sarah.[12]

Henry's growing wealth was driven by his rising legal star during these years; he became particularly well known for his work in criminal cases in which his appeals to juries almost always won the day. Henry was later unfairly criticized for representing criminals for large fees, but he was earning a living for his family while allowing juries to see things from his clients' perspective – exactly what an attorney is supposed to do. He had learned to mix legal learning and his common touch, and apparently few (if any) lawyers could match his skills. By 1771, when the conservative and accomplished treasurer of Virginia, Robert Carter Nicholas, decided that his public duties required him to give up the private practice of law, he asked that Henry take over his practice (after the young and talented Thomas Jefferson had declined) – a sure indication that Henry was seen as one of the leading lawyers in Virginia and that his legal reasoning and training, as well as his drafting of legal documents, were far from inadequate (as Jefferson and others would later claim).

* * * * *

RELIGIOUS FREEDOM AND SLAVERY

Legal work also exposed Henry to many important cases; some of the most notable were in the area of religious freedom.

In the 1760s, Virginia faced growing tension concerning its restrictions on religious liberty. The colony's official church was the Anglican Church or Church of England, with the King of England as its nominal head. All citizens paid taxes for Anglican ministers' salaries and to maintain the Church's buildings. Monthly attendance at the Anglican Church or a licensed meetinghouse was required; failure to attend could result in a fine (one of the most common crimes prosecuted in eighteenth-century Virginia). Politics were also controlled by Anglicans. Henry had tangled indirectly with the Church during the Parsons' Cause, but a more direct confrontation was brewing. Dissenters from the Church of England, mostly Presbyterians, Baptists, and Quakers, found it difficult to get their meetinghouses and ministers licensed, and many objected on principle to the idea that the government could deny a minister a license much less collect taxes to support one church. Yet, in spite of the restrictions, the number of dissenters in Virginia grew as the British colonies experienced the evangelical revival known as the Great Awakening. By the latter part of the 1760s, dissenters probably accounted for between one-fifth and one-third of Virginia's population, and their growth challenged the Anglican Church.

Some members of the established Church reacted to the challenge by increasing the discrimination and persecution of dissenters. Dissenters were whipped, dunked in ponds and rivers, chased with hounds. In 1768, dissenting ministers, particularly Baptists, began to face jail time for preaching without a license, disturbing the peace, or similar trumped-up charges. By the beginning of the Revolution, this would be an epidemic, with over half of the Baptist ministers in Virginia having been jailed for preaching. The arrests would evaporate with the Revolution, when the new state needed the support of all of its citizens for effective mobilization, but in the meantime, many Virginians, Henry among them, were outraged. Remember that Henry had often accompanied his mother to hear the preaching of Samuel Davies, the first Presbyterian minister in Virginia licensed by the General Court, and Henry's grandfather was fined for allowing preaching by a dissenter on his property. The firebrand lawyer was not likely to let this persecution go unanswered, and Henry offered his services *pro bono* to some of the ministers who faced jail for preaching.[13]

Over the years, many stories have been told about Patrick Henry's representation of dissenting ministers in court, some of them are probably myth. In one story Henry strode into the Spotsylvania Courthouse and picked-up the prosecution's indictment, turning to the court and courtroom he asked what the men were charged with. Waiving the indictment above his head, and answering the question himself, he bellowed "these men . . . are charged with, – with – what? – preaching the Gospel of the Son of God? Great God! Preaching the gospel of the Son of God – Great God!" As the story goes, the magistrates quietly left the bench unwilling to face Henry's wrath. The story may be apocryphal – William Wirt Henry says that while Henry did successfully defend the preachers in Spotsylvania, the speech was made-up later – but the sentiments are accurate.[14]

Other instances of Henry's defense of persecuted ministers are better documented. For example, John Weatherford, a Baptist minister, was jailed in Charlotte County for preaching without a license. While there, preaching from a jail window with his arms outstretched in prayer, he was cut with a knife by ruffians standing outside his cell hoping to discourage his preaching; he carried the scars to his death. When Weatherford's case finally came before the county court, Henry was able to get the charge dismissed, but the local jailor refused to release Weatherford until he paid the cost of his food while in jail (a common eighteenth-century practice). Weatherford had no money, so he remained in jail. Later he was released when an anonymous donor paid his fees. Only years later did Weatherford discover that Henry had paid the fees. Henry, a deeply religious man, was certainly moved by the plight of the dissenting ministers and the need for greater religious freedom. Henry's concern for freedom of conscience was to continue for the rest of his life and would become a significant issue both in 1776, as Virginia set itself on the road to independence, and again in 1786, when Henry supported a return to government support for religion (see Chapter 3).[15]

Henry was also confronted in this period by the issue of slavery. Of course, he had lived in a slave society his entire life and owned and profited from enslaved people. He participated in the buying and selling of slaves. As an inquisitive young man interested in ideas of freedom and liberty, he could not help but to see that slavery was an affront to many of the principles which he advocated. In the early 1770s, since Henry's fame as a defender of liberty had grown through the Parsons' Cause and his attacks on the Stamp Act, he was approached by Virginia Quakers to join in their growing opposition to slavery. One of the earliest letters historians have from Henry is a remarkable response to a Virginia Quaker, Robert Pleasants, after Pleasants sent Henry a copy of Anthony Benezet's attack on the slave trade. (Pleasants would later free his own slaves, over the strong opposition of his family, and become a major figure in the nascent abolitionist movement.) Henry's response, from January 18, 1773, is worth quoting at length:

> It is not a little surprising that the professors of Christianity ... should encourage a practice so totally repugnant to the first impressions of right and wrong ... Is it not amazing, that at a time, when the rights of humanity are defined and understood with precision, in a country, above all others, fond of liberty; ... we find men professing a religion the most humane, mild, gentle and generous, adopting a principle as repugnant to humanity, as it is inconsistent with the bible and destructive of liberty? ... Would anyone believe I am the master of slaves of my own purchase! I am drawn along by the general inconvenience of living here without them. I will not, I cannot justify it ... I believe a time will come when an opportunity will be offered to abolish this lamentable evil. Everything we can do is to improve it, if it happens in our day; if not, let us transmit to our descendants, together with our slaves, a pity for their unhappy lot, and an abhorrence of slavery. If we cannot reduce this wished-for reformation to practice, let us treat the unhappy victims with lenity.[16]

Here, Henry recognizes the hypocrisy of his support of slavery and "the rights of humanity ... in a country, above all others, fond of liberty." (Claims that historians impose twenty-first-century standards on eighteenth-century people when they condemn slavery are simply inaccurate.) One is also immediately struck with how the very religious Henry lamented the inconsistency of slavery with Christianity – a debate that would unfortunately rage in the nineteenth century as many southerners sought to defend slavery as being Biblical. Henry notes not only the abhorrent nature of slavery, but also the inherent wrong of his continued participation in the bloody institution. Over the course of his life, however, Henry did nothing to end his enslavement of scores of people or slavery generally. At the time of his death, by then a wealthy man, Henry owned 67 slaves, but his will does not free any of them, providing only that "If [his wife] chooses to set free one or two of my slaves, she is to have full power to do so." By comparison, many other Virginians, seeking to implement the principles for which they had fought, manumitted (freed) their slaves after the Revolution or at their death or refused to participate in the buying and selling of slaves, including George Washington, Robert Carter III (who freed 500), and Edward Coles (a relative of Henry and neighbor of Jefferson who freed his slaves in the Illinois territory in 1819 and provided them with farms). What, then, can be made of Henry on the issue of slavery?[17]

Certainly nothing should hide the immorality of slavery or the reprehensibility of Henry's participating in the institution. Still, one should recognize some of the factors that would have weighed on Henry as he considered the issue. Henry undoubtedly recognized what an integral part of the southern economy and culture slavery had become. He certainly recognized that slavery played an important role in his own growing wealth. Ending slavery would impose a large economic cost (although various plans existed to minimize that cost or spread it over a number of years). Importantly, like other southern slave owners who knew what they had done to the people they treated as chattel, he was deeply afraid of what would happen when the slaves were freed. And, of course, racism also allowed plantation owners, in their own minds, to minimize slavery and oppose emancipation. Given these factors, Henry and others saw no practical alternative that would protect their interests. In the end, on this issue, Henry fails, and he knew that he failed. He could not, he would not, remove himself from the slave plantation system or publicly and actively fight it. He would, instead, have to recognize the incoherence of slavery and his demands for liberty the rest of his life. Like many planters, he tried at least to soften somewhat the lot of his own slaves (the term "amelioration" would be used to describe this practice). He revisited the issue in 1786 when writing a letter to his daughter Anne upon her marriage to Spencer Roane. Using the common southern euphemism for slaves of "servants," he wrote: "Your servants, in particular, will have the strongest claim upon your charity; let them be well fed, well clothed, nursed in sickness, and let them never be unjustly treated."[18]

When it came to slavery, Henry, Jefferson, and many other of the Founding Fathers, had feet of clay (and pockets of gold).[ii]

---

ii While Henry undoubtedly was not among the most abusive masters in eighteenth-century Virginia, he participated in and profited by this brutal and inhuman practice. One question is how to treat Henry historically in light of these facts. If the question is whether Henry should be idolized as an untarnished paragon of virtue, his use of enslaved people would clearly disqualify him. As historians, however, while Henry participated in this abomination of the eighteenth century, he still has much to teach us about the American Revolution and the founding of the republic, not to mention his own struggles to overcome adversity.

In another sense, Henry's support of and participation in the institution of slavery is emblematic. One of the greatest, and saddest, ironies of American history is that the existence of slavery played a critical role in the coming and success of the American Revolution. While British poet and essayist Samuel Johnson famously asked: "How is it that we hear the loudest *yelps* for liberty among the drivers of Negroes?," there was a perverse logic in this. First, patriots often spoke passionately and effectively about the "slavery" that was being imposed by Britain on American colonists. Henry was a master of this rhetoric as is evident in his "Liberty or Death" speech. Hypocrisy notwithstanding, slave-owning patriots were not misusing the term; they knew better than anyone what "slavery" was – when others made decisions for you over which you had no control. This was very frightening to white Americans. Second, few actions of the British government did more to rally support for the patriots than when British officials threatened colonists that, if they did not cease rebellion, Britain would free the slaves. When Lord Dunmore, the last royal governor of Virginia, issued an edict in November of 1775 offering freedom to all slaves of patriot masters who would fight against the rebelling colonists, southerners flew to the patriot cause. (Notably, Dunmore did not offer freedom to all enslaved persons.) Third, and critically, the wealthy and influential patriots who led the American Revolution would have been far less likely to have supported such social upheaval if they believed that the Revolution might undermine their status as the "upper" class. (Compare the class implications of the French or Russian Revolution.) The existence of an identified underclass in Virginia which would not share (at least not immediately) in the benefits of the Revolution (enslaved African-Americans) allowed wealthy patriots to support the cause with some confidence. Lower-class whites could be convinced to support the social structure by allowing them to participate in the privileges of their race against blacks, and any possibility of class warfare was largely suppressed. White solidarity against blacks, then, was, sadly, an essential element of support for the patriot movement. (The implications of the great paradox of American liberty are, of course, still being felt today.)[19]

Interestingly, a note found among Henry's papers apparently written in this time period has him speculating about the impact of slavery and religious intolerance in Virginia on the colony's future prospects and economic growth. "How comes it that the lands in Pennsylvania are five times the value of ours?" he writes. Answering himself he explains that "Pennsylvania is the country of the most extensive [religious] privileges with few slaves." Jefferson would make similar comparisons to other states, particularly the relative religious freedom in Pennsylvania, in his famous *Notes on the States of Virginia*. Neither would find a solution to the problem of slavery, but they would famously clash in the years after the Revolution on the question of how broadly to define religious freedom.[20]

While occupied with his legal practice and plantations, Henry was maturing philosophically and politically during the decade after the Stamp Act crisis. No longer an obscure, poorly dressed member from the backcountry, an influential Henry now attended sessions of the House of Burgesses in the finest fashion, wearing a dark wig and a peach blossom-colored coat in one report.

In Virginia, the period from 1765 until the Boston Tea Party in December 1773 was relatively politically quiet. Virginians, with Henry often in the lead, continued to protest British taxes in the form of the Townshend Duties and British interference in internal matters, but in 1770, the duties were removed on all the products except tea. While this tax was still viewed as an affront in principle, with only one small tax, it was increasingly difficult to coordinate an effective response to British taxes across the colonies. Most resistance seemed to be in New England, where colonists suffered from the presence of Redcoats to enforce British customs law, the seizure of ships and goods, and the "Boston Massacre" of March 1770.

Still, Henry was politically active in the period, and he and many of his colleagues kept a wary eye on British actions. Before most of the Townshend Duties were withdrawn, in 1769, Henry had helped to lead opposition in the House of Burgesses with another set of resolutions opposed to Parliament's authority to tax the colonies. He was among a small group of Burgesses, including Thomas Jefferson, Dabney Carr, and Richard Henry Lee, who gathered at Raleigh Tavern after House of Burgesses' sessions to discuss ideas and possible actions. In March 1773, based upon a resolution proposed by this small group, the Virginia House of Burgesses sent a suggestion to the other colonial legislatures that they create Committees of Correspondence "to communicate from time to time" concerning threats to colonists' "legal, and constitutional Rights" and to coordinate responses. These Committees of Correspondence would prove increasingly important as conflict with the mother country again exploded. Fifty years later, in reminiscing about the Revolution, Jefferson would say "it is not now easy to say what we should have done without Patrick Henry. He was far above all in maintaining the spirit of the Revolution."[21]

In spite of the vigilance of Henry and his supporters, with the Townshend Duties all but eliminated, the tax on tea might not have resulted in an early, explosive response but for the Boston Tea Party of December 16, 1773, and the reaction of the British Parliament.

The British Parliament was incensed when colonial protesters filled Boston Harbor with 92,000 pounds of tea (worth almost £10,000 at the time, the equivalent of millions of dollars today). Determined to punish

such wanton destruction of private property and to clamp down on growing political opposition to British policies, Parliament responded with the
Coercive Acts (which Americans called the Intolerable Acts) in the spring
of 1774: Boston's port would be closed; members of Massachusetts' council
(the upper house of the legislature) would be appointed by royal officials
instead of elected in Massachusetts; sheriffs, who were responsible for finding jurors in all criminal cases, would be appointed by the royal governor;
royal officials accused of serious crimes could be transferred to London
for trial, and if colonies failed to provide housing for Redcoats stationed
in their midst, unoccupied buildings could be used without their owners'
permission. In short, until Boston agreed to pay for the tea that had been
destroyed, London intended to control its political life. At about the same
time, Parliament passed the Quebec Act which guaranteed Catholics in
Canada the right to practice their religion (a grave concern to many American Protestants who still feared and hated Catholicism) and announced
that the government in Quebec would be responsible for administering the
lands west of the Allegheny Mountains and north of the Ohio River, lands
which had been claimed by Virginia (and other colonies) and in which Patrick Henry, George Washington, and other colonial leaders had engaged in
land speculation.

Massachusetts called on its sister colonies for support.

The question facing Henry and his colleagues was how they would
respond to the Intolerable Acts. Would Virginia and the other colonies rally
to Massachusetts' defense? After all, while few colonists defended the tax
on tea, many believed that the people of Massachusetts had acted wrongly
in December by destroying the tea, which was private property, and many
were concerned that Massachusetts was rushing needlessly into a conflict
with Britain.

Yet times had changed since 1765 when Henry first announced a direct
challenge to British authority in the House of Burgesses. Jefferson later
explained that "The lead in the house on these subjects [was] no longer left
to the old members." In Virginia, Henry was a leader among the group of
younger, more radical members who quickly came to the defense of Massachusetts, setting a course for what we now know was a coming revolution. Realizing that any direct support for Massachusetts would result in
the royal governor dissolving the House of Burgesses (sending all the representatives home), Henry joined Thomas Jefferson, George Mason, Richard
Henry Lee, and Francis Lightfoot Lee to devise a plan to support Massachusetts in a manner that would be difficult for the governor to oppose: They
convinced conservative Robert Carter Nicholas to propose to the House
of Burgesses that June 1, 1774 be set aside as a day of fasting and prayer
throughout the colony to protest the closing of the Boston Port and support

Massachusetts. The plan was "conducted and prepared . . . by a very few members; of whom Patrick Henry is the principal." Once again, Henry was among those who recognized that adept political maneuvering required consideration of both official action and public opinion. Their choice of a day of fasting and prayer to rally support for Massachusetts' patriots was supported by even the most conservative of Virginia legislators who might otherwise have been hesitant to support the Massachusetts' radicals. Unimpressed, the Royal Governor, Lord Dunmore, dismissed the House of Burgesses anyway, but even Dunmore must have felt the winds of change. The gathering of colonial leaders on June 1 in prayer to support Massachusetts presaged the battles yet to come.[22]

* * * * *

CONTINENTAL CONGRESS

With support for Massachusetts growing throughout the British mainland colonies, and with Committees of Correspondence in active communication about a united colonial response to the Intolerable Acts, the colonies agreed that a Continental Congress should meet in September 1774 in Philadelphia to discuss how best to respond to British actions. Since Governor Dunmore had dissolved the House of Burgesses, the First Virginia Convention – an "unofficial" meeting which very closely resembled the recently dismissed House – elected Virginia's delegation to the First Continental Congress: George Washington, Peyton Randolph, Patrick Henry, Richard Henry Lee, Edmund Pendleton, Benjamin Harrison, and Richard Bland. Some indication of the role that Virginians expected Henry to play in the congress can be gathered from a private letter written at the time in which Henry was described as personally "moderate and mild, and in religious matters a saint; but the very d[evi]l in politics, – a son of thunder. He will shake the Senate."[23]

The Virginia Convention also issued a series of resolutions calling for a boycott of British imports and a prohibition of exports if the Intolerable Acts were not repealed. Most ominously, the Convention's instructions to its delegates to the Continental Congress warned that any action by General Gage to enforce his proclamation against citizens assembling "to consider their grievances" would "justify resistance and reprisal." This was a threat, and it was recognized as such in Britain where the idea of active resistance to a royal official was understood to be treason and a prelude to military conflict.[24]

Henry's election to the Continental Congress was no surprise. He was a spokesman for the people, "the instrument by whom the big-wigs were to be thrown down, and liberty and independence established," William

Roane, a member of the House of Burgesses, told his son Spencer (who years later would become a son-in-law of Patrick Henry). Still, as he rode toward Philadelphia, leaving Virginia for the first time in his life, Henry found himself entering onto a larger stage. The delegates faced a difficult task and were quickly approaching open rebellion.[25]

In Philadelphia, Henry met many of the leading political figures from 12 American colonies and quickly became an active member. Very early in the congress, he warned that British "Fleets and armies and the present state of things show that government is dissolved," that British oppression had returned the colonies to a "State of Nature." When Henry insisted that "The distinctions between Virginians, Pennsylvanians, New Yorkers, and New Englanders, are no more. I am not a Virginian, but an American," he cemented his position as a vigorous defender of American liberties. (As explained in the Introduction, he was also arguing, unsuccessfully, that colonies with large populations, including Virginia, should receive more weight in voting than smaller states.)[26]

Henry's work at the Continental Congress, though, was not limited to powerful oratory. Initially he was appointed to a committee reviewing the impact of British commercial and trade laws upon America. After that committee produced its report, Henry was added to the committee preparing a report on colonial rights. Henry also served on the important committee preparing a petition for the King. The first report from that committee, though, had to be rewritten; apparently some delegates thought it too forceful in its demands. Later, based on hearsay, Jefferson used this incident as evidence of Henry's alleged incompetence, saying that Henry had prepared the original draft that was rejected. The truth of the matter is more difficult to discern. In any case, while Henry's written documents might have lacked the eloquence of Jefferson or the diplomacy of John Dickinson, there is little question that Henry's support for aggressive opposition to British efforts to enforce taxes in America and, more broadly, to control the colonists was greatly appreciated by other delegates.

Still, there was a fundamental tension at the Congress about how far the colonies would or should go in their opposition to Britain's policy. Henry was an early advocate of firm measures and, by the end of the Congress, was coming to the conclusion that independence might be the ultimate result of the conflict. He was undoubtedly pleased when, on September 17, the Continental Congress received a copy of resolves from Suffolk County, Massachusetts, adopting a boycott of British goods and urging the colonies to arm to oppose British repression militarily if necessary. (He would take up the topic of military preparation in his most famous speech a few months later.) Most delegates, however, continued to favor some reconciliation with Britain which preserved American rights.

On September 28, 1774, Joseph Galloway, a moderate delegate from Pennsylvania (who would become a British loyalist during the Revolution), proposed to the congress a "Plan of Union" with Great Britain. The plan provided for an American council which would function much like Parliament. The council would be responsible for internal matters in the colonies and would cooperate with the Parliament in London on external matters. The King would continue to be the head of the government. (The proposal was not unlike the Commonwealth System that Britain adopted in the nineteenth century for governance of its colonies, such as Canada and Australia.) Had it been adopted by the Continental Congress, and it apparently failed by only one state vote, this plan might have moved the colonies to take a far more conciliatory approach. The radicals in the Congress, one might say the realists, vigorously opposed the plan because if adopted it would put a hold on the boiling opposition to British restrictions, eliminating the patriots' momentum, and there was little chance that Parliament would actually accept the proposal. Historians often see the rejection of Galloway's plan as a turning point for the colonies (although, even had it been adopted, it is almost inconceivable that the British Parliament would have accepted the plan).

The only recorded speech in opposition to Galloway's compromise was from Patrick Henry. He insisted that if Britain wished to impose taxes in America, Americans should have all the rights of British citizens. For example, he knew that British Navigation Acts decreased the price that could be obtained for American products and increased the price of consumer goods; as a result, he specifically included the right to trade freely with the entire world among the rights that Britain should provide America if it wished to resolve the dispute. He also opposed other aspects of Galloway's plan. Echoing concerns that he would express 14 years later in debates over the federal Constitution, he simply could not agree that a powerful but distant government should control Virginia or any other colony. During his time in Philadelphia, Henry certainly established himself as a leader among the radicals.[27]

With Galloway's plan rejected, the most important substantive action to come out of the First Continental Congress was adoption of an "Association" by which its members pledged to stop imports and consumption of products from Britain or the East India Company, to stop the importation of slaves (a lucrative business for Britain), and after some delay which would allow southerners to ship their current crop of tobacco, to stop exports as well. Critical to its success, the Congress asked that county committees be formed to enforce the Association. Henry was soon to demonstrate how crucial such local organizations would be to the revolutionary movement.

By the end of October the Congress was over, and the delegates were pleased with their work. Many believed, or certainly hoped, that their firm stance would result in Britain withdrawing the Intolerable Acts and the duty on tea. Realists were less convinced. As the delegates prepared to leave Philadelphia, John Adams, a leading radical from the leading radical colony, Massachusetts, shared with the Virginian from Hanover County a letter from another Massachusetts patriot, Joseph Hawley. Hawley, who had helped to lead opposition in Massachusetts to the Stamp Act, had written to Adams that "We must fight if we cannot otherwise rid ourselves of British taxation . . . It is evil against right, – utterly intolerable to every man who has any idea or feeling of right or liberty." Henry listened as Adams read Hawley's letter and then declared: "By God, I am of that man's mind." (Henry would repeat the admonition "we must fight" in his famous "Liberty or Death" speech in early 1775.) From that time forward, Adams felt that Henry was a reliable supporter of Massachusetts' and America's struggle. Years later, in recollections about the start of the Revolution, John Adams wrote that "In the Congress of 1774 there was not one member, except Patrick Henry, who appeared to me Sensible of the Precipice or rather the pinnacle on which he stood, and had candour and courage enough to acknowledge it." Henry may have lacked the formal education of some other patriots, the finesse of their arguments over political theory and diplomacy, or their eloquent writing style, but few contemporaries could match Henry for a piercing vision and voice.[28]

Upon returning to Virginia, Henry joined the colony's most popular leaders in supporting the continental boycott of British goods and the restrictions on exports to Britain, as well as the Congress' suggestion that this "Association" be enforced by county committees of safety. In Virginia, as at the Continental Congress, there was little question of Henry's leading role and where his sympathies lay. Henry reportedly confided to Hanover County neighbors that he thought war with Britain inevitable, and "A desperate and bloody touch it will be." That concern was evident in the decision of Hanover men in November 1774 to form a company of volunteers, a military unit separate from the county militia that was still ostensibly controlled by the royal governor. Henry's involvement with the Hanover Volunteers would prove important in the events to come.[29]

Unfortunately, the intervening months had done nothing to ease tensions with Britain. British officials were largely ignoring American petitions, and responding to reports that Americans were arming themselves, British governors were ordered to seize excess ammunition and armaments and prevent importation of gunpowder and military supplies from other nations. Given conditions in Massachusetts, including several thousand Redcoats occupying the town of Boston, General Thomas Gage, the British governor of Massachusetts and military leader in the colonies, was sitting on a powder keg. It seemed that a spark was inevitable.

* * * * *

LIBERTY OR DEATH

In March 1775, the Second Virginia Convention met in Richmond's St. John's Episcopal Church (see Document 1). The Virginia Conventions were technically unofficial bodies, but they were quickly becoming the only effective government in the colony. The key issue facing the Convention in early 1775 was the question of preparation for a possible military conflict. The topic had been introduced into the First Continental Congress when it received the Suffolk (Massachusetts) Resolves urging that local militias be raised in response to the Intolerable Acts. With the congress' endorsement of those Resolves, the question was obviously spreading. Several Virginia counties had joined the call for military preparation, but many of the Convention's members were initially unwilling to take such a momentous and provocative step.

On March 23, Patrick Henry rose to propose that Virginia be put in a "state of defence [sic]" and to make his most famous speech. Rejecting the hope that a reconciliation could be achieved short of open conflict, Henry referred to the troops and ships patrolling Boston's streets and harbor: "what means this martial array, if its purpose be not to force us to submission?" England was not compromising or retreating; it was sending troops and ships. American patriots had no choice. Henry told the delegates "we must fight! – I repeat it, sir, we must fight!!!" Henry recognized that many Virginians supported American rights but were afraid of an open break with Britain, the eighteenth-century's superpower. Responding to the meek of heart, he insisted that America, "armed in the holy cause of liberty, and in such a country as that which we possess," could bid defiance to the world. Besides, Henry insisted that men who cared about freedom had no choice. Less than four weeks before the Battle of Lexington and Concord, Henry mocked his opponents: "Gentlemen may cry, peace, peace – but there is no peace." Then he thundered: "The war is actually begun!" Henry's ringing speech seemed prophetic: "The next gale that sweeps from the north will bring to our ears the clash of resounding arms! Our brethren are already in the field! Why stand we here idle? What is it that gentlemen wish? What would they have?" The great orator concluded with words that would be famous shortly after their echo died in St. John's: "Is life so dear, or peace so sweet, as to be purchased at the price of chains, and slavery? Forbid it, Almighty God! – I know not what course others may take; but as for me, give me liberty, or give me death!" (see Document 5).

Henry's declamation was initially met with stunned silence; the delegates were thunder-struck. It was a call to arms against Britain, the mother country and greatest military power in Europe. Henry's imagery and words left an indelible mark on those who witnessed the event. One observer said: "The sound of his voice, as he spoke these memorable words, was like that of a Spartan paean on the field of Plataca [sic] . . . He stood like a Roman senator defying Caesar, while the unconquerable spirit of Cato of Utica flashed from every feature;[iii] and he closed the grand appeal . . . with the awful cadence of a hero's dirge, *fearless* of death."[30]

After a moment's hesitation, Richard Henry Lee rose to second Henry's call for military preparation, and Thomas Jefferson, Thomas Nelson, Jr., and others joined-in. Compelled forward by the force of Henry's words, the Convention voted to prepare Virginia for a possible war. Two days later the Convention elected Henry, along with Washington, Jefferson, Lee, Peyton Randolph, and others, to the Second Continental Congress.

It is worth pausing to consider several important aspects of this famous speech. As with other Henry speeches, the text was not recorded at the time, and what is now remembered – what was memorized by thousands of school children over two centuries – is only a synthesis of memories written years after the fact (see the Appendix). There can be no doubt, though, that Henry stirred listeners; his speech was overwhelming. Jefferson remembered that Henry "was impressive and sublime beyond what can be imagined." Edward Carrington, soon to be a Revolutionary War officer and representative to the Confederation Congress, was listening at a window in St. John's Church and was so moved that with Henry's words ringing in his ears he struck the ground and declared "Let me be buried at this spot!" – a wish later granted. One Virginia Tory wrote "You never heard anything more infamously insolent than P. Henry's speech." By June 20, word had reached the president of Yale in Connecticut that "Every Member of the House of Burgesses has cloathed himself in Homespun & has each on the breast of his Coat these words wrote with Needlework or painting LIBERTY OR DEATH . . . There is a grand & noble spirit in Virginia!" In the days ahead, Virginia minutemen from Culpeper and surrounding counties would march into battle with "Liberty or Death" emblazoned across their hunting shirts and flag.[31]

These words from Henry were not new; Henry was almost certainly borrowing from the very popular eighteenth-century play "Cato," a favorite of George Washington, in which the Roman republican hero, Cato, fighting

---

iii A paean is a victory song of praise. Plataea was the critical battle when Greeks expelled a Persian invasion in 479 BC. Cato was a senator in the Roman republic who defied Caesar's rise as a dictator and chose death to living under tyranny.

the dictator Julius Caesar, declared that it was time to speak of nothing but "liberty or death." This type of use of striking phrases from earlier authors was well accepted in the eighteenth century; in fact, it was a mark of the learning of the speaker.

It was not merely the words, though, that made Henry's speech so powerful. Both the force of his presentation and the logic of his political arguments drove men forward. With respect to the former, some sense of the stylized nature of Henry's speaking can be gained by the detailed reports of how he delivered the famous ending to this speech. While Henry had, as he often did, started speaking in a low and moderate tone, his oration rose to a crescendo. Asking "Is life so dear, or peace so sweet, as to be purchased at the price of chains, and slavery?" Henry bowed down with his wrists together as if bound in chains. Declaring "forbid it almighty God," he seemed to burst the chains and rise to his whole height. Taking an ivory letter opener, he turned on opponents of military preparation and, warning: "I know not what course others may take, but as for me, give me liberty," he lifted the letter opener above his chest and with his conclusion, "or give me death," appeared to plunge the blade into his chest as Cato had done rather than living under a tyrant. Today, such melodramatics would be seen as almost comical, but eighteenth century listeners – not influenced by the drone of television, movies, and the internet – sat dumbstruck. Henry "by his imagination, which painted to the soul, eclipsed the sparklings of art," Edmund Randolph explained. He knew "what chord of the heart would sound in unison with his immediate purpose, and with what strength or peculiarity it ought to be touched." No one knew better than Patrick Henry how to move an audience to action – be they members of the legislature or jurors.[32]

Even after Henry's speech, strong opposition to arming against Britain was evident; Henry's resolutions passed the Convention only by a vote of 65 to 60. Still, the weight of that opposition should not be overstated; once the decision to arm was made, Henry and his firebrands were appointed to head the committee drawing up plans for mobilization, an important concession that was not missed by British leaders. Henry had led Virginia across a Rubicon.

Incensed by reports of the Convention meeting in Richmond, Virginia's royal governor, Lord Dunmore, decided to execute his orders to seize munitions. On the evening of April 20, just one day after the battle of Lexington and Concord (although with the state of communications no one in Virginia at the time could be aware of that battle), Dunmore sent marines from the British schooner, *HMS Magdalen*, to seize the gunpowder stored in the public magazine in Williamsburg. When the night watch saw the sailors taking the powder early in the morning of the 21st, the town was alerted, and a violent attack on the Governor's Palace – perhaps a second Lexington and Concord – was prevented only by the call for calm by local colonial leaders like Peyton Randolph (also the president of the Continental Congress).

Patrick Henry was not to be so easily satisfied.

When news reached Hanover County of the Governor's seizure of the gunpowder in Williamsburg, Henry called together the local volunteer companies to discuss a response. By the time that the Hanover Volunteers met on May 2, news of the Battles of Lexington and Concord on April 19 had been published in the *Virginia Gazette* (April 29), and the people were mightily agitated. Seeing what lay ahead, Henry was already quietly talking to friends and family about the need for American independence. Henry reminded his neighbors of the farms at Lexington and Concord where spring plowing had been interrupted by British attacks and fields had been watered with the blood of Americans fighting in the common cause. He warned that the theft of the gunpowder was part of the same program of subjugation. Appealing to God, Henry assured the men of the justice of their claim and that with firmness they would succeed: "the same God . . . still reigned in all his glory, unchanged and unchangeable – was still the enemy of the oppressor." A decision was quickly made to take action. With many of the volunteers on horseback and armed, their normal officer resigned, and Henry was elected to lead them into Williamsburg to demand return of the powder. It is noteworthy that a similar gathering of volunteer companies in Fredericksburg dispersed after receiving assurances from Peyton Randolph that the incident was being addressed; Henry and his followers were not so easily dissuaded. Marching slowly toward the colonial capital, each mile that they moved east increased the concern of the royal government and those in Virginia who still hoped to avoid an open conflict. The miles also increased the size of Henry's force as men from around the region joined his ranks. Reportedly he left Hanover with 150 well-armed men, but by the time he reached Doncastle Ordinary, about 15 miles from Williamsburg, the force had swelled. A military confrontation seemed inevitable until Henry received a promissory note (essentially a check) from the colonial Receiver-General of taxes, Richard Corbin, for the value of the powder that had been taken. These funds were then turned over to the Virginia delegates to the Continental Congress for assisting in the defense of the colony. Henry had demonstrated that royal officials could not simply seize American property and that a firm military response to royal over-reaching was possible. For Henry, one biographer explained, the march on Williamsburg was a great opportunity, it "would rally the apathetic and rout the cautious." And so it proved. Counties from throughout Virginia sent notes of thanks and congratulations to Henry. Governor Dunmore, not surprisingly, declared Henry a rebel on May 6, but he was a local hero, and the governor could not seriously think that he could actually seize Henry.[33]

Henry made his second (and final) trip outside of Virginia in the spring of 1775 to attend the Second Continental Congress where he joined in the actions that prepared for a war, including formation of the Continental Army and appointment of George Washington to command. Henry and Washington seemed to share a special confidence at this time; after his appointment as general, Washington transmitted his first questions for the congress through Henry. In spite of some strains which developed over the years (or were encouraged by political rivals), Henry's support of Washington would not waiver, and they would maintain a close and important relationship through 1799, the year in which both died.

In terms of the day-to-day business of the Second Congress, Henry was appointed to several committees, but his involvement in Philadelphia in 1775 was undoubtedly less noted than in 1774. Jefferson, writing years later after their bitter political feud had erupted, claimed that "I found mr Henry to be a silent, & almost unmedling member in Congress" in 1775. Jefferson thought that the time of "splendid eloquence" was past, replaced by "cool-headed, reflecting, judicious men." According to Jefferson, in such an environment, Henry knew that he had little to add to the work of congress. By comparison, John Adams, who could be a sharp critic, knew Henry in the First and Second Congresses and told his biographer that he found him a man of "deep reflection, keen sagacity, clear foresight, daring enterprise, inflexible intrepidity and untainted integrity." Although Henry was undoubtedly not the accomplished legal draftsman that Jefferson was, the continued appointment of Henry to important committees suggests that his colleagues shared Adams' views. Still, with the congress seemingly inactive, Henry was likely pleased to return to Virginia in August when the Continental Congress recessed; back home, he was elected commander-in-chief of Virginia's incipient military forces by the Virginia Convention.[34]

This military post, Henry's only formal military position, was to prove a serious disappointment for Henry. While the whole Convention had elected Henry to the position, the political leaders on Virginia's Committee of Safety responsible for directing day-to-day military action tended to be conservatives who still hoped to avoid a full-scale war. In their minds, they had several reasons not to trust Henry: He lacked military experience. He was too willing to embrace the military conflict rather than compromise. He had become too popular with the people to be safely trusted with military command. (In fact, suggestions that Henry might seize power swirled about Virginia off and on for the next ten years, but there is no evidence that Henry ever participated in or supported any such plans.)

In any case, as a result of their suspicions, the Committee of Safety kept Henry inactive while subordinate commanders were given the opportunity for military action, most notably at the Battle of Great Bridge on December 9, 1775 where Lord Dunmore's "Ethiopian Regiment" (made up of formerly enslaved recruits who had fled to British lines in response to Dunmore's promise of freedom) and a group of Redcoats, marines, and Tories were soundly defeated by patriot volunteers wearing hunting shirts declaring "liberty or death." (Ironically, the uniforms for the Ethiopian Regiment declared "liberty for slaves.") Adding insult to injury, the Committee of Safety encouraged Henry's subordinate commander to report directly to the Committee rather than through their commanding officer, leaving Henry ill-informed of what his own men were doing. Later, when it appeared that the Virginia regiments would become part of the Continental Army, the Committee nominated someone else to be a brigadier general for Virginia's troops, leaving Henry a colonel. This was a clear insult to the honor of a proud eighteenth-century gentleman. Angry and embarrassed, in February 1776, Henry resigned his commission as commander-in-chief in Virginia and returned to the House of Delegates in April, in time for some of the most important political decisions of the war.

Many of the men serving under Henry were deeply disappointed by his resignation; some threatened to leave the service given his shabby treatment by conservative political leaders. Henry, dedicated to the cause more than his own position, met with the men to urge them to continue to support the patriots as he turned back to politics. His efforts were critical in preserving Virginia's military companies.

Henry would never again have a military position, and while it is certainly true that the Committee of Safety had treated him poorly, one cannot be too disappointed that he was sent back into politics. George Washington perhaps summed-up the situation best in saying that Virginia had "made a Capitol mistake when they took Henry out of the Senate to place him in the Field." Back in the Virginia Convention, Henry's great skills would continue to shine.[35]

Notes

1. For a discussion of the interrelationship of the tax and control issues, see Jack P. Greene, *The Constitutional Origins of the American Revolution* (New York: Cambridge University Press, 2011).

2. One way in which such taxes worked was for government to issue paper money to pay debts and make necessary purchases; then a tax could be imposed payable in the paper currency. When those taxes were collected, the paper currency would be destroyed – the paper currency allowed the government to buy what it needed, and the tax ensured that the paper currency maintained its value. Robinson had been lending paper money that had been collected for destruction.

3. Thomas Jefferson to William Wirt, August 14, 1814, *The Papers of Thomas Jefferson* (Digital Edition), eds. Barbara B. Oberg and J. Jefferson Looney, vol. 7 (Charlottesville: University of Virginia Press, Rotunda, 2008–2015): 545.

4. When Robinson died in 1766, the loan scheme was discovered. The scandal rocked Virginia. Many of the borrowers faced additional financial distress, and Robinson's estate would not be settled until 1808. The colony sought to avoid a similar occurrence by preventing one person from acquiring such political power; at a minimum, the Speaker of the House of Burgesses and the Treasurer would be different people in the future.

5. At least one newspaper reported that members had left Williamsburg because they did not want to confront likely proposals for action against the Stamp Act. See, e.g., *South Carolina Gazette*, August 24, 1865: "many of the members, I suppose knowing what was to come on, and irresolute on how to act, – retired, – so that there was but a very thin house." Most historians note simply that members left early because of the spring planting season.

6. See Jefferson's autobiography, quoted Meade, *Patrick Henry*, I: 173.

7. Letter from Edmund Pendleton to James Madison, April 21, 1790, in Edmund S. Morgan, ed., "Edmund Pendleton on the Virginia Resolves," *Maryland Historical Magazine* XLVI: 2 (June 1951): 75.

8. *Journal of the House of Burgesses of Virginia, 1761–1765*, ed. by John Pendleton Kennedy (Richmond, 1907): lxviii. Jefferson gives us the quote from Randolph, although Jefferson's recollections demonstrate the necessity of viewing eye-witness reports, even from famous Founding Fathers, with some caution. Over the years, Jefferson reported both that Randolph would have given 100 guineas for a vote and, at another time, it was 500 guineas. Compare Letter from Thomas Jefferson to William Wirt, August 14, 1814, *Papers of Thomas Jefferson*, 7: 547 and *Journals of the House . . ., 1761–1765*, lxvi. Either would have been a princely sum. A guinea was a gold piece initially worth 1 pound sterling.

9. Henry, *Patrick Henry*, I: 99. The best treatment of the crisis continues to be Edmund S. Morgan and Helen M. Morgan, *The Stamp Act Crisis: Prologue to Revolution* (Chapel Hill: University of North Carolina Press, 1953).

10. Henry, *Patrick Henry*, I: 90.

11. Henry, *Patrick Henry*, I: 148. John Adams' Diary (August 22, 1770), *The Adams Papers* (Digital Edition), ed. by C. James Taylor (Charlottesville: University of Virginia Press, 2008–2015).

12. Mark Couvillon, *Patrick Henry's Virginia* (Red Hill, VA: Patrick Henry Memorial Foundation, 2001): 50.

13. See generally Ragosta, *Wellspring of Liberty*.

14. Henry, *Patrick Henry*, I: 118–119.

15. William Henry Foote, *Sketches of Virginia Historical and Biographical* (1850, reprint, Richmond: John Knox Press, 1966): 161.

16. Henry, *Patrick Henry*, I: 152–153, II: 309.

17. Morgan, *True Patrick Henry*, 458. See generally Paul Finkelman, *Slavery and the Founders: Race and Liberty in the Age of Jefferson* (Armonk, NY: M.E. Sharpe, 1996).

18. Letter from Patrick Henry to Anne Henry Roane, 1786, Henry, *Patrick Henry*, II: 309.

19. See generally Edmund S. Morgan, "Slavery and Freedom: The American Paradox," *The Journal of American History*, 59:1 (Jun., 1972): 5-29.

20. Henry, *Patrick Henry*, I: 114.

21. *Journal of the House of Burgesses*, March 12, 1773, 23. Notes of Daniel Webster, Curtis, *Life of Daniel Webster*, I: 584–85.

22. *Papers of Thomas Jefferson*, I: 106. "Letter from George Mason to Martin Cockburn," May 26, 1774, *Virginia Register and Literary Note Book* (January 1850): 3: 28.

23. Letter from Roger Atkinson to Samuel Pleasants, in Bishop William Meade, *Old Churches, Ministers and Families of Virginia*, 2 vols. (1857, reprint, Baltimore, MD: Geneological Publishing Co., Inc., 1978): 1: 220.

24. Henry, *Patrick Henry*, I: 201–202.

25. Memorandum of Spencer Roane to William Wirt, Morgan, *True Patrick Henry*, 442.
26. Burnett, *Letters of Members*, I: 12 (James Duane). William Wirt Henry, *Patrick Henry: Life, Correspondence and Speeches*, vol. I (New York: Charles Scribner's Sons, 1891): 221–222 (quoting John Adams diary). Georgia initially did not send delegates to the First Continental Congress largely because it needed military assistance from Britain to address Indian conflicts, and it could not afford to antagonize officials in London.
27. *Letters of Members*, I: 53.
28. Henry, *Patrick Henry*, I: 239, quoting John Adams' Diary. Letter from John Adams to Thomas Jefferson, November 12, 1813, *Papers of Thomas Jefferson* (Retirement Series), 6: 612.
29. Robert Douthat Meade, *Patrick Henry: Practical Revolutionary*, vol. 2 (Philadelphia, PA: J. B. Lippincott Co., 1969): 3.
30. Fontaine, *Corrections*, 27 (emphasis original).
31. Curtis, *Life of Webster*, I: 584. Henry, *Patrick Henry*, I: 270. Meade, *Patrick Henry*, II: 36. Franklin Bowditch Dexter, ed., *The Literary Diary of Ezra Stiles, D.D., LL.D.*, vol. 1 (New York: Charles Scriber's Sons, 1901): 574–575.
32. Fontaine, *Corrections*, 27. Edmund Randolph, *History of Virginia*, ed. by Arthur H. Shaffer (Charlottesville: University of Virginia Press, 1970): 179.
33. Wirt, *Sketches*, 106. Henry, *Patrick Henry*, II: 241, 279–280. Henry Mayer, *A Son of Thunder: Patrick Henry and the American Republic* (New York: Franklin Watts, 1986): 252. By early 1775, a bill introduced into the English Parliament offered a full pardon to American rebels who would renew their loyalty to Britain; about 20 Americans were excluded from the offer, one of them being Patrick Henry. Henry, *Patrick Henry*, I: 254.
34. Jefferson's Notes on Patrick Henry, April 12, 1812, *Papers of Thomas Jefferson* (Retirement Series), 4: 602. Tyler, *Patrick Henry*, 110.
35. Letter from George Washington to Joseph Reed, February 26–March 9, 1776, *The Papers of George Washington* (Digital Edition), Revolutionary War Series, ed. by Theodore J. Crackel (Charlottesville: University of Virginia Press, 2008): 3: 374.

CHAPTER 3

WAR GOVERNOR AND LEGISLATOR

In American history, the period between 1776 and 1783 is generally remembered for the fighting of the Revolutionary War. George Washington and the Continental Army maneuvered across the former colonies, losing more battles than they won, until they captured General Charles Cornwallis and his army at Yorktown, Virginia, in October 1781. Other commanders rose and fell with the fortunes of war: General Horatio Gates, supported by thousands of New England militiamen, famously captured General John Burgoyne's army at Saratoga, New York, late in 1777 before Gates infamously ran from a resounding defeat as his army disintegrated at Camden, South Carolina, in 1780. General Benjamin Lincoln surrendered Charleston to the British in 1780, before Generals Nathaniel Greene and Daniel Morgan ran the Redcoats ragged across the south in 1781. In 1783, the Paris Peace Treaty was finally signed.

While the military conflict was certainly important, it is easy to forget the difficult work of nation-building and governance that was going on at the same time across the fledgling country. Providing soldiers and supplies, maintaining civil peace and a functioning government and economy, preventing or suppressing Loyalist insurrections, and protecting the frontiers from Britain's Indian allies were all equally essential to the success of the United States and presented new problems that were no less complex than those facing Washington and his soldiers. Patrick Henry was in the midst of those battles on the home front.

* * * * *

On May 15, 1776, the Virginia Convention unanimously adopted resolutions calling on Virginia's delegates to the Second Continental Congress to file a formal motion for independence. When introduced in congress a few weeks later, this resolution provided a key stepping stone to the Declaration of Independence adopted on July 4, a story which is well told elsewhere. Years later, Edmund Randolph reported that the critical Virginia resolution for independence "was drawn by [Edmund] Pendleton; was offered in Committee by [Thomas] Nelson; and was sustained, against all opposition, by Henry, with that unbounded energy and eloquence of which he was master." Henry wrote to John Adams that he had hoped that the resolution would be worded more strongly, but the unanimity of the Convention was critical evidence of Virginia's resolve. Henry believed that only by declaring independence would America gain the foreign allies which were essential to success against Britain; continued hesitation threatened to undermine the war effort. After Virginia's independence resolution was adopted, a relieved Henry wrote to Richard Henry Lee that "Moderation, falsely so called, hath nearly brought on us final ruin."[1]

If Virginia and the other states were to be independent, though, they would need new and effective governments. The famous May 15 independence resolution adopted by the Virginia Convention also called on Virginia to draft a new plan for its own government and a bill of rights. In June of 1776, after several weeks of frenzied activity, the Convention adopted Virginia's Declaration of Rights and a new constitution for the independent Commonwealth of Virginia.

As one of the foremost members of that Convention, Henry was placed on the critical drafting committee for the Virginia Constitution of 1776 and was deeply involved in the debates leading to its adoption. Jefferson (who was in Philadelphia attending the Second Continental Congress and writing the Declaration of Independence) saw these state constitutional debates as the essential element of the Revolution – formation of new governments being "the whole object of the present controversy," and he desperately wished that he could be in Virginia as the new government was formed. Unfortunately for historians, much of the work of the Virginia Convention occurred in the Committee of the Whole – a meeting of all of the members in which the proceedings and debates were not recorded. Still, Henry undoubtedly played a large role and is known to have been personally involved in at least two important aspects of the debates.[2]

First, the issue of religious freedom and of religious dissenters – those who were not members of the legally-established Anglican Church – continued to fester in Virginia. Many of Virginia's younger political leaders, including Henry, supported an end to legal discrimination and persecution on principle. Beyond that, with dissenters accounting for one-fifth to one-third of Virginia's population and their numbers still growing, something had to be done if their full support was to be obtained for the war effort. Unfortunately for these purposes, many of the Anglicans who had been deeply involved in the attacks on the dissenters were also leaders of the patriot movement. As a result, some dissenters asked why they should support a revolution for liberty led by those who had denied them religious freedom. The planned Declaration of Rights which was to preface the new state constitution had to address the issue.

The initial draft of the Declaration of Rights was prepared by George Mason, and he suggested that those dissenting from the Anglican Church should receive the "fullest tolerance in the exercise of religion." By the standards of the day, this was a very liberal provision. Yet, a new delegate, a young James Madison serving his first term in the legislature, thought that this was not good enough: Stating that different religions were only "tolerated" implied that the government had chosen a preferred religion but was willing (perhaps grudgingly) to permit dissenters to practice their religions. Madison insisted that government had no business choosing a preferred religion and that what was needed was religious freedom, a much broader concept than mere toleration. Being a new member (and always somewhat shy about public speaking), Madison sought the assistance of a more senior member to introduce an amendment to Mason's "tolerance" proposal. He turned to Patrick Henry who was immensely popular and known to sympathize with religious dissenters. Henry agreed to introduce a very broad proposal drafted by Madison: "all men are equally entitled to the full and free exercise of [Religion] . . . and therefore that no man or class of men ought, on account of religion to be invested with peculiar emoluments or privileges."[3]

Unfortunately, after introducing this amendment, when asked whether it would mean the disestablishment of the Anglican Church, Henry was apparently caught unprepared and said that it would not – although the words clearly suggested otherwise; the confusion killed the amendment. Madison was forced to enlist another delegate, Edmund Pendleton, to propose a somewhat weaker, but still important proposal that "all men are equally entitled to the free exercise of religion." When adopted, this was the first written guarantee of religious freedom (as opposed to toleration) in a foundational government document. In spite of the fumbling of the original amendment, Henry's support was undoubtedly significant (although some earlier historians mistakenly credited Henry with Madison's contribution).[4]

Ensuring religious freedom was important to the war effort, and Henry was active, both before and after the adoption of the Declaration of Rights, in successfully encouraging dissenters to support the war. Nonetheless, in the years ahead, the proper role of religious freedom would continue to be debated, and over time, Henry and Madison would become opponents on the issue as Madison sought an even clearer separation of church and state.

The second issue presented by Virginia's new constitution in which Henry played a particularly prominent, but less successful role was the question of executive authority. Fighting a revolution against the King of England, many patriots were particularly reluctant to give a new governor "kingly" powers; in particular, there was a strong opposition to giving the governor any veto authority over the popularly-elected legislature. Henry, who, to no one's surprise, would become the first governor of the new Commonwealth, was not afraid to express the unpopular view that the governor needed some veto authority if he was to function effectively and maintain reasonable checks and balances on the legislature.

Two things about this episode are interesting: While most of his colleagues were so obsessed with their battle with King George that they lost sight of the need for a balanced government, Henry seemed to see more clearly and relied on better political science. For example, in early 1776, foreseeing the task of government formation ahead, John Adams produced an essay called "Thoughts on Government," which was widely read by those working on state constitutions, including Henry. In his "Thoughts," Adams recognized the need for checks and balances, including some type of veto authority in a governor. Henry explained to Richard Henry Lee that "I own myself a democratic on the plan of our admired friend, J. Adams, whose pamphlet I read with great pleasure." Notably, Henry was not a supporter of a plan like that adopted in Pennsylvania which put all power in a single house, popularly-elected legislature, a radical democracy which would prove to be unstable. As with Adams, while no one was a stronger supporter of American independence, there was a certain conservatism in Henry's support of a balanced government. When communicating with Henry about the drafting of the Virginia Constitution, Adams was confident that Henry would ensure a good result. "I know of none so competent to the task as the author of the first Virginia resolutions against the stamp act, who will have the glory with posterity, of beginning and concluding this great revolution. Happy Virginia, whose Constitution is to be framed by so masterly a Builder!"[5]

Still, the debate over the executive veto raised sensitive political issues, with most of the delegates and people opposed to creating a powerful governor with king-like powers. Certainly Henry was no aristocrat; in the same letter to Richard Henry Lee he declared that "Perhaps I am mistaken, but I fear too great a bias to Aristocracy prevails among the opulent." Yet, his support for broad powers in the governor put many other patriots ill at ease. Only Henry's popularity and the trust of the people shielded him from claims that he was seeking to increase the governor's power knowing that he would be governor or, worse, that he supported monarchical powers. "No member but Henry," Edmund Randolph later explained, "could with impunity to his popularity have contended as strenuously as he did for an executive veto on the acts of the two houses of legislation." The bias against any significant executive power, however, could not be overcome, and Virginia's first constitution gave the governor no authority to veto legislation. Later developments would demonstrate that Henry's vision had been clearer.[6]

Immediately after the Virginia Constitution was adopted in June 1776, Henry was elected by the legislature to his first of three consecutive one-year terms as governor, the most permitted under the constitution. Not only would he face the challenge of being the first governor under a new constitution, plagued with necessary appointments and requests for office, but he did so in the midst of a difficult war requiring the governor's attention to numerous both mundane and monumental tasks. Henry deeply felt the weight of his new responsibilities. In accepting the position, he recognized that "from the events of this war the lasting happiness or misery of a great proportion of the human species will finally result." At times, the strain showed, and he was almost overwhelmed. His health suffered; in fact, Henry fought regular bouts with malaria as governor, his first very shortly after his inauguration. But he knew that if the war was lost, he and others would be treated as British traitors, and his efforts continued largely unabated.[7]

As the governor of the largest and most populous state, Henry corresponded with the Congress, General Washington and other military commanders, and domestic and foreign officials as Virginia struggled to support the war effort and maintain some semblance of a functioning economy. The most immediate and pressing of his duties was to ensure that Virginia met its obligations for troop requisitions from the Continental Congress and to facilitate the movement of supplies to the Continental Army. While the Revolutionary War was to prove a challenge for all of the new states, and none fully met the requisitions coming from the congress, Virginia under Henry was in the forefront of the Revolution.

Less than half way through Henry's initial three years in office, Washington's army found itself suffering and starving at Valley Forge. When Washington sent governors of nearby states pleas for emergency support, Henry immediately took action. Arguably overstepping his authority, Henry sent a flurry of letters intended to direct cattle and sheep to the army. He also directed shipments of clothing to Valley Forge. Not satisfied, he berated Congress for having allowed the supply situation for the Continental Army to reach such dire straits. These types of problems would plague the new wartime governor throughout his first three terms, and he would maintain a firm commitment to trying to provide for the troops who were fighting the Revolutionary War (perhaps influenced by his earlier, brief experience in the military).

Virginia's own resources, though, were also proving too thin for the extended war. Before the war, when questioned about how the colonies might defeat the world's strongest navy and army, Henry had soundly advised that the assistance of foreign nations – France, Spain, and Holland – would be needed. Once independence was declared, Henry thought that a foreign alliance should be made, but with the authority of the Continental Congress and the states unclear, foreign negotiations could not simply be left to the national government. Helping to encourage foreign nations to support the war effort became a particular interest of Virginia's first governor. By October 1777, Henry was corresponding with the governor of Cuba, a Spanish colony, to encourage trade for military supplies and other necessities. With Virginia's financial resources almost exhausted, the state, with Henry's support, was able to negotiate a crucial and timely loan from France in 1779. Henry also worked to ensure an effective alliance between France and the national government. When France signed a treaty of alliance with the United States in early 1778 after General Burgoyne's army of Redcoats and Hessians was captured at Saratoga, Henry was quick to urge support for that alliance. He was distressed when reports arrived in Virginia in early 1778 that Britain was sending peace commissioners to the United States in an effort to pre-empt the French treaty by offering concessions to the United States (but still refusing to grant full independence). In a letter to Richard Henry Lee, one of Virginia's representatives to the Continental Congress, Governor Henry fumed: "Surely Congress will never recede from our French friends. Salvation to America depends upon our holding fast our attachment to them. I shall date our ruin from the moment that it [the French alliance] is exchanged for anything Great Britain can say or do." Congress resisted Britain's efforts to bring the United States back into the British Empire, and Virginia's governor continued his tireless efforts trying to ensure that the war would be a success.[8]

Three other episodes which deeply involved Governor Henry during the war are worth considering. First, as the governor of the largest state, Henry found himself unavoidably involved in the political intrigues surrounding Congress and the army. By the end of 1777, some in Congress had lost faith in George Washington's ability – after all, he had lost New York and Philadelphia. At the same time, Horatio Gates had secured a spectacular victory at Saratoga, capturing the British army under Burgoyne by effectively rallying local militia. Perhaps Gates should be made commander of the main Continental Army some suggested, and Washington-skeptics began to lobby for his removal. While historians can today dismiss the so-called Conway Cabal as only a limited threat to Washington's leadership, at the time, with confusion and consternation over American defeats, the risk seemed very real; certainly, Washington was deeply upset by the episode.

If the cabal was going to be successful, however, it would need the support of key leaders in the states. Thus, in January 1778, Governor Patrick Henry received an anonymous letter suggesting that Washington had failed and should be replaced by Gates. Shocked, Henry immediately forwarded the letter to Washington. "I am sorry," the governor wrote, "there should be one man who counts himself my friend who is not yours . . . I really think your personal welfare and the happiness of America are intimately connected." Washington wrote back to express his appreciation: "Your friendship, Sir, in transmitting to me the anonymous Letter you had received, lays me under the most grateful obligations." Washington recognized the handwriting on the letter to Henry as that of Benjamin Rush, a former member of Congress from Philadelphia and an erstwhile friend of Washington's. With notice of the efforts against him, General Washington easily protected his command. Washington, though, never forgot Henry's cooperation and support during this crisis, and their mutual respect and admiration were cemented. Years later, when Washington was president and political opponents tried to stir up disagreements between Henry and him, Washington wrote that "I have always respected and esteemed him [Henry]; nay more, I have conceived myself under obligations to him for the friendly manner in which he transmitted to me some insidious anonymous writings that were sent to him in the close of the year 1777, with a view to embark him in the opposition that was forming against me at the time." Henry played an important role in Virginia with his steadfast support for Washington and the Continental Army.[9]

Second, while the focus of the war was on the east – battles for New York City, Philadelphia, Charleston, and the Hudson Valley – the first governor of Virginia was also deeply concerned about the west. Not only did he have to ensure that western frontiersmen were adequately organized and supplied to fight Britain's Native American allies, but he bristled at the fact that Redcoats controlled most of what was called the Northwest Territories (today the states of Ohio, Indiana, Illinois, Michigan, and Wisconsin), territory that Virginia claimed. Initially, the patriots seemed to be entirely on the defensive in the west. Complicating matters, ongoing conflict between settlers and Indians often inflamed relations with the Native Americans and provided fuel for British recruiting efforts among the Natives. For example, in November 1777, when American militiamen in present-day West Virginia murdered Cornstalk, a Shawnee chief who had tried to maintain Shawnee neutrality in the war, it understandably enraged many Indians in the area. Henry, watching from Williamsburg, was equally outraged and, with limited options, made every effort to bring the murderers to justice. Realizing that the Shawnee were likely to join the British after the murder, Henry wrote to one of the local militia commanders:

> I must tell you, Sir, that I really Blush for the occasion of this War with the Shawaneese. I doubt not but you detest the vile assassins who have brought it on us at this Critical Time, when our whole Force was wanted in another Quarter. But why are they not bro' to Justice? . . . Some say the people of your Country will not suffer the apprehension of the murderers. I desire it may be remembered

that if the Frontier people will not submit to the Laws, but thus set them at defiance, they will not be considered as entitled to the protection of Government; and were it not for the miserable condition of many with you, I should demand the delivery of the offenders previous to any other step.

Henry told the commander that the military aid requested by the frontiersman would be provided "In the confidence that what I now press, I mean bringing the Murderers of the Indians to Justice, will be done." Unfortunately, while some men were arrested for the murder, no one would testify against them, and they were released.[10]

At about this time, Governor Henry realized that attacks would continue in the west, and western conflict would continue to divert resources from the eastern war, if something was not done to drive the British from the Northwest Territories and prevent them from supplying Native Americans with arms and ammunition. In December 1777, when George Rogers Clark of Kentucky approached Henry about the possibility of military action against Redcoats and their Native allies in what had been "French Country," the governor seized the opportunity. Henry realized that secrecy and prompt action were necessary and that presenting the proposal to either the Virginia legislature or the Continental Congress would undermine its chances of success. After consulting secretly with a select group of legislators, including Thomas Jefferson, George Mason, and George Wythe, Henry obtained authorization from Virginia's Council on January 2, 1778 to supply Clark with the money and commission, as well as the secret orders needed to launch his campaign. In those orders, Henry urged Clark forward, reminding him that "great things have been done by a few men." Clark's success in capturing the British forts at Kaskaskia, Cahokia, and Vincennes (in what would become Illinois and Indiana) would prove important in relieving pressure from Indian attacks on the frontier and breaking up a major British-Native offensive that had been planned for 1779. Long term, the consequences were even greater as Clark's conquest would be an important factor in the decision of the peace commissioners in 1783 to make the old northwest part of the new United States.[11]

Once the conquest was made, ensuring that the region would become loyal to the United States was equally critical. By the end of 1778, Governor Henry was writing to John Todd, the new Illinois County Lieutenant (a militia official appointed by Virginia), urging him to work with the local French and Spanish to consolidate authority and to try to stop additional Indian attacks. Always the revolutionary spokesman, he suggested that the French and Spanish settlers who lived in the territory be reminded of the advantages of being incorporated into the United States. "A free and equal representation may be expected by them in a little time," Henry assured them, "together with all the Improvements in Jurisprudence which the other parts of the State enjoy." Writing to George Rogers Clark the same day, Henry urged his support of Todd's mission and included for Clark a copy of the Virginia Constitution, the Declaration of Rights, and the treaty with France "to show our new friends the ground upon which they are to stand." Not forgetting that injustice had contributed to the Indian warfare on the frontier, Henry implored the Illinois County lieutenant to "discourage every attempt to violate the property of the Indians, particularly in their lands. Our enemys [sic] have alarmed them much on that score."[12]

The third interesting episode during Henry's wartime terms as governor involved the problems resulting from the breakdown of authority. War often contributes to lawlessness, but the problem is particularly acute in a civil war. This is especially true where, as in the American Revolution, there is a significant population loyal to the old regime, in this case the King and Parliament of Britain. While Virginia had one of the smallest contingents of loyalists among the new states during the war, there were still those in Virginia who sought to undermine the war effort or who used the war as cover for criminal behavior or to settle old scores. Bandits could rob and pillage while claiming to do so in support of Britain (in the hopes that they would be treated as military prisoners rather than criminals if caught and that they might gain some protection from the British). The state was left with a thorny problem of civil rights: how to stop criminal behavior masquerading as acts of war? While fighting for liberty and protection of rights, could the new state undermine the rights of others?

The most serious challenge in Virginia in this regard came from a notorious bandit named Josiah Philips who claimed that the marauding by his gang in the Norfolk area was authorized by the (former) royal governor, Dunmore. Frustrated with the inability of the local militia to catch Philips and concerned that failure to take action against an active outlaw band posed a risk to the state, Henry supported an "attainder," a legislative decision of outlawry. Under an attainder, if caught, Philips could be hung without the benefit of trial.[i] When Philips was eventually caught, there was apparently a good deal of hesitation about applying an attainder and hanging the man and several members of his gang without a trial. While the record is not perfectly clear as to what happened or why, evidently to avoid any questions, Virginia's Attorney General, Edmund Randolph, had Philips brought to trial for theft through regular procedures, after which he was duly convicted and hung.

---

i Bills of attainder are unconstitutional in the United States, but the U.S. Constitution, adopted in 1789, obviously did not apply to Virginia in 1778. Still, the principle that attainders were an affront to civil rights certainly was known.

One of the reasons that this episode became so infamous, and a potential black mark on Henry's governorship, is that it was brought up ten years later during the 1788 Virginia Convention that was considering ratification of the U.S. Constitution (the centerpiece of the next chapter). At that time, Randolph used the fact that Henry had supported the act of attainder, even though it had never really been used, to attack the former governor's character and suggest that he was not a consistent advocate of civil rights. Adding substance to Randolph's attack, Henry had opposed outlawing attainders in the 1776 Virginia Constitution, believing that unexpected circumstances could arise during the Revolution making it necessary to take extreme measures.

Given wartime conditions, Randolph's criticism rang a bit hollow. Even Jefferson, hardly a Henry ally by that point, reported in 1814 that "The censure of mr. E. Randolph on mr Henry in the case of Philips, was without foundation . . . Philips was a mere robber, who availing himself of the troubles of the times, collected a banditti . . . plundering and maltreating the neighboring inhabitants, and covering himself, without authority, under the name of a British subject." (Of course, Jefferson himself had cooperated in the legislature's decision to enact the attainder and may have been unduly defensive about the process.) In the end, while some of the details seem to be lost to history, this was at best a minor scar on Henry's very successful career as Virginia's wartime governor, but it appears regularly in biographies, and it is a good example of the daily difficulties faced by Henry as he attempted to launch Virginia's first government independent of Britain and maintain order in a state at war.[13]

These three actions – Henry's support of Washington, his effort to invigorate the western war effort, and the problem of maintaining civil order – are emblematic of the extraordinary troubles that Henry faced as Virginia's first governor during what was a cataclysmic war. Overall, he acted energetically and wisely in a difficult and complicated position. Not surprisingly, though, he also experienced his share of failures.

Beyond his important administrative duties, being the state's first governor demanded that Henry set a proper tone and establish appropriate protocols and precedents for the chief magistrate in the new state (an issue that George Washington would grapple with 20 years later as the first president under the U.S. Constitution). Realizing that he had been seen as a bit of a backwoods legislator, Henry made a point to project the dignity of the office of governor. Living in the former royal governor's palace in Williamsburg (see Document 1), Henry was certainly living in more style than that to which he had been accustomed. His dress also improved. Judge Spencer Roane (a son-in-law) reported later that, as governor, Henry "rarely appeared in the streets, and never without a scarlet cloak, black clothes, and a dressed wig." While Henry never lost his warm feelings for his country neighbors, an astute politician, he did learn to act the part of governor.[14]

After Henry's governorships ended in 1779 (the 1776 Virginia Constitution permitted only three consecutive one-year terms in a seven-year period), Virginia's General Assembly elected Henry to be a representative to the Continental Congress, but he declined, saying that his health would not allow him to take on such a strenuous job so far from home. Henry hoped that he would have some rest and time with his family. He had sold the Scotchtown Plantation in Henrico County in 1777 and the next year bought a majority interest in the massive Leatherwood Plantation (16,650 acres) in southern Virginia's Henry County (named after the governor). It was there that he moved in late 1779 after leaving Williamsburg. The war was still raging, however, and Henry's new neighbors would not allow him to withdraw from public service. In the spring of 1780, he was elected to the Virginia General Assembly and returned to the public debates, now being held in Richmond. (In 1779, Jefferson, the second governor, had urged the legislature to move the capital to Richmond in what would prove to be a vain hope that a more inland location would be safer from British raids.)

In the General Assembly, Henry immediately became a leading member and continued his hard work to support the struggling patriot cause. By 1780, both the Continental Army and the economy seemed to be on the verge of collapse. Among Henry's notable efforts in the General Assembly was his work to prop-up the crumbling currency.

Some background is needed to understand this issue. One of the most serious problems facing the new nation as it attempted to wage the Revolution was how to pay for it: How were soldiers to be paid? How were supplies to be purchased? Where would the money for ships and armaments come from? The Continental Congress and various state legislatures had cobbled together answers to these questions as best they could. While taxes would be the obvious answer, it was notoriously difficult to collect taxes in the midst of a war, especially since much of the trade throughout America had been cut off; politically, it was equally difficult for legislators to impose high taxes when the people were facing economic hardships and many were being asked to enlist. France made several generous grants, and money was borrowed from France, Spain, and the Netherlands, but this could not meet all of the needs. By default, the essential means to finance the war became the printing of paper money.

The idea was that the governments would print paper money and use it to purchase what they needed; people would accept the paper currency expecting that at some point the government would impose taxes which could be paid with the paper. If a person was confident that taxes would eventually be imposed payable in the paper currency, he or she would continue to value the new paper and be willing to accept it as payment for goods or services. If taxes were not collected, over time, the paper supplied by the government became increasingly worthless. The worry was that if you accepted the paper currency in return for goods or services, you might not later be able to get others to accept the paper when you needed to buy something. As a result, many people insisted upon species (gold or silver) or some other form of payment. Adding to the problem, counterfeiting was rampant (and encouraged by the British). As the war dragged on, as a result of counterfeiting and loss of confidence in the governments, the value of the money that had been printed to pay soldiers and buy supplies was quickly dropping.

In 1777, at Governor Henry's urging, Virginia passed a tax to support its paper currency, but tax collection was not consistent and taxes were not large enough to fund the war. This resulted in a downward spiral in the value of Virginia's paper currency. The same occurred to currency printed by the Continental Congress and the other new states. The longer the war continued without adequate efforts to collect taxes, the more paper currency was printed, and the more value the currency lost. By 1780, the currency had effectively collapsed; the paper was becoming almost worthless (leading to the phrase "not worth a Continental," referring to Continental currency). This was especially painful for the soldiers and small farmers who relied upon the paper money that they had been paid for fighting in the patriot cause or for providing supplies.

Congress was aware of the problem and proposed to the states that the crisis be addressed by requiring the states to collect the "old" paper currency through taxes (or pay $1 of gold or silver for every $40 of paper money outstanding); Congress would then issue "new" paper currency, but only one-twentieth of the amount of the old paper currency. When the plan came before the May 1780 Virginia Assembly, Henry opposed it, thinking that this would hurt farmers and soldiers the most. Recognizing that something had to be done to support the value of the old money, he encouraged a taxation scheme that would give stability to the funds by allowing the state's paper debt to be retired over 15 years. While there had initially been overwhelming support for the congressional plan (which seemed the easy way out of the predicament), given Henry's argument and his immense popularity, he convinced the delegates to reject Congress' plan and to adopt the tax scheme. Unfortunately, after that vote, Henry had to return to Leatherwood for his health, and shortly after Henry left Richmond, the legislature reversed itself and adopted the proposal of the Continental Congress to pay only $1 for $40 in paper money and to replace the existing paper money with "new" paper money. As Henry had anticipated, this scheme did not work, and the currency continued to depreciate.

This is not the place for a thorough review of the intricacies of Revolutionary War finance, but several things stand out about this incident: Henry's concern for soldiers and small farmers, Henry's leading role in the legislature, and his willingness to push politically-unpopular ideas (like taxes) when sound policy dictated. As Virginia continued to struggle with the war effort, his colleagues clearly saw Henry as a leader. (Even in ceremonial matters, Henry was given special consideration. For example, he was given the honor of nominating Jefferson for a second one-year term as governor in June of 1780, returning a favor as Jefferson had re-nominated Henry several years earlier.) It also again demonstrates that while Henry has sometimes been characterized as a demagogue without understanding or appreciation of complex policy matters, his actions as a legislator in the final years of the war and the first years of peace tell a different story.

As Jefferson's second year as governor began, the war continued to go poorly. In January 1781, Virginia was invaded by British forces led by the hated traitor, Benedict Arnold. By early May, General Cornwallis arrived from North Carolina with additional British troops, and Virginia, after six years of supporting a war that was being fought primarily elsewhere, seemed too exhausted to mount an adequate defense. Richmond was easily taken, and Virginia's government was pushed to Charlottesville. In June, Cornwallis sent the infamous Colonel Banastre Tarleton – known as "Bloody Ban" after his troops pillaged large areas of South and North Carolina – to capture the Virginia Assembly in Charlottesville and Jefferson at his hilltop home, Monticello. On June 4, warned at the last minute of the approach of British troops by Jack Jouett, "Virginia's Paul Revere," Jefferson fled with his family toward his Poplar Forest home in Bedford County, 70 miles southwest, as British troops climbed his little mountain. The legislators, with Henry among them, fled precipitously to Staunton, 40 miles west.

An amusing story about Henry's rather unfortunate flight from Charlottesville to Staunton survives. Reportedly Henry and several other hungry, disheveled members of the General Assembly fleeing over the mountains toward Staunton stopped to ask for food and shelter at a rustic home in the woods. The woman of the house, suspicious of the strangers when she answered the door, heard their story and tried to shoo the vagabond politicians on their way, lecturing them that her husband and son had joined the militia gathering west of Charlottesville to defend the Assembly and that they were cowards to have run. Henry tried to explain that the Assembly had to flee; their capture would have been a serious loss for the war effort. "Here is Mr. Speaker Harrison," Henry said, "you don't think he would have fled had it not been necessary?" "I always thought a great deal of Mr. Harrison," the woman said, "till now," she added, turning to close the door. Henry continued to plead from the door that Judge John Tyler and Colonel William Christian were with him, but he received no better response. Finally, Tyler spoke up: "What would you say, my good woman, if I were to tell you that Patrick Henry fled with the rest of us?" The indignant woman turned to confront the legislators: "Patrick Henry! I would tell ye there wasn't a word of truth in it; Patrick Henry would never do such a cowardly thing." A sheepish Henry was left to introduce himself at which the matron yielded. "Well, then, if that's Patrick Henry, *it must be all right.* Come in, and ye shall have the best I have in the house." As with many Henry stories, it is hard to determine the accuracy of the tale, but both the image of a disorganized flight of the legislature and the love and respect for Henry among the common folks of Virginia are certainly true.[15]

When the legislature reconvened in Staunton, Henry again took the lead on several measures, one of which was to lead to Jefferson's lasting and bitter animosity.

When the British attacked Charlottesville, Jefferson's second term as governor was just expiring, and Jefferson had expressed the view that the next governor should have military experience. While no new governor had yet been appointed, Governor Jefferson did not travel to Staunton where the legislature was schedule to reconvene, but left for Poplar Forest; as a result, the state was left without a governor for almost a week as it faced the invaders. Jefferson was probably correct that the new governor should have military experience that he was lacking. The legislature also had to take action to give the governor the tools needed to respond to such crises. Throughout his two terms, Jefferson had struggled to respond forcefully in the face of a war-weary state and the very limited authority given to Virginia's governor by the 1776 constitution. Still, many have criticized Jefferson for not staying on until a successor could be appointed; hindsight certainly suggests that he should have joined the legislature in Staunton. In any case, the first order of business for the legislature once it reconvened was to elect a new governor. Agreeing with Jefferson about the need for military experience and increased powers, the legislature appointed Thomas Nelson, Jr., the commander of Virginia's militia from the "lower" (coastal) counties, and gave the new governor expanded powers to seize supplies and call out the militia – powers that would prove essential as Virginia finally rallied to assist in the defeat of Cornwallis at Yorktown. Patrick Henry could testify from personal experience about the problems of being a wartime governor with very limited authority, and it was significant that he was on the committee that recommended expanding the governor's powers.

Unfortunately, the frustrated Virginia delegates did not stop there. Embarrassed at the failure of Virginia's militia to make any reasonable stand against the invading Redcoats, and questioning Jefferson's flight from Monticello and seeming abdication of the governorship, George Nicholas, a new member of the Assembly and a supporter of Henry's, offered a resolution calling for "an inquiry . . . into the conduct of the Executive of this State for the past twelve months." The motion was actually seconded by Jefferson supporters so that he might have the opportunity to defend himself directly, and the investigation was launched. Nothing in the official record shows that Henry was involved in calling for this investigation, and some historians have questioned it, noting that Henry and Jefferson had been allies and that Henry would be more circumspect knowing better than anyone else the difficulties of governing during wartime with very little power. "There is no evidence to support the accusation, and considerable reason to doubt it," historian Henry Mayer concludes. On the other hand, in the heat of the moment, the fact that Henry was familiar with the difficulties of governing in wartime with limited power, but had not abandoned his post or failed so conspicuously, could have encouraged his support for an investigation. It is noteworthy that among the charges leveled by Nicholas was that Jefferson had failed to accept offers by Colonels Campbell, Christian, and McDowell (two of whom were Patrick Henry's brothers-in-law) to help raise troops for defense. More to the point, while Henry and Jefferson had clearly drifted somewhat apart before this incident, it seems highly unlikely that Jefferson would have blamed Henry without reason to do so, and Jefferson had numerous friends in Staunton who could be expected to report on developments. By December, Jefferson was dismissing the role of Nicholas as "trifling" while apparently referring to Henry as "the whale himself [who] was discoverable enough by the turbulence of the water under which he moved." Years later, during a new political battle between Jefferson and Henry, John Taylor, who was a delegate in Staunton, wrote to James Madison of his anger at Henry for his "conduct respecting Mr. Jefferson at Stantown." Jefferson's conclusion that Henry was behind the investigation, or at least an important supporter of it, is almost certainly correct.[16]

Ultimately, nothing formal came of the investigation. Jefferson prepared a detailed defense, but before the investigation really got underway, the Continental Army, its French allies, and the Virginia militia (led by Governor Nelson) captured Lord Cornwallis' army at Yorktown. While it would take two more years for the official treaty of peace to be signed, everyone understood that the war had been won. The investigation of Jefferson now seemed petty, and perhaps ill-advised in the first place. The inquiry was quietly dropped and the Assembly (including Henry) unanimously voted Jefferson its thanks for his years of service as governor, stating "in the strongest manner . . . the high opinion which they entertain of Mr. Jefferson's Ability, Rectitude, and Integrity as cheif [sic] Magistrate."[17]

In spite of the legislature's decision to withdraw the investigation and offer its thanks, the proud Jefferson was genuinely hurt, and he blamed Henry. He moaned to James Monroe that the investigation "inflicted a wound on my spirit which only will be cured by the all-healing grave." Given the other political and personal battles that Jefferson fought throughout his life, this is a remarkable statement; this assault on his honor wounded deeply. Perhaps Jefferson felt personally betrayed; as a young man, Jefferson had seen Henry as a leader of the patriot movement, someone whom he sought to emulate. Whatever the cause, he would never forgive Henry. This is certainly one of the critical elements of Jefferson's aggressive effort to smear Henry's reputation for almost 50 years. Within a year, Jefferson is writing that Henry is "all tongue without either head or heart." Mayer, although wrongly discounting Henry's role in the investigation, was correct that "a wounded Jefferson nursed his grudge for a long time, went out of his way to cast aspersions on Henry's character, and implied that Henry had sought 'dictatorial' powers himself," an issue addressed below. (Interestingly, George Nicholas later acknowledged that he had acted wrongly in seeking the investigation, and Jefferson and he became good friends and political allies.)[18]

While the details of how the aborted investigation was launched are not entirely clear, and while Henry and Jefferson (and Jefferson's friend, James Madison) would clash in the 1780s on other important issues, it is certain that Jefferson's deep antipathy of Patrick Henry existed after 1781.[19]

Before leaving Henry's role in Virginia's government during the Revolution, one must confront a persistent criticism of Henry's role: After the war, there were several reports that Virginia, faced with revolutionary crises, considered the temporary appointment of a dictator, a plan that some thought Henry supported.

One might begin by putting loaded terms into context: The Roman Republic had been known to appoint a "dictator" with extensive powers for a short period of time when the safety of the city was threatened, and after safety was restored, the dictator was expected to step down. (The famous Cincinnatus was made Roman dictator in a crisis, but after defeating an invading army, he stepped-down to return to his farm. In memory of his example, George Washington is often referred to as the American Cincinnatus.) If someone suggested the appointment of a dictator in eighteenth-century Virginia, it would have been understood that the suggestion was not for a leader with unlimited power or tenure. In fact, it was later argued that the extensive powers given to the commander-in-chief by the Continental Congress in 1781 essentially made Washington a dictator for a period of time. Yet, in spite of classical precedents, providing such extensive power to one individual in the midst of a revolution against monarchical and aristocratic power would certainly have raised serious issues, and the threat of abuse of power was always present.

There is very little detail concerning reports that the Virginia General Assembly considered appointing Henry a dictator in 1776. Apparently accepting the stories, Henry's first biographer, William Wirt, repeats the legend that Archibald Cary, the first speaker of Virginia's Senate, one day accosted Colonel John Syme, Henry's half-brother, about the reports. "I am told that your brother wishes to be dictator," the volatile Cary fumed. "[T]ell him from me, that the day of his appointment shall be the day of his death – for he shall feel my dagger in his heart before the sunset of that day." Tradition has it that Syme responded heatedly that Patrick Henry was not involved in any such efforts and that there was nothing more foreign to his character. Governor Henry was granted some additional powers in December of 1776 to assist with the war effort, but these fell far short of anything that could be termed dictatorial. Greater powers, for example, were given to Jefferson, the second governor. Nor did the members of the Assembly seem to think that Henry had abused his powers. In fact, Henry was re-elected two times after 1776 with overwhelming support (the first time without opposition, the second time unanimously), and under Henry's leadership, the state and its new constitution seemed to function relatively well.[20]

There is more information concerning the proposals to give the governor extensive powers, arguably dictatorial powers, in 1781 after the British had chased the legislature and governor out of Richmond and out of Charlottesville. Apparently, George Nicholas (the same delegate who launched the investigation of Jefferson) proposed to recall George Washington and make him a dictator during the crisis. (While Washington was busy with the Continental Army near New York City, a number of Virginians had pleaded with him to return to Virginia to protect it from invasion, which he would eventually do by trapping Cornwallis at Yorktown with the assistance of the French army and navy.) General Nathaniel Greene was also apparently discussed as a possible dictator. Henry seconded the suggestion made by Nicholas, while noting that the title of the post was unimportant, it might be called dictator or a governor with expanded power. Still, there is no evidence that Henry assumed that he would be chosen (although he certainly was aware that, other than Washington, the post would likely be his for the asking). As things turned-out, Thomas Nelson, Jr., was elected governor, and while not receiving the title of dictator, he was given extensive powers to deal with the crisis. As a general matter, the proposal was quickly forgotten after the victory at Yorktown. There is little if any evidence that Henry ever sought "dictatorial" powers and seems to be very little reason to censor Henry for his role in the affair.[21]

Others have argued that the charge that Henry wished to assume dictatorial powers originated with Thomas Jefferson after his falling-out with Henry in 1781 and that Henry was never named as a supporter of such efforts until after his death, when he could no longer defend himself.

Henry's great grandson wrote that "The only contemporaneous evidence which has been brought to establish the charge, is that of Thomas Jefferson . . . [who] was not with the Legislature, on either occasion." This is true with respect to the 1776 episode; but in the second instance, in 1781, the legislature undoubtedly contemplated extending the governor's powers, although evidence that Henry expected to assume that role is far from clear. It is evident, though, that reports on these episodes were significantly influenced by personal and political battles. For example, Louis Girardin – a great Jefferson devotee who wrote the final volume of Burk's *History of Virginia* under Jefferson's guidance – is another leading source of the story that Henry was involved. Girardin wrote that in 1781, in order to support the plan to appoint a dictator, "it was necessary to place Mr. Jefferson *hors de combat.*" Yet, it was Jefferson who took himself *"hors de combat"* (outside the fight) when he fled with his family to Poplar Forest rather than meeting the legislature in Staunton. Perhaps the best summary of these episodes comes from the traditional story of the response of John Syme, Henry's half-brother, to Archibald Cary: there is no evidence that Henry himself sought dictatorial powers, even temporarily.[22]

* * * * *

One cannot pass from the war years without recognizing that Henry's family life took on a new and happier complexion even in the midst of the Revolution's trials. After being devastated by the death of Sarah in 1775, Governor Henry found a new love, the beautiful and well-connected Dorothea Dandridge. On October 9, 1777, Henry (41 years old) married the young Dorothea (different sources give her age as 20 or 22). Dandridge brought to the marriage not only considerable wealth (e.g., increasing Henry's ownership of slaves from 30 to 42) but also important family connections. (The Dandridges were an old and wealthy Virginia family. Dorothea was a first cousin once removed of Martha Washington and a granddaughter of former Governor Spotswood.) The young Dorothea was immediately propelled into a highly visible, public position and had to take on the responsibility of raising Henry's six children from his first marriage, the youngest only six years old. In time, Dorothea and Patrick would have 11 children of their own, the first three – Dorothea, Sarah, and Martha – born while the war continued. Curiously, Henry likely met the very young Dorothea at the Christmas party at her father's house in 1759, the same party at which he met Thomas Jefferson traveling on his way to college.

The match, while a very happy one for the governor, was not without its difficulties. It appears that Henry's eldest son, John, then a captain in the

Continental Army, had also been enamored with Dorothea Dandridge and had by some reports hoped to marry her. John had a mental breakdown after walking the corpse-strewn battlefield at Saratoga in October 1777, where he had fought with distinction; his breakdown may have been related to receiving word of his father's marriage to Dorothea, a report that Governor Henry apparently believed. (John's life would continue to be troubled. He eventually married Susannah Walker, but died in 1791 at the age of 34; see Document 2).

In any case, his new wife certainly must have brought a great deal of joy to the war-weary governor. The marriage would also have a dramatic impact upon Henry's future. The very substantial growth in the size of his family, and the need to provide for his growing brood, would eventually encourage Henry's decision to leave office and to return to the law and to large-scale land speculation to earn money.

* * * * *

After 1781, with the war apparently won (although the formal peace treaty would not be signed until 1783 and some combat would continue until then), Henry continued to play a dominant role in Virginia politics and was the force behind many developments in the General Assembly. Much of the Assembly's work in this period related to day-to-day government operations and economic issues as the states struggled to pay their war debts and grapple with a post-war economy. Henry, of course, continued to support Virginia's small, hard-working farmers.

Henry also became an active proponent of healing the wounds that separated people in society, in particular seeking the reintegration of loyalists into the new nation and the assimilation of Native Americans. (Henry and many others, including George Washington, Thomas Jefferson, and Henry Knox, thought assimilation would be the best for Natives who were being pushed out of their traditional homes and hunting grounds by settlers; in reaching that conclusion, they apparently did not consult the Natives.) Unfortunately, Henry was not successful on these matters, although they do speak to Henry's principles. At the same time, Henry became a leading advocate of denying British creditors their rights to sue for pre-war debts, a topic that would engage his efforts well into the 1790s.

In early 1783, a debate erupted in the General Assembly over what to do about loyalists who had fled Virginia during the Revolution. Henry, the Trumpet of the Revolution, rose to argue in favor of permitting loyalists to return with the full rights of citizens. John Tyler, speaker of the House of Delegates, was astonished that Henry, of all people, would be advocating for loyalists, but Henry explained that his personal feelings had nothing to do with the question. "On the altar of his country's good he was willing to sacrifice all personal resentments, all private wrongs." His logic was powerful: "We have, sir, an extensive country, *without population*," Henry explained; "what can be a more obvious policy than that this country ought to be peopled? – *people*, sir, form the strength, and constitute the wealth of a nation." Henry chided his opponents who seemed to fear allowing people who might still be loyal to Britain to return; with independence won, there was nothing to fear from the loyalists. "Afraid of *them*! – what, sir, shall *we*, who have laid the proud British *lion* at our feet, now be afraid of his *whelps*?" In the same session, Henry supported a resolution to repeal the prohibition on trade with Britain.[23]

Henry also proposed that the state seek a treaty to encourage amicable relations with Native Americans in the vain hope of ending conflict on the frontier. In the same vein, he encouraged intermarriage of Native Americans and those of European ancestry, introducing a bill that would pay a bounty for intermarriage and for each child of a Native-white couple, as well as specifying that the children of such couples would have all of the rights of white citizens. Henry's proposal applied both to white men marrying Indian women and white women marrying Indian men. He likely thought that such intermarriage would increase the population of the state while integrating Natives into Virginia's culture and reducing the risk of frontier wars. While Henry's goals may have been laudable, he was still clearly a man of his time, and Natives seem to have had little interest in assimilation. In any case, the bill failed to become a law after Henry was again made governor in 1784, removing the bill's strongest advocate from the legislature.

While Henry proposed liberal terms for British loyalists who had been born in America and fled during the war, he was a firm supporter of wartime confiscations of loyalist property and was opposed to allowing British creditors to enforce debts from before the war which had been "confiscated" under Virginia law. This was an issue with a long history. For many years, large debts owed by many Virginians to English and Scottish merchants (referred to as "factors") had been a sore subject. Before the war, there had been a pattern of tobacco planters (large and small) buying British goods on credit based upon the expected value of their next tobacco crops, and when the money received for their crops fell short, they ran up debt. The causes were myriad: Certainly many Virginians spent beyond their means, buying luxuries that they could not afford. Henry had warned against such extravagance as early as 1765. At the same time, British mercantilist policies – demanding shipment on British ships and direct sales only to Britain (subject to a large tax) – dramatically reduced planters' incomes and increased the price of imports. Henry understood this to be unfair. Some historians believe that mounting debt owed by Virginians and other colonists to British merchants actually encouraged the war; the theory being that as it became apparent that the debts could not realistically be paid, war became a convenient excuse to disavow debts to British merchants. This was certainly not Henry's view, but the war did change things in his eyes.[24]

Henry believed that British tyranny had forced America into a bloody and costly war. He blamed Britain for devastating losses, for example the burning of Norfolk and the loss of trade. As a result, and given the dire financial straits of the new state, by mid-1776, "a general confiscation of Royal and British property" was urged by Henry. He supported laws which "confiscated" any debt owed to British merchants and permitted Virginians to pay those debts to the Virginia government rather than to the British creditor (and to use depreciated paper currency to do so). Unfortunately for Virginians who took advantage of that law, the Paris Peace Treaty of 1783 guaranteed British merchants the right to collect their debts. This would continue to be an issue for another dozen years, and Henry would be one of the lead attorneys on the British debts case which eventually made its way to the Supreme Court (where the Court sided with the British creditors, a case discussed more fully in Chapter 5). In any case, in the immediate post-war years, Henry was a known advocate of the confiscation laws which claimed to have eliminated debt to British merchants, and he sought to defend those laws in the legislature.[25]

* * * * *

In addition to these legislative battles, in 1784, Henry became deeply involved in another critical debate over religious freedom. This time, unlike the situation in 1776, Henry found himself in conflict with James Madison and Jefferson (although Jefferson was at the time ambassador in Paris). The debate involved the proper role of government in supporting religion, and the debate that these Founders joined in 1784 continues in key respects to this day.

Over the course of the Revolutionary War, the taxes which had paid Anglican ministers' salaries and maintained Anglican churches were eliminated, and dissenters from the Church of England (Presbyterians, Baptists, Quakers, Lutherans, and others) received progressively more rights. At the end of the war, though, there was some confusion on how best to proceed with respect to religion and religious freedom. The Anglican Church (soon to be the American Episcopal Church) still benefited from several legal advantages: In most counties, Anglican vestries were still responsible for poor relief and care of orphans (and sometimes discriminated in favor of Anglicans); non-Anglican ministers were now permitted to perform marriages, but only in the county in which they were licensed, and the question of the official role of the Anglican Church had not been resolved.

Henry, like most Americans in the era, supported some level of religious freedom, but there was a broad difference of opinion about what such freedom should mean. Many people, especially evangelical dissenters from the established church and Enlightenment rationalists like Jefferson and Madison, supported a strict separation of church and state. Others, including Henry, agreed that government should not discriminate among churches (or at least not among Christian, or perhaps Protestant, churches), picking one as a preferred church, but thought that government support for religion was appropriate, if not necessary. Still others, especially in New England, continued to support an established church but thought that dissenters (at least Christian or Protestant dissenters) should be tolerated. The question that presented itself in Virginia was how to define religious freedom more clearly. How far should church and state be separated?

Henry was a deeply religious man who believed that religious people would make better citizens; they would be concerned for their neighbors and nation and be willing to make the sacrifices needed for a well-functioning republic. In eighteenth-century terms, they would have virtue. As a result, Henry was very concerned by the apparent decline of religion during the war. Perhaps it was not surprising that Anglican churches had suffered during the war; the king of England was, after all, the head of the Anglican Church. With the end of official tax support many Anglican priests had to find other jobs; others returned to Britain. But many other churches also suffered from economic hardship and wartime dislocation and destruction. To many, it was no coincidence that speculation, hoarding, and other private vices flourished while churches declined. Henry feared that this decline in virtue threatened the new nation, and he sought some way to renew what was now called the Episcopal Church (of which he was a life-long member) and to support other churches.

Many people agreed with Henry that virtuous citizens were needed in a republic and shared his hope that religion would flourish in the young nation, believing that religion encouraged virtue. The question for Henry and other Virginia legislators was whether the government had an essential, or even appropriate, role in supporting the churches. Or could religion flourish – indeed, might it do better – if government left religion to private individuals?

In 1784, Henry became one of the most vocal supporters of a plan that he thought could achieve all of the desired ends: a general tax assessment to support Christian religious leaders and churches. The idea was to impose a tax on all citizens, but to allow each to specify which minister would receive his or her tax dollars. For Henry, such broad support of religion would be fair, promote virtuous citizens, and not interfere with religious freedom because it did not discriminate among Christian churches.[ii] Many other leaders supported the General Assessment as well, including Richard Henry Lee, John Marshall, and Benjamin Harrison. In essence, Henry supported non-discriminatory government aid to religion. (Today, such direct aid to religion would violate the First Amendment separation of church and state, although several justices, notably Justices Scalia and Thomas, would support such aid.)[26]

Opposing Henry, Madison and his allies wanted religious freedom to be defined broadly to mean more than just non-discrimination. While Madison agreed that a republic needed virtuous citizens and that religion promoted virtue, he believed that government could best promote religion by leaving it alone. On principle, he insisted that government had no business supporting religion or taking a position on such personal matters; the proper position was a separation of church and state. Importantly, most of Virginia's evangelicals (primarily Presbyterians and Baptists at this time) joined Madison in opposing the religious General Assessment. Based on their experience with an officially-established church, and with strong theological reasons against government interference in faith, they believed that mixing church and state would corrupt both. Like Madison and Jefferson, they preferred a strong separation of church and state best reflected in Jefferson's proposed Bill for Establishing Religious Freedom.

The conflicting positions resulted in complicated political maneuvering and what was a massive (by eighteenth-century standards) petitioning campaign in support of separation of church and state. Henry initially led the legislators who supported a general assessment, but in the midst of the heated battle over the issue, Henry was again elected to the post of governor, removing him from the General Assembly. Many believed that removing Henry, the Assessment's most effective supporter, was an important factor in the ultimate defeat of the General Assessment and adoption of Jefferson's Statute for Establishing Religious Freedom in 1786. (Some historians go so far as to say Henry was glad to be removed from the Assembly so that he

---

ii There was an exception for Quakers, who lacked a formal ministry, and if citizens failed to specify a minister, their taxes would be allocated to support education, although most schools at the time were religiously-affiliated. Although Catholicism was repressed during the colonial era, there were a few Catholics in Virginia, and while there were no Catholic priests in the state, on its face, the law also applied to Catholics. (After the Revolution several states continued to restrict religious freedom to Protestants.)

One question is whether Henry and others would have supported a General Assessment that applied to all places of worship, not just Christian churches. While almost all the people in Virginia in 1784 would have described themselves as Christian, there was a small Jewish community and leaders were aware of other religious traditions. Richard Henry Lee, for example, thought that the law should apply to all religions, not just Christianity. Ragosta, *Religious Freedom*, 95. The debates over the General Assessment did not focus on this issue.

could avoid voting on what was becoming the unpopular Assessment proposal, but there is little evidence to support that argument.)

While Henry suffered defeat in this legislative battle, it was to prove to be an epic victory for religious freedom. Most historians, and most members of the U.S. Supreme Court, see the Virginia experience of defeating the religious General Assessment proposal and adopting Jefferson's Statute for Establishing Religious Freedom as an important foundation for the First Amendment of the U.S. Constitution and for America's commitment to separation of church and state. Henry, who had been a leading advocate of eliminating discrimination against non-Anglican religious dissenters early in the Revolution, was not willing to go so far. Many also see this as another important and somewhat bitter division between Henry and Jefferson (and Madison).

Even after the defeat of the General Assessment and adoption of Jefferson's Statute, Henry continued to be very concerned about the condition of religion in America and the Episcopal Church. While he remained in the legislature, he was critical of the successful efforts in Virginia to protect the property of the Episcopal Church, which had been bought with tax dollars, from being seized by the government and sold. (A law to seize glebe farms and churches no longer used by the Episcopal Church would be adopted after Henry retired.) As discussed in Chapter 5, his broader concern to protect religion swelled after the French Revolution became increasingly violent and the revolutionaries attacked Christianity. This issue would continue to influence Henry for the rest of his life, and the division with Jefferson, while not the root of their feud, was significant.[27]

* * * * *

Other personal matters also occupied Henry after the victory at Yorktown. By the time he was again elected to the governorship in 1784, he had four children with Dorothea, and more were on the way. Henry believed that to provide for his growing brood he needed to arrange advantageous marriages for his daughters and acquire adequate land and money so that he could leave his sons reasonable plantations and his daughters substantial legacies. (Henry did not see large pieces of land as being necessary for daughters who were well married.) After his fifth term as governor, Henry would return to his practice of law to provide for his growing family and their future.

Given his personal obligations, Henry's acceptance of a fourth term as governor in 1784 might be surprising. Some have suggested that Henry's willingness to return to the governorship was related to his desire to find appropriate suitors for his older daughters, Anne and Elizabeth. Richmond, and the social life of a governor, would be far more conducive to doing so than his home in rural Henry County. Moving from Henry County, the new governor settled at Salisbury in Chesterfield County, several miles west of the new capitol that was being built in Richmond (having been designed by Jefferson). By the time that Henry declined to run for a sixth term as governor in 1786 so that he could return to his farm, both of the young women were engaged to up-and-coming young men in Richmond.

During this period, Henry also suffered some of the inevitable tragedies of life. On November 22, 1784, his mother, to whom he had always been close and devoted, died. Earlier that spring, a favorite brother-in-law, William Christian, died, and his older brother, William, died in 1785. In understanding and honoring Henry's great contributions in public life, it is necessary to remember the substantial commitments that he was facing in his private life at the same time.

Henry's two terms as governor in the mid-1780s were relatively uneventful, but his administration seemed sound. He continued his efforts to encourage peace on the frontiers, issuing a proclamation on January 6, 1785 in an effort to end surveying and settlements in Indian territory north of the Ohio River. The surge of white settlers into Indian lands seemed unstoppable, however.

Henry also took the opportunity of being governor to encourage some criminal law reform (also an important goal for Jefferson). At the time, most serious crimes (including theft) were capital offences: a convicted criminal could be hung. Henry, an experienced criminal lawyer, understood that the punishment often did not fit the crime, and he tried to address the problem by offering some criminals a governor's pardon which required them to serve hard labor. The courts, however, concluded that the governor did not have such authority; the authority to pardon in the Virginia Constitution was an "all or nothing" tool. In response, the legislature gave Henry the authority to issue conditional pardons on all crimes except treason and murder. In this, Henry's humanity put him at the forefront of important penal reforms.

With several daughters married and some legislative victories achieved, in 1786, Henry declined an appointment for a sixth term as governor, in part because the expense of running a home and entertaining as governor "greatly exceeded the salary."[28]

At the same time, the post-war years posed a great challenge for the country as a whole, a challenge that would culminate in the adoption of the U.S. Constitution in 1788, a debate in which Henry would be intimately involved.

Notes

1. See generally Pauline Maier, *American Scripture: Making the Declaration of Independence* (New York: Alfred A. Knopf, 1997). Henry, "Patrick Henry: A Vindication," *Historical Magazine*, 272 *et seq.* See also *Virginia Gazette and General Advertiser* (Richmond), November 2, 1803. *Adams*

Papers, 4: 201. Letter from Patrick Henry to Richard Henry Lee, May 20, 1776, Henry, *Patrick Henry*, I: 411.

2. Letter from Thomas Jefferson to Thomas Nelson, May 16, 1776, *Papers of Thomas Jefferson*, 1: 292.

3. John Ragosta, *Religious Freedom: Jefferson's Legacy, America's Creed* (Charlottesville: University of Virginia Press, 2013): 60–61.

4. Ibid.

5. Letter from Patrick Henry to Richard Henry Lee, May 20, 1776, Henry, *Patrick Henry*, I: 411. Letter from John Adams to Patrick Henry, June 3, 1776, ibid., I: 414.

6. Ibid., I: 411. Randolph, *History of Virginia*, 255.

7. Henry, *Patrick Henry*, I: 447.

8. Letter from Patrick Henry to Richard Henry Lee, June 18, 1778, ibid., I: 565.

9. Letter from Patrick Henry to George Washington, February 20, 1778, *Papers of George Washington*, Revolutionary War Series, 13: 609. Letter from George Washington to Patrick Henry, March 27, 1778, ibid., 14: 328. Letter from George Washington to Henry Lee, August 26, 1794, ibid., Presidential Series, 16: 603.

10. Letter from Patrick Henry to William Preston, County Lieutenant of Montgomery, February 19, 1778, Henry, *Patrick Henry*, III: 146–147.

11. Letter from Patrick Henry to George Rogers Clark, January 2, 1778, in Patrick Henry, *The Secret Orders & . . . Letters of Patrick Henry and George Rogers Clark* (Indianapolis: Indiana Historical Society, 1974).

12. Letter from Patrick Henry to Colonel John Todd, December 12, 1778, Henry, *Patrick Henry*, III: 214–215. Letter from Patrick Henry to George Rogers Clark, December 12, 1778, ibid., III: 210.

13. Letter from Thomas Jefferson to William Wirt, August 14, 1814, *Papers of Thomas Jefferson*, 7: 548. See generally W. P. Trent, "The Case of Josiah Philips," *The American Historical Review*, I: 3 (April 1896): 444–454.

14. Judge Spencer Roane's Memorandum to William Wirt, Morgan, *True Patrick Henry*, 438.

15. The story is recorded in *The Life of John Tyler, President of the United States* (New York: Harper & Brothers, 1843): 10–11.

16. Henry Mayer, "Patrick Henry and Thomas Jefferson," in James M. Elson, ed., *Patrick Henry and Thomas Jefferson* (Brookneal, VA: Patrick Henry Memorial Foundation, 1997): 3. Letter from George Nicholas to Thomas Jefferson, July 31, 1781, *Papers of Thomas Jefferson*, 6: 106. Letter from Thomas Jefferson to Isaac Zane, December 24, 1781, ibid., 6: 143. Letter from John Taylor to James Madison, March 4, 1799, *The Papers of James Madison*, Digital Edition, J. C. A. Stagg, ed. (Charlottesville: University of Virginia Press, 2010): 17: 245.

17. *Journal of the House of Delegates of Virginia*, December 12, 1781, in *Papers of Thomas Jefferson*, 6: 136. Recognizing that he faced enormous problems and did so with limited authority, still, the end of his governorship was not Jefferson's finest hour. The matter is analyzed carefully in Michael Kranish, *Flight from Monticello: Thomas Jefferson at War* (New York: Oxford University Press, 2010).

18. Letter from Thomas Jefferson to James Monroe, May 20, 1782, *Papers of Thomas Jefferson*, 6: 185. Letter from Thomas Jefferson to George Rogers Clark, November 26, 1782, *Papers of Thomas Jefferson*, 6: 205. Mayer, "Patrick Henry and Thomas Jefferson," 3.

19. Some antipathy toward Henry may have antedated the 1781 investigation. For example, after Henry was elected Virginia's first governor, Francis Eppes, Jefferson's brother-in-law, wrote "What a stra[n]ge infatuation attends our Convention. At a time when men of known integrity and sound understanding are most necessary they are rejected and men of shallow understandings fill the most important posts in our country." Letter from Francis Eppes to Thomas Jefferson, July 3, 1776, *Papers of Thomas Jefferson*, 15: 576. Jefferson, wisely, did not respond in writing to this apparent attack on the new governor.

20. Wirt, *Sketches*, 13.

21. Henry, *Patrick Henry*, II: 148. See generally *Papers of Thomas Jefferson*, 6: 85 note, discussing Letter from Archibald Stuart to Thomas Jefferson, September 8, 1818.

22. Henry, "Patrick Henry: A Vindication," 348, 351.

23. Wirt, *Sketches*, 167, 169. Unfortunately, Henry's proposal to permit loyalists to return was defeated. Richard R. Beeman, *Patrick Henry: A Biography* (New York: McGraw-Hill Book Co., 1974): 122.

24. Experience with British trade restrictions was one reason why Henry, and others, became advocates of free trade. In the May 1783 legislative session, Henry argued "Fetter not commerce, sir – let her be as free as the air – she will range the whole creation, and return on the wings of the four winds of heaven, to bless the land with plenty." Henry, *Patrick Henry*, II: 192.

25. Letter from Patrick Henry to Richard Henry Lee, May 20, 1776, Henry, *Patrick Henry*, I: 410.

26. Discussion of the triumph of a Jeffersonian separation of church and state can be found in Ragosta, *Religious Freedom* and works cited therein.

27. Meade, *Old Churches*, I: 221. See generally Ragosta, *Wellspring of Liberty*, 135.

28. Spencer Roane, quoted in Henry, *Patrick Henry*, II: 303.

CHAPTER 4

FIGHTING THE CONSTITUTION

After the American Revolution, the United States faced numerous complex issues and day-to-day problems related to governing a new nation. Thousands of veterans returned from war, many wounded or crippled; most were still owed money for back-pay or enlistment bonuses. They found an economy under stress, an economy that would continue in turmoil for several years after the 1783 Treaty of Paris that settled the war. Some problems resulted simply from demobilization; others resulted from the war's realignment of commercial and trade relationships. For example, before the war, American ships (which were, after all, part of the British Empire) could transport goods to Britain and British colonies; after the war, because of British trade restrictions, U.S. farmers, sailors, and merchants suffered from the inability to ship directly to some of the world's largest markets. Southern plantation owners faced rebuilding after losing tens of thousands, perhaps as many as 100,000, enslaved people, many of whom fled to the British during the war seeking their freedom. Some estimate that by June 1784 American output had shrunk as much as 50 percent, bringing on a deep recession. In the midst of these problems, the loans that France, The Netherlands, Spain, and American citizens had provided to finance the war were due, with precious little money available to pay them. By 1785, the new United States could not pay the interest due on its foreign loans; by 1787, it was in default.[1]

The new nation was also plagued with problems of governance: Loyalists were returning to the country and challenging confiscation laws that had been passed during the war. Many leaders wanted to open the frontier for settlement to satisfy land grants made to soldiers and to fund the government with land sales, but British forces still occupied forts in the Northwest which they had agreed to surrender (including Detroit and Niagara), and their presence encouraged Native resistance. Natives still skillfully defended their lands, and there was no Continental Army capable of pushing them out. States argued over who would control the Northwest; Virginia did not cede its claim to the territory to the United States until 1784.

Equally disturbing to many wealthy politicians and merchants, during and after the war, some states expanded the representation of western farmers and tradesman (the "lesser sort"), meaning that legislatures were less likely to be controlled by the eastern, wealthy elite. As a result, many laws were passed that some thought threatened business. For example, some states allowed debtors to delay payment of their debts; in others, the printing of paper money was continuing and laws mandating that paper money be accepted by businessmen in the place of specie (gold or silver coins) were resulting in rapid inflation and undermining the value of contracts. Laws that favored debtors at the expense of creditors had become popular with new legislators, many of the "middling sort," who owed their elections to small farmers and tradesmen.

In the midst of these challenges, the national government was largely impotent. The Continental Congress had seen the war to a successful conclusion, thanks in no small part to the Continental Army and Washington's leadership, but the army was almost entirely disbanded after a near rebellion among officers at Newburgh, New York, in March 1783, over past-due pay. Washington resigned his commission on December 23, 1783 at Annapolis, Maryland, where Congress was meeting, and returned to Mount Vernon to farm – earning his title as the American Cincinnatus. Under the Articles of Confederation, formally adopted only in 1781, Congress had very few powers to cope with the problems that beset the new nation. It had no authority to prevent states from passing laws that violated the Paris Peace Treaty, discriminated against citizens of other states, interfered with commerce, undermined business, or contributed to inflation. Often the Confederation Congress could not even muster a quorum to conduct official business. Most critically, the national government had no power to tax or to regulate commerce, having to rely on the states to voluntarily pay tax assessments in a timely manner – something which they rarely did. The national government seemed virtually powerless; it was bankrupt.

There had been efforts to amend the Articles of Confederation to address the obvious problems, but amendment of the articles required unanimous agreement of the states, something that proved impossible to achieve. The most notable proposal was to allow the Confederation Congress to impose a 5 percent impost, a tax on imports, so that the Confederation could pay its bills. In 1781, this proposal was almost adopted, but was blocked by Rhode Island. (In fairness to Rhode Island, Virginia rescinded its acceptance in 1782, and other states also objected that tax collectors would work for the Congress rather than the states.) In 1783, an amendment was introduced to allow an impost of no more than 5 percent for no more than 25 years and only to pay old debts; this compromise proposal also would have allowed the states to make initial appointments of tax collectors, although collectors would have reported to the Confederation. Henry, still dominant in the Virginia legislature, was concerned about increasing the power of the central government, but eventually supported the 1783 proposal. In spite of Virginia's support, though, this proposal failed when New York refused to ratify it, imposing a bevy of conditions that made the proposal unworkable. (Among the reasons that New York refused to ratify was a concern that a federal impost might cut into its own import taxes.) At mid-decade, there seemed to be little prospect of gaining fiscal independence for the Confederation government.

By the latter half of the decade, things were arguably looking-up. The economy seemed to be improving. Crop prices were rising, and yields were good. Most states were slowly paying their wartime debt, and several states began to run budget surpluses (although they continued to be delinquent in paying requisitions from the Confederation Congress).

Still, the overall picture seemed gloomy to most politically active observers, particularly the elite. State governments seemed more than willing to interfere with business in favor of debtors – acts that James Madison would later call "frequent and . . . flagrant" injustices, and the national government seemed almost moribund. In early 1787, a deeply concerned Madison wrote to Edmund Randolph, Virginia's governor:

> No money comes into the federal Treasury. No respect is paid to the federal authority; and people of reflection unanimously agree that the existing Confederacy is tottering to its foundation. Many individuals of weight particularly in the eastern district [New England] are suspected of leaning toward Monarchy. Other individuals predict a partition of the States into two or more Confederacies. It is pretty certain that if some radical amendment of the single one [the Confederation] cannot be devised and introduced that one or other of these revolutions, the latter no doubt, will take place.[2]

Some of this was predictable. From their inception, many had thought that the Articles of Confederation were too weak. When the country was faced with the emergency of the Revolution, the Confederation could organize the effort, but it had almost no power to compel the states to follow its lead. During the war, this resulted in repeated crises with recruiting and supplying the army and financing the war. Living with the problem first-hand, General Washington became an early and leading advocate of increasing the power of the central government. The necessity of fighting the American Revolution ensured a modicum of cooperation among the states, but after the war, problems seemed to get worse. By the middle of the decade, especially after the effort to amend the Articles again failed, calls for reform and for creating a more powerful national government grew louder and more persistent.

By 1785, many of the most important national leaders recognized that reform was necessary. It seemed that no one thought more deeply, nor worked more actively, on the problem than James Madison, and he had concluded that a much stronger central government was needed. As he would later tell Thomas Jefferson, "It was generally agreed that the objects of the Union could not be secured by any system founded on the principle of a confederation of sovereign States." When a farmers' revolt broke out in the fall of 1786 in western Massachusetts against high taxes, foreclosure lawsuits, and a political system in that state that still favored eastern elites at the expense of western farmers – Shays' Rebellion – many people seized on the apparent chaos to argue for a stronger national government. While the rebellion was easily crushed, Shays' and similar disturbances in other parts of the country fueled a fear of civil unrest and anarchy among the political elite like Washington and Madison. By 1787, Madison, Washington, James Wilson, Alexander Hamilton, and other leaders all wanted to strengthen the central government.[3]

After trying unsuccessfully to gather a conference to discuss commercial relations among the states in Annapolis in 1786, Madison and others settled on a plan and convinced the Confederation Congress to support a convention in Philadelphia in the summer of 1787 supposedly for the "sole and express purpose of revising the Articles of Confederation and reporting to Congress . . . such alterations and provisions therein as shall when agreed to in Congress and confirmed by the States render the federal Constitution adequate to the exigencies of Government." This became the Constitutional Convention. Critically important, Madison convinced George Washington, the greatest American hero of the age (along with Ben Franklin), to support the convention and attend. With Washington and Franklin in attendance, almost all of the states would send some of their top political thinkers as delegates. (Rhode Island, historically contrarian and concerned that its powerful status in the Confederation Congress – an equal vote with far larger states – might be compromised at Philadelphia, did not send a delegation.)[4]

As the state legislatures began to choose delegates to the Philadelphia Convention, no one knew quite what it would do. Nominally, the convention was to propose amendments to the Articles of Confederation, but everyone understood that amendments would require unanimous consent of the states and might never be implemented. Some politicians, notably

Madison and Alexander Hamilton, were discussing proposals that clearly went beyond mere amendments.

And what of Patrick Henry – the most popular politician (excluding Washington, who had nominally retired) in the most populous state? What was he thinking during these important events and debates?

After the war, Henry had continued his public service, but he was anxious to be home. In 1786, as his fifth term as governor drew to a close, Virginia's General Assembly would have happily elected Henry to a sixth term, but he declined the honor, telling the Assembly that he did not need any additional political honors or titles; "the approbation of my country is the highest reward to which my mind is capable of aspiring," he said. Yet, while he could retreat from the governor's office, Henry could not long stay out of the political spotlight.[5]

In 1787, soon after he moved to Prince Edward County, the voters returned Henry to the General Assembly. When the Virginia legislature chose delegates to attend the Philadelphia convention that spring, no one was surprised to see Patrick Henry's name on the list (along with George Washington, James Madison, Edmund Randolph, George Mason, George Wythe, and James Blair). Henry, though, would not attend. Later reports surfaced saying that Henry was concerned that the convention would create a strong national government and that he wanted nothing to do with it. "I smelt a rat," he allegedly declared – still a popular story today. Perhaps. The historic record is unclear (there appear to be no written references to this quote before 1853 and the source is questionable), and Henry's family obligations certainly gave him adequate reasons to stay home. Governor Randolph told Madison that he had been unable to persuade Henry to attend because he was "distressed in his private circumstances" – he needed to earn some money. All that the official record shows is that Henry, "with much concern," declined the appointment. While anxious about the nation's problems and the possible results from the Convention, perhaps he simply felt that he had devoted enough time to public service and that he was not needed in Philadelphia. (This leads to one of the inevitable "what ifs" of history: What if Patrick Henry had been in Philadelphia at the constitutional convention? Would the final proposed U.S. Constitution have ever been agreed upon? Or, perhaps the Constitution would have provided for a more limited federal government and stronger states' rights – and ratification of the Constitution, with Henry's help, might have been that much easier.)[6]

By March 1787, Madison, who had recently locked horns with Henry over religious freedom, had become skeptical of the former governor's actions. Perhaps politics were at play. Perhaps Henry wanted to avoid the convention so that he could later oppose the result if he disliked it. Seemingly bitter, Madison wrote to Washington that if Henry was not part of drafting any proposals for reform, it would "leave his conduct unfettered on another theatre [during ratification] where the result of the convention will receive its destiny from his omnipotence."[7]

Henry had reasons to be cautious. Like most leaders who had helped to spark and win the Revolution, Henry was well aware of the shortcomings in the Articles of Confederation. Having struggled during the war, not always successfully, to provide the Continental Congress with Virginia's share of assessments of money, troops, and supplies, Henry had direct experience with the problems of trying to support a national government based on "voluntary" contributions by the states. Trying to convince Henry to accept appointment to the Philadelphia Convention, Governor Randolph reminded him of those problems and warned him that the new nation might yet dissolve into squabbling states or small confederacies: "From the experience of your late administration," Randolph explained, "you must be persuaded that every day dawns with peril to the United States . . . You will therefore pardon me for expressing a fear that the neglect of the present moment may terminate in the destruction of Confederate America."[8]

Henry understood that changes were needed in the Articles of Confederation to increase the power of the central government and, at least initially, he could be characterized as a moderate nationalist. Henry wanted to see the power of a national government expanded, but he did not want that power to grow so large that it would undermine the states. In May 1784, as Madison began to contemplate more seriously the need for a stronger central government, and before his open warfare with Henry over religious freedom broke out, the future president wrote to Jefferson, serving as ambassador in Paris, that Henry was "strenuous for invigorating the federal Government, though without any precise plan." William Short, a member of Governor Henry's council (and later Jefferson's personal secretary), agreed that Henry "saw Ruin inevitable unless something was done to give Congress a compulsory Process on delinquent States" – that is the power to collect taxes if the states would not pay requisitions.[9]

In addition to the inability to raise revenue, other aspects of the Confederation's weakness concerned Henry. He had a longstanding commitment to the frontier and the Northwest Territories – arguably only a part of the United States because of Henry's critical support for George Rogers Clark's efforts during the American Revolution; but he was deeply concerned for the future of those territories given the inability of the Confederation Congress to protect settlers or even to force Britain to abandon its forts on U.S. soil. Frontiersmen, including many of Henry's kin, were anxious to obtain government support against Native Americans (who were being supplied by the British). After one brother-in-law was killed by Natives in a frontier clash in April of 1786, Governor Henry complained that national aid was needed and that it was "extremely unjust" to expect Virginia to carry the cost of defending the frontier after it had turned-over the land to the national government. He wrote to the president of Congress about his "apprehensions of the neglect or mismanagement which I am inclined to think has taken place in the Department of Indian Affairs." Henry and western settlers were distressed by "the seeming inattention which appears in this Department of the Public Business." Henry wished that "Congress in their wisdom will provide a remedy for these Evils, & prove the rectitude of that policy which vested that hon'ble Body with management of the Business," but he well knew that significant movement by the national government on protecting the frontier was unlikely unless the powers of the national government were expanded.[10]

Then, however, an incident occurred that seemed to pit the southern and western states against the northeast and middle states, and Henry's natural caution about increasing governmental power flared up. The incident related to the frontier and, particularly, the right to navigate on the Mississippi River.

After the Revolution, as thousands of settlers poured over the Appalachian Mountains, western farmers needed commercial outlets for their crops. Even the most self-sufficient farmer needed to earn some money in order to buy items that could not easily be made on the farm (guns and gun powder, tools, etc.) and to pay taxes. This posed a quandary for settlers: It was far less costly to send tobacco, wheat, corn, and other products down local rivers to the Mississippi and through New Orleans for shipment to U.S. coastal cities or elsewhere in the world rather than trying to ship them by horse or wagon back over the mountains. Yet, the lower Mississippi, the land around New Orleans, was controlled by Spain.

In 1785, as the frontier population exploded, John Jay was tasked with negotiating a commercial treaty with Spain on behalf of the Confederation Congress. The Congress wanted improved commercial relations with Spain and an open Mississippi River, but Spain was concerned about the surge of settlers coming over the mountains and toward Spanish territory. In particular, Spain wanted to maintain a very large buffer between American settlers and its extremely profitable silver mines in northern Mexico. As a result, Spain proposed to close the Mississippi to shipments from American farmers for 25 to 30 years in return for giving the United States improved trade opportunities elsewhere, concessions that would have provided significant benefits to U.S. merchants and seamen (mostly in New England and the middle states) at the expense of western farmers. In August of 1786, Jay urged the Confederation Congress to accept Spain's offer – the Jay-Gardoqui Treaty – as, on balance, a good deal for the nation; northern and middle states were ready to do so. If this proposal had been adopted, it would have strongly discouraged westward migration. It also posed a serious threat that some westerners might start a war with Spain to secure New Orleans, or seek to leave the United States and join British Canada in hope that Britain would force the Mississippi open, or even join Spain to preserve their ability to ship their farm produce.

For some, the political battle that broke out was further evidence of the necessity of a stronger national government. John Marshall, a member of the Virginia House of Delegates and future chief justice, wrote to Arthur Lee, then a member of the Confederation's Treasury Board, that "I very much fear that the conduct of some unthinking men in the western country will embroil us with Spain unless there be some more vigorous interposition of government than we seem disposed to make."[11]

On the other hand, most southerners, including Henry, were outraged that the Confederation would so readily sacrifice essential interests of westerners (who at the time came mostly from southern states). Henry, who had always been first and foremost an advocate for his state and region, wrote to family and friends in Kentucky warning them of the danger of the proposed treaty, but he urged western settlers to act with caution because they needed the support of the United States to force Spain to open the Mississippi. In early 1787, as plans for the Philadelphia Convention proceeded, Edmund Randolph wrote to Madison that losing navigation of the Mississippi would "throw the western settlers into an immediate state of hostility with Spain," and warned that absent an emphatic rejection of the proposal by Congress it would be impossible to "secure Mr. H[enr]y to the objects of the convention at Phila." John Marshall reported that Henry, previously a supporter of increasing the power of the national government, said that "he would rather part with the confederation than relinquish the navigation of the Mississippi." Marshall recognized that Henry's strong reaction was political posturing, adding that "but as we have been fortiter in modo, I dare say we shall be suaviter in re," which is to turn on its head the idiom "*fortiter in re, suaviter in modo*" ("strongly in deed, gently in manner"); in other words, he expected that Henry's actions would be gentler than his strong language. Still, it was clear that Henry was incensed by the suggestion of sacrificing the interests of western farmers in favor of eastern merchants. In December of 1786, Madison warned Washington that:

> I am entirely convinced . . . that unless the project of Congs [to give up navigation of the Mississippi] can be reversed, the hopes of carrying this State into a proper federal System will be demolished. Many of our most federal leading men are extremely soured with what has already passed. Mr. Henry, who has been hitherto the Champion of the federal cause, has become a cold advocate,

and in the event of an actual sacrifice of the Misspi. by Congress, will unquestionably go over to the opposite side.[12]

Southerners ultimately blocked the proposed Jay-Gardoqui Treaty in the Confederation Congress because it required 9 of 13 states for approval (the vote was 7: 5 in favor of the treaty, with all of the southern states in opposition), but their deep suspicion of a strong national government was to be long lasting and became a major factor for many in souring their interest in expanding the central government's power.

So, Patrick Henry recognized that the power of the Confederation had to be increased. At the same time, he was concerned with the problem of how to control power in the hands of government officials, and the larger, the more powerful, and the more distant the government, the greater the problem. Like many leaders in the Revolution, he saw men as corruptible, and government officials – operating with public power – were especially subject to the corruption of power. For the deeply religious Henry, this was both a political and a religious reality. The political machinations of eastern politicians and merchants concerning the Jay-Gardoqui Treaty tended to confirm Henry's suspicions and put him on-guard against a broad extension of governmental power. Not only was he concerned that a similar treaty could be adopted by a new, more powerful national government, but it demonstrated a central problem – the ability of the national government to take actions that would benefit one particular region (or one particular interest) while harming another, for Henry, particularly Virginia, the south, or the west. More than any other single factor, this turned Henry from a moderate supporter of increasing the power of the national government to a strong skeptic.

* * * * *

The story of the drafting of the Constitution is told elsewhere. Today we know that the long, hot summer in Philadelphia produced a masterful and widely-revered document, the longest active written constitution in the world. In September of 1787 when the proposed Constitution was released to the public, however, many people, Henry among them, were shocked, some outraged. The Philadelphia Convention did not adopt specific, limited amendments to the Articles of Confederation as it had been asked to do but instead proposed an entirely new strong central government. Many were deeply concerned that the Constitution would create a government that was far too powerful and that it lacked express protections for important rights (such as freedom of religion, speech, and press – these were only added later when the Constitution was amended with the Bill of Rights). Adding to the problem, the proposed Constitution specified that ratification required approval by only 9 states (rather than all 13 as was required to amend the Articles of Confederation). Given these and other concerns, it was not at all clear that it would be adopted. There was particularly serious opposition in Virginia, Massachusetts, New York, New Hampshire, North Carolina, and Rhode Island. Many claimed that had there been a popular vote, the majority of the people in the United States actually opposed the Constitution.[13]

Knowing that Henry would play a central role in ratification in Virginia (still the largest state), George Washington, the chairman of the Philadelphia Convention, sent Henry a copy of the proposed Constitution as soon as he could. "In the first moment after my return" from Philadelphia, the Convention's chairman wrote that he would let Henry make up his own mind on the Constitution; but Washington was clearly lobbying the influential former governor. Washington stressed the difficulty that the Convention faced in trying to reach a compromise acceptable to all the states: "[Y]our experience of the difficulties, which have ever arisen when attempts have been made to reconcile such a variety of interest and local prejudices, as pervade the several States, will render explanation unnecessary." Washington conceded that he wished the Constitution "had been more perfect," but the alternative may well be "anarchy." "I sincerely believe," Washington assured his Revolutionary compatriot, "it is the best that could be obtained at this time." Washington advised Henry that amendments could be adopted later to address any serious problems as they arose.[14]

Henry responded cautiously to his hero. Thanking Washington for his service to his country in Philadelphia, the "arduous Business of the late Convention," Henry had "to lament" that he could not bring himself to embrace what he felt was a seriously flawed document. He told Washington that "The Concern I feel on this account is really greater than I am able to express." Holding out a thin possibility that he might change his mind with further reflection, Henry concluded: "I beg you will be persuaded of the unalterable Regard & attachment with which I shall ever be, dear Sir, your obliged & very humble Servant." This would be the last direct communication between Henry and Washington for many years.[15]

While politely cautious with Washington, Henry was coming to the conclusion that he would have to oppose ratification of the U.S. Constitution. Henry thought that the Constitution would create a strong government too distant from the people to reflect their concerns. Powerful, wealthy people would control the Congress and the presidency. While not denying that the Articles of Confederation should be strengthened somewhat, Henry reminded people that the Confederation, controlled by the states, had "carried us through a long and dangerous war . . . with a powerful nation" and that the country was at peace and increasingly prosperous.

Was a fundamental change to the entire system really needed? With the Jay-Gardoqui experience in mind, Henry thought that the Constitution could prove disastrous: Would a new federal government be controlled by New England elite and middle state merchants? Filled with these concerns, Henry accepted election to the Virginia General Assembly in 1788 and election to the state's ratification convention scheduled for June 1788.[16]

When Virginia's ratification convention began on June 2, 1788, eight states had already ratified, creating a great deal of momentum for ratification, but there was still a high risk that the Constitution would be voted down. Even after New Hampshire voted to approve the Constitution on June 21, becoming the ninth state ratifying (a fact not known in Virginia until after its June 25 vote), as a practical matter the new nation would be seriously-wounded if Virginia (the largest state) did not approve. And if Virginia voted against ratification, there was a strong chance that New York would as well; even without Virginia in opposition, North Carolina and Rhode Island continued to oppose ratification for over a year. Much hung on Virginia's decision, and all eyes were on Henry.

As Virginia's ratification convention assembled, it became evident that Patrick Henry would lead the assault on the proposed Constitution. Anti-federalist opponents of the Constitution also included George Mason (a delegate to the Philadelphia Convention who refused to sign the final document), Richard Henry Lee (who remained in New York City during the convention as a representative to the Confederation Congress), James Monroe (a future president), and former governor Benjamin Harrison. Jefferson, still acting as U.S. ambassador to France, predicted that with such powerful opposition, Virginia would not ratify. Others had similar concerns. Henry Knox, a strong federalist, and soon to be the first secretary of war under the Constitution, wrote that "I fear that overwhelming torrent, Patrick Henry."[17]

Crowds flocked to the General Assembly to watch the convention debates. With anti-federalists Henry, Mason, Monroe, and Harrison, and federalists Madison, Randolph, Edmund Pendleton, and John Marshall locked in battle, the contest would prove to be not only important, but entertaining (these were the days before radio, television, and the internet). Soon crowds became so large that meetings were shifted to the New Academy (the largest building in Richmond). Observers understood that the fate of the nation hung in the balance.[18] It may be difficult today to understand what so disturbed Henry about the Constitution. The U.S. Constitution is the oldest written national constitution in the world, and many countries have modeled some of its key aspects. In America, it has developed a status almost of scripture. Henry's concerns, though, would lead to one of his greatest and most important political battles. That battle would have lasting influence on the way in which the American people understand their Constitution even today.

Henry's objections were far-ranging, but his more important concerns fell into three overlapping categories. First, he joined George Mason's concern that the Constitution absolutely required a Bill of Rights spelling-out critical protections against excessive governmental power. Second, and most importantly for Henry, he wanted structural changes to the Constitution to limit the power of the national government in key respects, protecting the sovereignty of the states. He wanted to deny the national government authority to tax individuals directly, requiring Congress to requisition states for their share of needed funds (and punishing states if they failed to meet the requisitions), and he believed that a super-majority of Congress should be required to make laws concerning commerce, thus protecting southern interests. Henry was also concerned that the president would be too powerful, especially with respect to treaty negotiations and control of the army. Third, and more generally, Henry expressed a deep concern that the entire Constitution was built on a premise that the United States would be, had to be, a powerful and expansive empire. Yet, from Henry's perspective, a government powerful enough to create such an empire was a threat to the states and to liberty. While Henry had always favored growth of the United States – fighting the Jay-Gardoqui Treaty, for example, because it threatened westward expansion – when faced with the possible loss of liberty, Henry was willing to forego a powerful empire. Each of these concerns can be considered briefly in turn.

Anti-federalists throughout the country focused on the fact that the proposed Constitution had no Bill of Rights. While federalist supporters of the Constitution said that a Bill of Rights was not needed because the government had limited, express powers, Henry had the better part of this debate (and, as discussed below, a Bill of Rights was added to the Constitution shortly after ratification). "The rights of conscience, trial by jury, liberty of the press, all your immunities and franchises [voting rights], all pretensions to human rights and privileges," Henry warned the delegates in Richmond, "are rendered insecure, if not lost." Given the increased power and size of the proposed government, "the necessity of a bill of rights appears to me to be greater in this government than ever it was in any government before." Scoffing at those who opposed a bill of rights, Henry asked why it could not be added before a final vote: "Is it because it will consume too much paper?"[19]

More time was spent in the Virginia Convention on Henry's larger concern with excessive federal power. The point that got the most attention was the plan to give the new federal government direct authority to tax people. Everyone recognized that the government needed revenue, but anti-federalists argued that the federal government should rely first on import duties and if those would not cover all the necessary costs, simply ask the states for their allotted share of the funds needed, requisition the sums as under the Confederation. State and local officials would be in a better position to determine how the taxes could be collected efficiently and with the minimum amount of disruption; they would also be directly affected by any taxes that they agreed to impose, tending to guarantee restraint. More broadly, Henry recognized that the power to tax could be easily abused and that this was an area requiring particular caution.

Another serious concern related to the authority to regulate commerce among the states and with foreign governments. Here, too, Henry recognized that some authority had to be given to the national government; but the Jay-Gardoqui Treaty had alerted him to the danger of regions of the country with a particular commercial interest forming voting blocs and acting against the interests of other regions. He believed that the threat could be largely eliminated if laws regulating commerce required a super-majority vote in Congress, perhaps two-thirds.

The creation of a centralized executive also was a concern, especially the fact that there were no term limits on the presidency (a serious concern for Jefferson as well). By comparison, even with very limited authority, a governor in Virginia could only serve for three of seven years. How would a president elected again and again differ from a king, Henry asked? It seemed to him that the presidency had "an awful squinting; it squints toward monarchy."[i] Then there was the problem of treaties, a sensitive subject given Jay-Gardoqui. With the Constitution providing that treaties would be negotiated by the president and confirmed by the Senate, Henry objected that the House of Representatives, the branch most directly representing the people, was not involved and that ratified treaties would be able to trump domestic law, even with respect to largely domestic concerns such as commerce.[20]

Beyond these specific concerns, Henry was apprehensive that the new national government would effectively impair the power of the states in ways that might not have been foreseen. The proposed Constitution not only gave Congress a list of specific powers, but also far-reaching and undefined authority to take actions "necessary and proper" to effect its stated purposes. Henry recognized that this power could be used to justify almost any federal action, a fear largely confirmed by later actions. Caution was needed.

The third broad area of concern for Henry looked beyond any particular provision in the proposed Constitution in isolation and related to the

i The concern with term limits was evidenced in the voluntary decision of Washington and every president thereafter – until Franklin Delano Roosevelt during the Depression and World War II – to step down after no more than two terms. In 1951, the 22nd Amendment to the Constitution restricted the president to two terms.

underlying question of governmental power and what the United States, as a nation, could or should be. The fundamental question for Henry was why was a government needed? For him, the answer was clear: A government was needed to protect the people's liberty (e.g., against crime or Indian or foreign assaults); any additional powers were unnecessary and dangerous. He wanted a federal government of strictly limited authority. Henry was not opposed to the United States growing, expanding through the west; indeed, he undoubtedly expected that and opposed Jay-Gardoqui in part because it would have interrupted westward expansion. Yet, philosophically, he did not seek a powerful government for the sake of being able to project power elsewhere. Perhaps his hopes were unrealistic – an expansive nation with a strictly limited national government; but they were based on his experience and shared by many of his contemporaries, especially farmers and tradesman.

Many delegates to the Philadelphia Convention seemed to have been focused in an entirely different direction. Federalists like Washington, Madison, and Hamilton were concerned that the weak United States under the Articles of Confederation was not living up to its potential. The new nation could easily extend to the Mississippi River and beyond, build an empire, an empire of liberty they thought. Such a nation could have an enormous influence around the world. Henry, they might conclude, was thinking small. Historians, with 20:20 hindsight, have made much the same argument, concluding that it was "hard to avoid depicting Henry as one of history's losers, as one too short-sighted to see beyond the bounds of his own native state to glimpse the promise of national greatness embodied in the Constitution."[21]

Henry railed at this argument, essentially questioning what it meant for a nation to be "great." He warned the delegates that they were being seduced by visions of power and were asking the wrong questions. "You are not to inquire how your trade may be increased, nor how you are to become a great and powerful people, but how your liberties can be secured; for liberty ought to be the direct end of your government." Decrying the danger of the lust for power, even for a powerful nation, much less an empire, Henry was at his most eloquent: "Liberty, the greatest of all earthly blessings – give us that precious jewel, and you may take everything else!" With a strong grasp of history and the nature of power, he warned in terms that still resonate today that "those nations who have gone in search of grandeur, power and splendor, have also fallen a sacrifice, and been the victims of their own folly. While they acquired those visionary blessings, they lost their freedom."[22]

While Henry's arguments were eloquent, he faced a near insurmountable problem: What did he really want delegates to do? By the time of the Virginia ratification convention, with eight states already having ratified (and New Hampshire ratifying during the Virginia Convention, although no one in Virginia knew that), realistically, what could the delegates in Virginia do? With hindsight, it is clear that anti-federalists should have scheduled ratification conventions in their strong states earlier. Had Virginia (or New York or North Carolina) rejected the Constitution before other states (or most other states) had voted, things might have been very different. Lacking effective prompt communication, and having been caught a bit "flat-footed," the anti-federalists were out-maneuvered by better prepared and better organized federalists.

Henry's answer was that Virginia (and other states that had not yet ratified) should reject the Constitution until amendments were made addressing the key concerns. He was even able to produce a letter that Jefferson had written from Paris to a Virginia friend suggesting that nine states should ratify and four should reject the Constitution until amendments were made (a position that would prove an embarrassment to Madison when it was used by the anti-federalists). To accomplish this, Henry urged that a second convention be called to fix the proposed Constitution: a Bill of Rights should be added; limitations on the power to tax and regulate commerce should be made; the president should have term limits. Henry explained that "If Virginia be for adoption [before amendments were added], what States will be left, of sufficient respectability and importance, to secure amendments by their rejection?"[23]

Federalists, of course, responded to these arguments, sometimes very effectively. The idea of a second convention might seem plausible at first, but calling a new convention would result in endless squabbling as delegates coming to such a meeting would have hardened positions and be even less open to compromise. Washington wrote to one friend explaining that this alternative was entirely unworkable; "if another federal convention is attempted the sentiment of the members will be more discordant [sic] or less Conciliator than the last . . . they will agree upon no gen[era]l plan." The specific anti-federalist proposals were also problematic. Requiring Congress to request states to provide funding before imposing taxes, for example, would result in delays and arguments over whether states had complied; then, federal taxes would be imposed anyway (in some states, causing further confusion). Requiring a two-thirds vote on commercial regulations was a proposal that had been rejected in Philadelphia (as part of a negotiation between northern and southern states that gave slavery additional constitutional protections), and who would define when a super-majority was needed? The power of the government and states' rights had already been debated thoroughly at the Philadelphia Convention, and many compromises had been made to protect the states. Perhaps Henry now realized that he should have been in Philadelphia.[24]

The central substantive problem for the anti-federalists was that once it was admitted that the Articles of Confederation were flawed and that the national government had to be made more powerful – a point which Henry seemed to concede, the anti-federalists did not have a specific, workable alternative to the Constitution. Simply rejecting the Constitution until amendments were adopted, and continuing in the meantime with the unsound Articles posed serious problems. Federalists were effective in arguing that the vote was essentially for the Constitution or nothing, potentially chaos. "[T]here is no alternative between the adoption of it [the Constitution] and anarchy," Washington warned.[25]

Facing these issues, and with a very strong anti-federalist contingent of its own, Massachusetts had ratified the Constitution but included a list of proposed amendments that it hoped the first federal Congress would consider. Of course, these were just proposals, and even if Congress gave them serious consideration, whether or not those amendments were adopted would depend upon votes in the Congress and later state ratification.

Federalists in Virginia and elsewhere did not agree with many of the amendment proposals presented by Massachusetts' anti-federalists, but they saw the Massachusetts' approach as a reasonable means to get the new government up and running. They began to endorse the proposal for consideration of amendments subsequent to ratification. Henry pointed out that it made little sense to adopt a new Constitution that most people thought was essentially flawed with the hope for subsequent amendment. "Evils admitted in order to be removed subsequently, and tyranny submitted to in order to be excluded by a subsequent alteration, are things totally new to me," he concluded. This "proposal is an idea dreadful to me." Henry tried to turn the argument around, urging that "I acknowledge the weakness of the old confederation. Every man says that something must be done . . . Is not this the most promising time for securing the necessary alteration?" But the practical alternatives were limited.[26]

As the ratification convention continued for weeks, often with long days filled with Henry speeches, Henry may have sensed that the convention was turning against him. Seeking to stem the tide, he made an ugly speech in which he warned the slave owners who dominated the convention that if the Constitution was adopted a northern majority in the federal Congress might mandate abolition. (Clearly there were limits to the democratic principle of majority rule beyond which most southern slave owners, including Henry, would not pass.) Henry conceded that slavery was wrong: "Slavery is detested. We feel its fatal effects – we deplore it with all the pity of humanity." Yet, he could not, would not, accept the possibility of emancipation, and certainly not by a distant government that might be unfamiliar with conditions in Virginia. The Virginia economy had been built on the backs of enslaved men and women and freeing them would cost the state (and its slave owners) dearly. In addition, like many slave holders, he knew how horrendous the treatment of enslaved people had been and, as a result, was deeply afraid of what freed slaves might do. He played on these fears. "As much as I deplore slavery, I see that prudence forbids its abolition." As one scholar noted, Henry "used any argument he could find to oppose the Constitution."[27]

As the crucial vote in Virginia approached, the anti-federalist leader made one of his most compelling speeches. Henry reminded his listeners that the issues faced were momentous; decisions made about how to frame the U.S. government, the first modern republic to throw off a colonial monarchy, would have implications for nations around the world and millions yet unborn. Responding to the arguments of Madison, the leading federalist, Henry warned the delegates:

> He tells you of the important blessings which he imagines will result to us and mankind in general, from the adoption of this system. I see the awful immensity of the dangers with which it is pregnant. I see it. I feel it. I see beings of a higher order anxious concerning our decision . . . reviewing the political decisions and revolutions which, in the progress of time, will happen in America, and the consequent happiness or misery of mankind . . . Our own happiness alone is not affected by the event. All nations are interested in the determination.

Other reports of the speech suggest that the stenographer had only captured the outlines of Henry's oratory: the "awful immensity of the question to the present and future generations." Invoking religious imagery, he warned that there were "celestial beings who were hovering over the scene, and waiting with anxiety for a decision which involved the happiness or misery of more than half the human race." As this speech continued, an extremely violent summer thunderstorm broke out in Richmond, and Henry played to the storm, almost as if he was calling down the thunder and lightning himself. One awe-struck observer reported that "the spirits whom he called seemed to have come at his bidding . . . He seemed to mix in the fight of his ethereal auxiliaries, and 'riding on the wings of the tempest, to seize upon the artillery of Heaven, and direct its fiercest thunders against the heads of his adversaries.'"[28]

Henry's "thunder speech" is often remembered, and it and his speech several days earlier on the dangers of empire are impressive odes to the danger of excessive power, especially government power. For three weeks, Henry's rhetoric had masterfully defended the states against what he saw as federal usurpation, but equally important (and often overlooked) is what Henry said the next day as the Virginia Convention neared its end and the delegates prepared for the decisive vote. Seeming to know that the closely divided convention would likely ratify the Constitution, as he rose to address the convention one last time, Henry was very clear about his duty as an American. With the intensity of his arguments seemingly checked, Henry struck a tone of conciliation and asked to "beg pardon of this House for having taken up more time than came to my share, and I thank them for the patience and polite attention with which I have been heard." What, though, to do if the vote was for ratification?

> If I shall be in the minority, I shall have those painful sensations which arise from a conviction of *being overpowered in a good cause*. Yet I will be a peaceable citizen. My head, my hand, and my heart shall be at liberty to retrieve the loss of liberty, and to remove the defects of that system *in a constitutional way*. I wish not to go to violence, but will wait with hopes that the spirit which predominated in the revolution is not yet gone, nor the cause of those who are attached to the revolution yet lost. I shall therefore patiently wait in expectation of seeing that government changed, so as to be compatible with the safety, liberty, and happiness of the people.[29]

While some contemporaries, historians, and modern politicians have found it convenient to make Henry out to be an uncompromising opponent of all federal power, willing to risk secession to protect states' rights, the reality was far different. Henry had historically been an ally of increasing the power of the government. Contrary to reports from federalists that Henry would have preferred dissolution of the union or creation of several smaller republics to adoption of the Constitution, Henry was emphatic that he was not a secessionist; his push for greater states' rights did not go that far. In the political fighting leading up to Virginia's ratification convention, had he intimated that trying to force the Constitution on the people might result in the Confederation being broken into smaller sections and that he could live with that result – a claim often made by his opponents? The record is not perfectly clear; political protagonists in the eighteenth century (as well as the twenty-first) are capable of exaggerating or selectively editing the arguments of their opponents. John Marshall, a federalist, was one of the primary sources for the notion that Henry preferred a splintered union to the Constitution, but Marshall recognized that Henry was likely using exaggerated political rhetoric. While Henry was capable of engaging in heated political battles and some of his arguments at the convention suggested that small confederacies would be better than a tyrannical central government, he was careful not to advocate such a result. He explained that in focusing on liberty "I speak the language of thousands"; yet, he was equally emphatic that "I mean not to breathe the spirit, nor utter the language, of secession." In response to federalist arguments that anti-federalists wanted (or risked) the United States being broken up into several smaller confederations, Henry expressly denied any such interest, although, at the time, the denials themselves may have sounded to some like a threat. Now, as the debates drew to a close, he demanded obedience to the Constitution if it was ratified and rejected any talk of secession, an enormously important service that Henry performed for his country.[30]

As the Virginia ratification convention neared its end, one of the most effective and telling responses to Henry and the anti-federalists came from Zachariah Johnson, a delegate from rural Augusta County in the Shenandoah Valley (the type of delegate that Henry needed to convince if he hoped to block ratification). Johnson had been quiet through most of the convention. He said that he had listened attentively, and he agreed that the Constitution was imperfect. He also agreed with Henry that the question faced "may involve the felicity or misery of myself and posterity." Yet, he saw that the issue was, in part, a question of optimism or pessimism about his fellow man. He thought that opponents, including Henry, had made every possible negative assumption, assumed the worse of the new Congress, expected citizens to turn against citizens. This made little sense to Johnson. Perhaps speaking for the critical swing votes, Johnson said that he would vote for ratification and hope to see the constitutional system address any problems that did arise through amendment or sound governance. William Nelson, Jr., (brother of former Governor Nelson) reported to Jefferson's private secretary in Paris that "I heard a man of judgment declare, that Johnson's speech was the best which was delivered in the convention." Shortly after Johnson spoke, the debates meandered to an end.[31]

On June 25, 1788, Virginia ratified the Constitution in a relatively close vote, 89 to 79.

The Virginia Convention then adopted a series of proposed amendments, 40 in all, many drafted by Henry and his supporters. These included a long list of restrictions on the federal government, including the power to tax and regulate commerce, and a list of rights for a possible federal Bill of Rights. But these were only proposals; they would have no legal force unless the new federal Congress adopted them (by a two-thirds vote) and three-quarters of the states ratified them.

Henry, and the anti-federalists, had apparently lost.

Some anti-federalists, led by George Mason, gathered in Richmond immediately after the convention and discussed continued opposition and possibly active disobedience to the Constitution. More reasoned voices opposed that idea, saying that federalists had won the ratification vote and that honest citizens had to work within the system. There has been some disagreement as to what role Henry played at this meeting. Some (including some of his federalist opponents who were certainly not at the meeting themselves) insisted that he was among the radicals; others reported that he urged the moderate position. Once again, history is not entirely clear. Yet, given Henry's speech at the end of the convention, the latter seems more likely. According to one source, Henry told the assembled anti-federalists "The question had been fully discussed and settled, and that, as true and faithful republicans, they had all better go home; they should cherish it [the new government], and give it fair play." William Nelson, Jr. distinguished Henry's moderation, using his "influence" to support "good order," from Mason's radicalism, saying that the latter "is said not to have behaved with such temper." In the end, the anti-federalist meeting broke-up with no action taken. Before he died, Henry would again find himself in the midst of an epic battle over compliance or opposition to the Constitution and law. See Chapter 5.[32]

Still, while he recognized that a good citizen must live within the Constitution, Henry was far from being done. Open defiance of the Constitution was one thing, but working within the system to try to ensure serious reforms was another matter altogether. Re-elected to the Virginia House of Delegates after the Constitution was ratified, he vowed to do everything possible to have the proposed amendments adopted and to launch the new federal government in what he thought was the right direction. He was still one of the most powerful politician in Virginia. "He has only to say let this be Law – and it is Law," Washington warned Madison. Henry hoped to influence both the election of Virginia's congressional delegation and the project for amending the Constitution.[33]

The first challenge was election of Virginia's congressional delegation under the new Constitution, and Henry was violently opposed to having James Madison, the leading federalist in the ratification convention, as one of Virginia's first senators.[ii] He explained to other lawmakers that Madison, who said at the convention that the Constitution needed no amendments, could not be trusted to seek the changes that Virginia had proposed, especially the structural amendments that would strictly limit federal power. Henry believed that it would be better to have anti-federalists representing Virginia. The legislature agreed, appointing anti-federalists Richard Henry Lee and William Grayson as Virginia's first senators. Having kept Madison out of the Senate, Henry was also apparently behind the gerrymandering of electoral districts in an effort to deny Madison even a position in the House of Representatives (by including a number of anti-federalist counties in his district); Henry also encouraged James Monroe, a well-respected

---

ii Before the 17th Amendment to the Constitution (1913), state legislatures appointed members of the Senate.

anti-federalist, to run against Madison. Madison won the election only after promising that he would seek to have protections for personal liberty added to the Constitution, especially religious freedom.

Henry also continued to advocate for a new constitutional convention to propose major amendments, seeking to convince other states to join Virginia in demanding such a meeting.

So what happened? And did Henry, and his leadership of the anti-federalist movement, have any lasting importance for the country?

Of course, the effort to have a second constitutional convention failed; only New York responded favorably (and Pennsylvania and Massachusetts expressly rejected the proposal from Virginia). Who knows what the consequences might have been had the proposal succeeded?

More broadly, in assessing Henry's impact, the efforts of other anti-federalists must also be considered. After ratification, many anti-federalists seemed to sit back and allow the federalists to run the new system. As a result, even though anti-federalists were believed to outnumber federalists during the ratification debate, federalists dominated in the first federal Congress. Had anti-federalists in other states followed Henry's lead of working within the system to try to ensure reforms, encouraging election of anti-federalists to the new Congress, and insisting upon structural amendments (such as limiting Congress' taxing power and authority over commerce, and presidential terms), the results might have been very different. Instead, lacking effective means of communication and a national leadership, and having a varied group of overlapping concerns with the Constitution and no simple, agreed-to alternative, the anti-federalists proved ineffective at bringing the weight of their numbers to bear not only in ratification conventions, but afterwards. (The creation of an opposition political party in the 1790s, the Democratic-Republicans, would address many of these problems.)

Still, much was accomplished, and Henry's influence was substantial. The Bill of Rights was adopted by the first federal Congress in 1789 (ratified in 1791), answering perhaps the most consistent anti-federalist objection to the un-amended Constitution. James Madison, Henry's great opponent in the ratification debate, led the charge for the Bill of Rights in Congress when many federalist members wanted to ignore the issue and proceed with setting up the new government. In part, Madison was responding to a campaign promise. But by the time the first federal Congress met, Madison had also thought seriously about the objections raised by Henry and other anti-federalists. When arguing in Congress for the necessity of a Bill of Rights, Madison noted that the "necessary and proper" clause of the Constitution created the possibility of federal power being abused, a point that Henry had made forcefully at the Virginia ratifying convention. Another critical reason that Madison advanced for a Bill of Rights was that the

Supreme Court would use it to strike down congressional actions that violated the Constitution. Henry had made a similar point in the ratification debates. "I take it as the highest encomium on this country," Henry argued at the convention, "that the acts of the legislature, if unconstitutional, are liable to be opposed by the judiciary." (Jefferson made the same point to Madison.)[34]

Of course, today the tremendous importance of the Bill of Rights is clear.

Was Patrick Henry the father of the Bill of Rights as some historians claim? One of Henry's leading biographers, for example, concluded that "Without the pressure from him and his party, first in the Virginia Convention and then in Congress, it is doubtful if the United States would have had a federal Bill of Rights in its present form." This is not perfectly clear. Massachusetts and other states had urged rights amendments before the Virginia ratifying convention, and Madison was certainly more immediately involved in the process of adoption of the first ten amendments. On balance, it seems fair to say that Henry certainly influenced the effort significantly and without his effort and continued pressure on federalists after ratification, the Bill of Rights might have proven far more difficult to get passed in the Congress and far less likely to have been adopted by the states. Other conclusions are conjectural.[35]

The irony in all of this is that Henry was deeply dissatisfied with the Bill of Rights. Writing to one of Virginia's first senators before the Bill of Rights was drafted, Henry was pleased that a broad consensus had developed in favor of amendments: "Federal and anti [seem] now scarcely to exist; For our highest toned Feds say we must have the amendments." The amendments that were actually proposed by the federalist-controlled Congress, though, left out the greater part of the anti-federalist proposals, certainly all of the structural reforms that Henry had sought – "Direct Taxation Treatys Trade &c." Madison had recognized that adopting a Bill of Rights covering personal liberties might be useful in its own right, but it would also undermine much of the political support for Henry's call for a second convention and broad structural reforms to limit federal power. Madison had outmaneuvered Henry again. A frustrated Henry eventually, grudgingly, accepted the amendments that were made but thought that more were needed.[36]

On the broader point of governmental power and the desire that many had for a new American empire, Henry's thinking and forceful speeches seem to exemplify an important theme in American political thought, one which has waxed and waned over the years. Today, arguments continue about whether the United States should be focused on the liberty and well-being of its own citizens or on having a broader influence in the world, and how the two might be separated (a far more difficult task in the interdependent twenty-first century than in the eighteenth). Henry spoke for posterity in trying to get citizens to concern themselves with the risks that expansive government power, and an empire, posed.

Looking beyond the individual issues presented and debated during ratification, Henry played another important role, a role that he would revisit near the end of his life. He helped to frame a "loyal opposition"; he showed how to disagree strongly with a political decision but to continue to support the government and country nonetheless. After James Monroe, a fellow anti-federalist, was elected to be a senator from Virginia in 1790 (after the death of Senator William Grayson), Henry urged the new senator to work within the system. "[A]ltho' The Form of Govern^t into which my Countrymen determined to place themselves, had my Enmity, yet as we are one & all imbarked [sic], it is natural to care for the crazy Machine, at least so long as we are out of Sight of a Port to refit." Henry, a man of principle, recognized that compromise was often a critical component of living in a republic, but urged Monroe to continue to seek opportunities to "refit," to correct problems that Henry saw in the Constitution. As one historian noted, "The greatness of the anti-federalists ultimately was their willingness to work within the structure to oppose tyranny, rather than to take up arms against a government they feared."[37]

After ratification, as the new nation worked to get "on its feet," other important issues concerning the power of the government presented themselves as well, and Henry continued his efforts to keep the government within its bounds. Perhaps the most significant issue was Alexander Hamilton's expansive financial plans for the new government based upon an understanding that the federal government had broad powers implied in the specific grants of the Constitution. Henry joined Jefferson and Madison in strongly opposing this extension of government power. Explaining his concerns to Senator Monroe, Henry warned against the expansive constitutional interpretation implicit in the plan; "Government Influence, deeply planted & widely scatter'd by preceding Measures, is to receive a formidable Addition by this plan." He also opposed Hamilton's plan because it promoted sectional factions in Congress; it "seems to be a consistent part of a system which I ever dreaded. Subserviency of Southern to N[orther]n Interests are written in Capitals on its very Front."[38]

While Henry was no abstract political scientist, his work, and the work of the anti-federalists who objected to the Constitution, would prove to be an important foundation for political thought as the new Democratic-Republican party, led by Jefferson and Madison, started to form in opposition to expansion of federal power through a broad reading of the Constitution. While Henry would soon retire from politics, the battle over the authority of the federal government would continue, contributing to the creation of political parties in the 1790s and, ultimately, drawing Patrick

Henry back into politics for his final political campaign. By the end of 1791, though, having fought the battle over the Constitution, in declining health, and desperately hoping to have time to strengthen his finances and enjoy his family, Henry again withdrew from politics for what he hoped was the last time.

* * * * *

While the debates over the structure of American government and the U.S. Constitution are undoubtedly the most important aspects of this period of Henry's life, his family and professional life continued to develop as well. Before turning to Henry's retirement, a brief review of his personal affairs during the battle for the Constitution is appropriate.

When Henry retired from the governorship in 1786, he was 50 years old, tired of the strains of governance, and he had a young wife, a growing family (five more children since 1778), and concerns about how he would provide for them. His family continued to expand, as did his obligations. Alexander Spotswood Henry was born in 1788 (during the ratification convention), becoming the sixth child of Patrick and Dorothea, Henry's 12th (ranging in ages in 1788 from a newborn to a 33-year-old mother who already had six children of her own). Five more children would follow in the 1790s (see Document 2).

In 1786, leaving what seemed like the bustle of Richmond (although still a very small town by modern standards, less than 4,000 people), Henry moved to a simple home in Prince Edward County not far from present-day Farmville. There he ran a plantation of nearly 1,700 acres and managed other landholdings, including the 10,000 acre Leatherwood Plantation in Henry County where he had lived from 1779 to 1784. With some time and hard work, Henry expected to fix his finances, but he became concerned that he would not be able to do so with farming alone. When Henry expressed these concerns to a neighbor, reportedly the neighbor just laughed and told him "Go back to the bar; your tongue will soon pay your debts." Whether or not the story is true, Henry soon returned to the practice of law to help him pay debts and fund a legacy for his children, a topic that will be addressed in the next chapter.[39]

In addition to seeking to secure his family's financial future, Henry also wanted to give his sons the formal education that he lacked. (Alas, in this era, very few young women were given a formal education; rather, they were educated at home with the expectation that they would become home-makers or, in the case of southern gentry, plantation mistresses.) His desire to provide college educations for his sons encouraged Henry to support the creation of Hampden-Sydney College in Prince Edward County. When the College was incorporated in 1783, both Henry and James Madison were on its board of trustees. Over the years, seven of Henry's sons would attend Hampden-Sydney.

Unfortunately, the divisive debates over ratification of the Constitution would also interfere in Henry's relationship to the new college. The president of Hampden-Sydney in 1788 was John Blair Smith, a Presbyterian minister who had been deeply involved in the debate over Virginia's religious General Assessment. (Smith seemed initially to support the assessment advocated by Henry, but after the Presbyterian laity denounced any government involvement in religion, Smith changed his position.) Smith, a federalist, actively advocated support of the Constitution, a relatively unpopular position in the south side of Virginia (south of the James River). That alone would not likely have caused a significant rift with Henry. Smith, though, scheduled a campus debate among students at Hampden-Sydney on the question of ratification of the new Constitution. In that debate, Smith had one student mimic Patrick Henry's arguments against ratification (arguments that Smith had apparently had a student record during one of Henry's appearances opposing the Constitution). Smith then provided arguments in response to Henry for another student to deliver. Henry, coming to the college to witness what he thought was a student debate, was deeply angered – not only did he feel that his position had not been adequately presented, but he had no opportunity to respond to Smith's arguments. As a result, Henry refused to again attend church services when Smith was preaching; while the former governor did not end his support for Hampden Sydney, this episode may have had something to do with Smith's stepping-down from the college's presidency in 1789. Interestingly, Smith was equally annoyed over the ratification debate; for example, he later took the opportunity to snipe at Henry's prior support of a religious assessment in a letter to James Madison (an odd criticism for Smith to make given his previous support for the assessment).

All of this – the ratification of the Constitution, the growth in Henry's family and his farming and legal practice, and his efforts to educate his children and provide them with a material legacy – would play out in Henry's retirement years.

Notes

1. Peter H. Lindert and Jeffrey G. Williamson, "American Incomes Before and After the Revolution," *Journal Economic History*, 73: 3 (September 2013): 725–765. See generally John J. McCusker and Russell R. Menard, *The Economy of British America, 1607–1789* (Chapel Hill: University of North Carolina Press, 1985).
2. Letter from James Madison to Thomas Jefferson, October 24, 1787, *Papers of James Madison* (Congressional Series), 10: 212. Letter from James Madison to Edmund Randolph, February 25, 1787, ibid., 9: 299.
3. Ibid., 10: 207. See also Norman K. Risjord, *Chesapeake Politics, 1781–1800* (New York: Columbia University Press, 1978): 177 (similar disturbances in the Chesapeake region). Jefferson,

serving as Ambassador to France, thought people were too alarmed by Shays' Rebellion, leading to his famous comment that "a little rebellion now and then is a good thing." Many historians believe that fear of anarchy was overblown and that the elite were really more concerned about the threat to their status posed by increased democracy and more active participation of the "lesser sort" in government, including Madison's concerns with Henry's populism. Beeman, "Democratic Faith," 309. Also Woody Holton, *Unruly Americans and the Origins of the Constitution* (New York: Hill & Wang, 2008). For Shays' Rebellion, see, e.g., Leonard L. Richards, *Shays's Rebellion: The American Revolution's Final Battle* (Philadelphia: University of Pennsylvania Press, 2002).

4. *Journals of the Continental Congress*, vol. 32 (February 21, 1787): 74.

5. Henry, *Patrick Henry*, II: 304.

6. Letter from Edmund Randolph to James Madison, March 1, 1787, *Papers of James Madison* (Congressional Series), 9: 301. Letter from Patrick Henry to Edmund Randolph, February 13, 1787, Henry, *Patrick Henry*, II: 311.

7. Letter from James Madison to George Washington, March 18, 1787, *Papers of James Madison* (Congressional Series), 9: 316.

8. Letter from Edmund Randolph to Patrick Henry, December 6, 1786, Henry, *Patrick Henry*, II: 311.

9. Letter from James Madison to Thomas Jefferson, May 15, 1784, *Papers of Thomas Jefferson*, 7: 258. Letter from William Short to Thomas Jefferson, May 15, 1784, ibid., 7: 257. Some historians believe that it was Henry who introduced a resolution into the Virginia House of Delegates in 1784 arguing that the Confederation Congress had *implied* authority to force states to pay requisitions, an argument later made by Jefferson as well. See William C. Rives, *History of the Life and Times of James Madison*, vol. 1 (Boston: Little, Brown and Co., 1859): 565.

10. Letter from Patrick Henry to the Virginia Delegates in Congress, May 16, 1786, Henry, *Patrick Henry*, III: 351. Letter from Patrick Henry to the President of Congress, May 16, 1786, ibid., III: 353–355.

11. Letter from John Marshall to Arthur Lee, March 5, 1787, *The Papers of John Marshall Digital Edition*, Charles Hobson, ed. (Charlottesville: University of Virginia Press, Rotunda, 2014), 1: 206.

12. See Patrick Henry to Joseph Martin, October 4, 1786, Henry, *Patrick Henry*, III: 375, and Patrick Henry to Annie Christian, October 20, 1786, ibid., III: 380. Letter from Edmund Randolph to James Madison, March 1, 1787, *Papers of James Madison* (Congressional Series), 9: 301. Letter from John Marshall to Arthur Lee, March 5, 1787, *Papers of John Marshall*, 1: 206. Letter from James Madison to George Washington, December 7, 1786, *Papers of James Madison* (Congressional Series), 9: 200.

13. On the Convention, see Richard Beeman, *Plain, Honest Men: The Making of the American Constitution* (New York: Random House, 2009). The story of the ratification of the Constitution is told well in Pauline Maier, *Ratification: The People Debate the Constitution, 1787–1788* (New York: Simon & Schuster, 2010).

14. Letter from George Washington to Patrick Henry, September 24, 1787, Henry, *Patrick Henry*, II: 319–320.

15. Letter from Patrick Henry to George Washington, October 19, 1787, Henry, *Patrick Henry*, II: 320–321.

16. Speech of June 5, 1788, Jonathan Elliot, ed., *The Debates in the Several State Conventions on the Adoption of the Federal Constitution*, vol. III (Philadelphia, PA: J. B. Lippincott & Co., 1861): 46.

17. Letter from Thomas Jefferson to William Carmichael, December 15, 1787, *Papers of Thomas Jefferson*, 12: 425. Letter from Henry Knox to Rufus King, June 19, 1788, Meade, *Patrick Henry*, II: 342.

18. While a stenographer, David Robertson, transcribed convention speeches, the transcription does not do Henry justice. Often, Henry spoke too fast for Robertson to keep up; at other times, Robertson was so mesmerized by Henry's eloquence that he forgot to continue to

transcribe. Some suggest that Robertson, a federalist, may have dropped some of Henry's words or arguments. This may explain why Henry's recorded remarks sometimes seemed to wander. Others suggest that Henry was not as prepared as he might have been; federalists were naturally far more familiar with negotiation of the Constitution. Still, even the incomplete transcriptions of Henry's speeches fill over one-fifth of the record and demonstrate the power of his oratory.

19. Elliot, *Debates*, III: 44, 445, 448.
20. Ibid., III: 58.
21. Beeman, "Democratic Faith," 303.
22. Speech of June 5, 1788, Elliot, *Debates*, III: 44–45, 47.
23. Speech of June 12, 1788, ibid., III: 314.
24. Letter from George Washington to Charles Carter, December 14, 1797, *Papers of George Washington* (Confederation Series), 5: 492.
25. Ibid.
26. Elliot, *Debates*, III: 591, 595.
27. Speech of June 24, 1788, ibid., III: 590–591. Paul Finkelman, "Slavery and the Constitutional Convention: Making a Covenant with Death," *Beyond Confederation: Origins of the Constitution and American National Identity*, eds. Richard Beeman, Stephen Botein, and Edward Carter III (Chapel Hill: University of North Carolina Press, 1987), 193 n.
28. Speech of June 24, 1788, Elliot, *Debates*, III: 625. Wirt, *Sketches*, 209–210, quoting Judge Archibald Stuart (Federalist).
29. Speech of June 25, 1788, Elliot, *Debates*, III: 652 (second emphasis added).
30. Speech of June 5, 1788, ibid., III: 63. See also ibid., 57, 161.
31. Ibid., III: 644–649. William Nelson, Jr., to William Short, July 12, 1788, John P. Kaminski, ed., *The Documentary History of the Ratification of the Constitution*, vol. X (Virginia III) (Madison: State Historical Society of Wisconsin, 1993): 1701.
32. Henry, *Patrick Henry*, II: 412–413, citing "Manuscripts of David Meade Randolph," *Southern Literary Messenger* I: 7 (March, 1835): 332. *Documentary History of Ratification*, X: 1701. See also ibid., X: 1560–1563, 1697–1698.
33. Letter from George Washington to James Madison, November 17, 1788, *Papers of James Madison* (Congressional Series), 11: 351.
34. See Madison Speech, June 8, 1789, *Papers of James Madison* (Congressional Series), 12: 207. Henry Speech, June 12, 1788, Elliot, *Debates*, III: 325. See also Letter from Thomas Jefferson to James Madison, March 15, 1789, *Papers of James Madison* (Congressional Series), 12: 14.
35. Meade, *Patrick Henry*, II: 392.
36. Letter from Patrick Henry to William Grayson, March 31, 1789, *Virginia Magazine of History and Biography* 14: 2 (October 1906): 203.
37. Letter from Patrick Henry to James Monroe, January 24, 1789, Henry, *Patrick Henry*, II: 460. Paul Finkelman, "Antifederalists: The Loyal Opposition and the American Constitution," Review, "The Complete Anti-Federalist," ed. by Herbert J. Storing (Chicago: University of Chicago Press, 1981), 7 vols., *Cornell Law Review*, 70 (1984–1985): 206.
38. Letter from Patrick Henry to James Monroe, January 24, 1789, Henry, *Patrick Henry*, II: 460.
39. Ibid., II: 331.

CHAPTER 5

RETIREMENT

When Patrick Henry's term as a member of the Virginia House of Delegates expired in 1791, he did not have to retire from politics. He remained the most popular politician in Virginia (with the exception of George Washington, serving in Philadelphia as the first president under the Constitution). As further evidence of Henry's popularity, in 1790 the legislature had split Patrick Henry County (created in 1777) into two counties, named Patrick and Henry Counties. Having two counties in the state named for him was an unmatched honor.

But Henry, though only 55 years old in 1791, was feeling his age. His eldest son, John, only 34 years old, died tragically, apparently in 1791 (although the records are not perfectly clear on the date), and Henry was increasingly concerned about his ability to provide an adequate financial legacy for each of his children (12 living at the end of 1791, with 4 more to be born in his retirement; see Family Tree, Document 2). He hoped to leave plantations for his sons and reasonable security for his daughters, something from which he had not benefitted.

It had been over 25 years since Henry had entered public service at the time of the Stamp Act crisis. For almost all of those years, he had served in the Virginia legislature or as governor (although it should be noted that service as a state legislator was not a full-time job in the eighteenth century). Having entered public life without a great fortune, and with a very large and growing family, it was time for Henry to retire from the public scene. Writing to a daughter from his first marriage, he explained: "I am obliged to be very industrious & to take on me great Fatigue to clear myself of Debt – I hope to be able to accomplish this in a year or two if it pleases God to continue me in Health & Strength." Much of the debt had been incurred buying thousands of acres of land in Virginia, Kentucky, and North Carolina.[1]

As he left Richmond, Henry was determined to spend more time with his still-growing family, pursue farming and his legal career, and stay out of politics. Over the next eight years, he achieved two of those goals.

* * * * *

Removed from direct responsibility for public affairs and surrounded by his family, Henry was generally very happy in the period from 1791 until his death in 1799, and his demeanor showed it. Judge Spencer Roane, a son-in-law, wrote that "I am positive that I never saw him in a passion, nor apparently out of temper. Circumstances which would have highly irritated other men had no visible effect on him, he was always calm and collected."[2]

During his retirement, Patrick Henry's home was filled with small children and grandchildren, and Henry was exceedingly fond of spending time with them. Visitors often found him rough-housing on the ground with a group of offspring. He especially enjoyed entertaining family with music from his violin and flute, with the young children dancing happily about the old musician. He was known to write short poems and songs to amuse the children, especially "little sonnets for his daughters to sing and play." (These verses were intentionally destroyed after use because Henry, with some vanity, thought that "such compositions, if published, would injure his reputation, and lessen his influence with the people of Virginia.")[3]

Not all was fun and games, of course. There was much work to do. Raising his own children was expensive and time consuming, and Henry took on himself responsibility for many of his grandchildren, nieces, and nephews if one or both of their parents died prematurely. Henry was also a local community leader and was known to supply provisions for some of the needy in the area.

Education for his progeny continued to be a priority for Henry as well. While his education had been informal, although quite good, he wanted better for his sons. After receiving a basic education at home with tutors, many of his sons and grandsons attended Hampden-Sydney College. The old governor, though, did not leave their education solely to schoolmasters. Grandson Patrick Henry Fontaine told how the former governor would quiz him on his Latin lessons and that the oversight of his grandfather always proved far more intimidating than that of his college professors. Henry also trained some of his sons and grandsons in the law during his retirement, maintaining his law office at Red Hill for this purpose even after his own legal practice had largely ended (see Document 1).

Henry also had numerous social obligations in retirement, and he certainly continued to enjoy meeting people. While he preferred living in out-of-the-way locations, his home had always been a hospitable place, and in retirement he continued to honor Virginia's tradition of hospitality. He also encouraged sociability and hospitality among his children, telling them that he rarely met a man who did not tell him something of interest of which he had been ignorant.

The issue of Virginia hospitality and alcohol, though, was of some concern to Henry. It was reported that he had at least one whiskey still on his land, and consistent with the custom at the time, he likely provided hard liquor to guests. But, "[h]e rarely drank any wine or spirits," usually drinking water, although sometimes preferring Madeira wine. Reports that Henry completely abstained from alcohol appear to be inaccurate; still, in an effort to discourage the excessive drinking that was all too common in the eighteenth century, he supplied his table with home-brewed "small beer," a beer with a low alcohol content. He had done the same when serving his final terms as governor. Similarly, while Henry was a tobacco farmer for many years, as he grew older he developed a strong aversion to tobacco smoke. As a result, he banned smoking from his house and immediate dependencies. Stories were told that enslaved people who smoked would try to hide their pipes from Henry when he came around, often unsuccessfully. While Henry became a wealthy man in retirement and was known as a good host, his natural moderation in food, drink, and clothing was evident.[4]

Throughout this period, Henry continued to have a very substantial number of enslaved people working his plantations; at his death, he held over 100 on two plantations. While he recognized the horrors of slavery, Henry simply would not accept the cost of living without it (the financial cost and the cost in terms of his own comfort). He also apparently shared a deep, lingering fear among Virginia slave owners: slaves or free blacks would, if given the opportunity, exact an understandable revenge upon their "owners" because of years of often brutal oppression. During the ratification debates for the Constitution, he had noted that slavery was "detested" and had "fatal effects," but he argued to the slaveholders that dominated the convention that "prudence forbids its abolition." Racism undoubtedly fed his inaction. As a result, Henry took no action to encourage emancipation (although he reportedly supported the 1782 Virginia law which liberalized manumission – the voluntary freeing of enslaved people by masters), nor did he free any of his slaves nor make arrangements to free his slaves upon his death (as George Washington and numerous other Virginians did). Henry's will includes a detailed list of bequests of slaves to his wife and various children (and he only mentions that his wife may, should she choose, free one or two slaves). Henry was certainly not the most abusive slave owner in Virginia, but he did participate in the miserable institution and apparently somehow having "made his peace" with slavery as he grew older he did not express any particular antipathy to the practice nor, in his surviving writings, confront the hypocrisy of slavery flourishing among the patriots of '76.[5]

In spite of his lack of action on slavery, Henry became increasingly religious as he aged. Perhaps it is not uncommon for people to think more about issues beyond this life as they grow older, but challenges to religion in the French Revolution and among some Americans also drove Henry to increased religiosity (and had a significant influence on his political views as well). Initially, most Americans, including Henry, welcomed the French Revolution as the people of France rose up to oppose the tyrannical power of the monarchy and aristocracy; but the growing terror of repeated political purges and the beheading of King Louis XVI and Queen Marie Antoinette in early 1793 caused horror in America. The French Revolution had gone too far. Like many others, Henry was particularly outraged when Christianity, Catholicism for the vast majority of the French, was forcibly replaced by a state religion that worshipped the Goddess of Reason. (French revolutionaries correctly saw that the Church had worked in alliance with the monarchy and nobility to maintain power, but their solution was radical.) By the end of the 1790s, Henry had become concerned that revolutionary France, quickly becoming Napoleonic France, would destroy "the great pillars of all government and of social life . . . virtue, morality, and religion." Linking developments in France to Thomas Paine's unorthodox book, *Age of Reason*, Henry decried attacks on traditional Christianity at home and abroad. To his chagrin, after the first part of Paine's book was published in France in 1794, it had gone through 17 American editions from 1794 to 1796. Henry apparently went so far as to write a response to Paine but, deciding that others had already provided an adequate defense of Christianity, Henry had his unpublished manuscript destroyed. Instead, he continued to give away copies of Soame Jenyns's "On Internal Evidences of Christianity" (first published in 1776), which he had had printed at his own expense shortly after his last term as governor, saying a bit sheepishly that he hoped that recipients would "not take him for a travelling monk." (Ironically, Jenyns, a member of the British Parliament, had been a strong opponent of the American Revolution.)[6]

The increased influence of religion on Henry's personal life was also evident. In retirement, Henry reportedly always spent an hour late in the day in prayer and meditation. One neighbor told a story that he saw Henry reading the Bible one day when Henry held the book up saying "This book is worth all the books that ever were printed, and it has been my misfortune that I have never found time to read it with the proper attention and feeling till lately. I trust in the mercy of Heaven that it is not yet too late." In 1796, Henry wrote to his daughter Betsy, perturbed that it was "said by the deists that I am one of their number."[i] Undoubtedly with the French Revolution and Paine's deist tract in mind, he thought deism, by denying God's active involvement in the world, was just "another name for vice and depravity." While Henry had always been religious and a life-long member of the Anglican Church, his concern for religion undoubtedly increased in retirement and would again become evident at the time of his death.[7]

Still, some caution should be taken in evaluating Henry's religiosity. Before retirement, Henry had consistently been "remarkably tolerant of others," and "never obtruded" the topic of religion into a general conversation with friends or acquaintances. Evaluating his religiosity in the 1790s is complicated both by his increased interest in religion, which was undoubtedly real, and by the fact that his religiosity could be emphasized by both political allies and opponents. So, for example, Spencer Roane, a son-in-law and initially a political ally, expressed some skepticism about the purported change in Henry, saying that in the last several years of his life Henry's focus on religion was evidence of "some debility or gloom in his understanding"; that is, Roane thought he was becoming feeble-minded. Some biographers have seemed to agree with Roane's assessment. On the other hand, a more recent biographer has tended to see Henry in primarily religious terms, both in the 1790s and earlier.[8]

Both views seem to miss the mark. While Roane was certainly very familiar with Henry, he also was a rabid Jeffersonian republican; when he wrote about Henry's "debility," he was deeply discouraged with Henry's final political campaign as a Federalist (about which more later) and was trying to curry favor with Jefferson. In addition to questioning the source and consistency of Henry's religiosity, Roane tried to explain away Henry's mature political positions by claiming that his final years were marked by mental incapacity, which even a cursory review of the letters he wrote and his final political speech demonstrate not to be the case. At the same time, his correspondence also shows that religion did not dominate his life, nor either his business or political dealings during retirement. While undoubtedly religious, and increasingly so in retirement, Henry's developing political views cannot be dismissed as the ramblings of an overly-religious, feeble-minded old man.

Henry's retirement was also occupied with land acquisition. After leaving his governorship in 1779, Henry lived in Patrick Henry County in the

---

i   Deists believe that God created the world and the natural laws which control it, but believe that God does not intervene in the running of the world with miracles or by granting prayers. (The belief that God is active in the world is referred to as providentialism.) Deists often refer to God as the great clock-maker: God created and wound-up the system and allows it to run without interference. A number of the founders tended toward deism. Benjamin Franklin is perhaps the best example; Jefferson also had strong tendencies toward deism.

southern tier of the state on the 10,000 acre Leatherwood Plantation until 1784 when he was again elected governor and moved to Richmond. As governor in the mid-1780s, Henry moved his family to Pleasant Grove in Prince Edward County, not far from Richmond; but in 1792 he moved to Campbell County (almost 100 miles southwest of Richmond) and a large home on the Long Island Plantation (over 2,500 acres, with an additional 1,000 acres added before Henry's death). Even with that large acquisition, his fixation on land had not ended, and he began almost immediately to buy additional land in Virginia, Kentucky, and North Carolina. His land acquisitions would continue until his death; in fact, the month Henry died, he acquired a one-quarter interest in 25,000 acres in North Carolina. By the time of his death, Henry reportedly owned over 50,000 acres.

In 1794 Henry moved his home for the last time when he bought Red Hill Plantation (520 acres) in Charlotte County. While the 1.5 story family home at Red Hill was smaller than the home at Long Island, Henry was very comfortable there. He referred to Red Hill as the "Garden Spot of Virginia," and he would live there until his death in 1799.[9]

Henry acquired land for farming, for bequests to his children upon his death, and as an investment. He certainly had a farmer's love of his land. "As for *boasting*," one son-in-law told his biographer, "he was an entire stranger to it; unless it be that in his latter days he seemed proud of the goodness of his lands, and, I believe, wished to be thought wealthy . . . This I have accounted for by reflecting that he had long been under narrow and difficult circumstances as to property, from which he was at length happily relieved."[10]

Most of his land acquisitions were mundane business deals. One deal that was never finalized, though, became a bit of a political embarrassment to Henry and was used unfairly by his political opponents to try to tar his name. After ratification of the Constitution, Henry became particularly interested in land on the frontier and in the Deep South, thinking that if the new Constitution failed or if the government became tyrannical – a real concern for Henry at the time – it might be advisable to move from his beloved Virginia to more distant lands. Frontier lands were also a good investment which could be given to his children or be sold for profit. While it is not clear what, if anything, would have actually caused Henry to move from Virginia, he did seek to acquire a very large tract of land in what is now Mississippi (and was then part of Georgia) on the Yazoo River. The deal would prove to be a great disappointment and cause for much slander.

In 1789, the Georgia legislature gave the Virginia Yazoo Land Co., in which Henry was an investor, the right to buy over 11 million acres on the Mississippi River for $93,750 payable within two years. The Georgia legislature apparently believed that the lands were too distant and speculative to be developed by the state, but it initially welcomed private investment. Unfortunately, the transaction ran into multiple problems.

The investors understood that the land could be paid for with cash or with Georgia debt certificates surviving from the Revolution. Since they could be bought for less than face value, Henry and his partners bought up Georgia debt certificates. Unfortunately, in June 1790, the Georgia legislature passed a resolution saying that payment must be in specie (i.e. gold and silver); in 1791, when the investors offered debt certificates for the land, Georgia refused to accept them. By the time that Henry and his partners decided to sue Georgia, planning to take the case to the Supreme Court, the suit was prevented by the 11th Amendment to the Constitution (1795), which blocked the right of private individuals to sue a state.[11]

Complicating matters further, the United States and the Creek Indians entered into a treaty in 1790 returning control of the land that Georgia had promised to sell to the Virginia Yazoo Land Co. to the Creeks (land which Georgia claimed the Creeks had sold to the state). Henry was furious that the federal government was interfering with a state land transaction:

> If Congress may of Right forbid Purchases from the Indians of Territory included in the Charter Limits of your State, or any other, it is not easy to prove that any Individual Citizen has an indefeasible Right to any Land claimed under a State Patent. For, if the State territorial Right is not Sovereign & Supreme, & exclusively so, it must follow that some other Power does possess that exclusive Sovereignty: and every Title not derived from that other Power must be defective.

Apparently having not considered the extent of federal control of Native American relations, Henry saw this as the type of expansion of federal authority which he had warned against. As was not uncommon, Henry's political position aligned with his personal interests. (He made a similar objection to North Carolina's grant of what became Tennessee to the federal government without seeking approval of the territory's settlers – a deal which arguably interfered with some of Henry's land speculation.) With the Yazoo mess on his mind, he told another correspondent that "It is a Deception to urge, that Encroachments from the American Government are not dangerous." He encouraged the governor of Georgia to contact other states and to ask them to protest against federal efforts to control land within the states through Indian negotiations.[12]

This, though, did not cause the controversy. The real problem arose because, after reneging on the deal with the Virginia Yazoo Land Co., Georgia's legislature reached a different deal concerning the same land with several new groups of investors. Henry was not involved in this second set of transactions, but some of the investors that were had bribed every member of the legislature but one. When this became known, many of those who had been bribed were swept from office and a newly elected Georgia legislature changed directions again, abrogating the law that provided for the sale to the second group. Subsequent purchasers who had bought land from the second group and claimed that they knew nothing about the bribery sued. Finding a way around the 11th Amendment, they won their case at the Supreme Court – Fletcher v. Peck, 10 U.S. 87 (1810). This episode became a famous scandal, the Yazoo Land Fraud.

After his death, when he could no longer defend himself, political opponents, including Jefferson, attacked Henry's role in the Yazoo land deal for several reasons. First, they tried to tie Henry to the later fraud when he had nothing to do with the fraudulent transaction. In fact, Henry had studiously avoided land speculation while governor to prevent any suggestion that he was using his position for personal gain.[13]

Second, Henry was criticized for speculating in depreciated debt, speculation which had been rampant in this period. Speculators with deep pockets often bought debt certificates for a fraction of their face value from former soldiers who had been paid for their service with state "IOUs." When speculators did so based upon inside information about government policy not generally available to the public, serious ethical questions arose. In this case, however, while the partners apparently acquired the debt for far less than its face value from holders who were anxious to get some quick cash for their paper certificates, the transaction was entered into after 1788 (that is, after the Constitution was ratified and the value of such debt had begun to stabilize, although before Alexander Hamilton's plan for the federal government to fund the debt at face value had been introduced).

The claim that Henry "became wealthy" by speculating with soldiers' debt certificates is both untrue and unfair. Jefferson argued that Henry and his partners, since they could not buy the land with the debt certificates that they had purchased, found themselves benefitting from a windfall when Alexander Hamilton, the first secretary of the Treasury and Jefferson's great political antagonist, convinced Congress to adopt a plan which guaranteed the payment of state debt, as well as federal debt, at face value. Jefferson went so far as to tell Henry's biographer that Henry became a great supporter of Hamilton. This was simply not true: Consistent with his longstanding political principles, Henry was a strong opponent of Hamilton's finance plans because he believed that they exceeded the federal government's power expressed in the Constitution, and the Yazoo deal did not change his position. While Henry and his partners undoubtedly benefitted financially from Hamilton's scheme after it was introduced in Congress in January 1790 and adopted by the Congress in August 1790, they had bought debt after the Constitution was ratified and before the Hamilton scheme was proposed, and had planned to use it to purchase the property after Hamilton's plan was adopted. Thus, when they offered the certificates to Georgia, the certificates had risen to something approaching face value. In a letter to George Washington at the time, Jefferson admitted that the value of the debt certificates had increased before being offered to Georgia (and insisted that the buyers, including Henry, would drop the matter because of their profits on the debt). In fact, even after the certificates had increased in value, the investors decided to pursue a lawsuit against Georgia trying to get it to accept the payment. Still, it is true that they realized large profits from the debt that they held after the land deal fell through.[14]

Henry, of course, did not hear much of this criticism (since most of it was only voiced after his death when he could not defend himself), but he did always regret that he had been unable to purchase a large section of land in what would eventually become Mississippi.

While farming and land speculation occupied a great deal of Henry's time in retirement, his primary means of earning money was his legal practice.

* * * * *

After his fifth term as governor, Patrick Henry returned to the practice of law to help shore up his finances. While Henry may have needed the money, he also clearly loved being a lawyer. Given his abilities, it is no surprise that he soon regained his status as one of the most successful, and most highly paid, attorneys in Virginia. If one had an important case, particularly if your property or even life was riding on the outcome, Henry was the man to call upon. This period of his legal career was short – most of his legal work occurring from 1789 to 1793 – but it offers an interesting picture of Patrick Henry.

Some of his legal victories are the stuff of legend. In one case, a man happened to be traveling with a wagoneer on the road to Richmond when the driver knocked down a turkey that belonged to a local farmer and put it in the wagon. When a complaint was made to a justice of the peace, the driver accepted a whipping rather than go to jail. The other man, traveling with the wagoneer, was also whipped, but he then sued the justice of the peace insisting that he had nothing to do with the turkey. Henry represented the justice of the peace and was wrapping-up his defense when he turned to the jury: "this plaintiff tells you that he had nothing to do with the turkey – I dare say, gentlemen, not until it was *roasted.*" When Henry rolled the word "roasted" off his tongue with a knowing smile, the plaintiff was apparently the only one in court who was not convulsed with laughter.[15]

In another case, John Venable, an assistant commissary during the Revolution, took two steers from John Hook to supply the poorly provisioned American army on its way to Yorktown in 1781. Hook was a Scottish storekeeper and a suspected Tory. (It was not uncommon at this time for army commissaries to "impress" needed supplies, especially if the owner refused to accept the badly depreciated paper currency that was available, but as William Wirt observed, Venable's actions "had not been strictly legal.") After the war, Hook filed a lawsuit because he had not been paid for the cattle. Representing Venable, Henry told the jury the story of ragged soldiers – ill-clothed, ill-fed – struggling against one of the world's greatest military empires; he recounted the long and difficult war; he reminded jurors of the snow, dirt, and mud bloodstained by soldiers marching to battle without shoes. "Where was the man who had an American heart in his bosom, who would not have thrown open his fields, his barns, his cellars, the doors of his house, the portals of his breast, to have received with open arms, the meanest soldier in that little band of famished patriots?" Henry asked enraptured jurors. "Where is that man? There he stands [pointing at Hook] – but whether the heart of an American beats in his bosom, you, gentlemen, are to judge." Henry continued his story until he got to the glorious victory at Yorktown – a victory that brought universal rejoicing, fireworks, music, and parades. Interrupting his own story of celebration, Henry turned back to the jurors, "but hark! what notes of discord are those which disturb the general joy, and silence the acclamations of victory – they are the notes of *John Hook*, hoarsely bawling through the American camp, *beef! beef! beef!,*" Henry cried with a comical contortion of his face. Roaring with laughter the jurors seemed hardly to hear the plaintiff's attorney and retired to reach a verdict, by one report giving Hook a victory but damages of only one penny. Some reports noted that the plaintiff barely escaped the courthouse without being tarred and feathered. Was this fair to Hook? Perhaps not, but Henry had little sympathy for Tory's property (and an unmatched control of juries).[16]

Henry could also be serious when the case demanded it. In another case, a constable had been sent to a plantation to capture a slave accused of a minor crime, and he seized and bound the slave with the assistance of several colleagues and moved to take him away when the plantation mistress tried to intervene. Failing to convince the constable to release the slave, the woman ran to find her husband. He was seen entering the house and came out with a gun, some say he was seen to raise it, but the constable fired quickly and killed him. The constable was indicted for murder. At trial, extensive testimony from both sides took most of a day, and the jury seemed tired and ready to convict. Henry, one of the constable's attorneys, rose slowly, seemingly tired, and turned to the jury and entreated them: "I shall aim at brevity. But should I take up more of your time than you expect, I hope you will hear me with patience when you consider that *blood is concerned.*" Gripped by Henry's appearance, tone, and argument, the jury and the court fell silent. Henry proceeded, reminding them that the plantation owner had not come out of the house with a club or stones that the constable might have avoided, he asked the jury: "How wide is the difference between sticks or stones and *double-triggered, loaded rifles, cocked at your breast?*" The constable was acquitted. There are many such stories.[17]

Within a few years, Henry became one of the undisputed leaders of the Virginia bar. Archibald Alexander, a Presbyterian minister, explained that "The power of his eloquence was felt equally by the learned and the unlearned. No man who ever heard him speak, on any important occasion, could fail to admit his uncommon power over the minds of his hearers." Some of the most telling testimonies to his persuasiveness came from those who were initially skeptical. Before the famous British Debts case (discussed below), Justice James Iredell, a strong Federalist, had dismissed reports of Henry's abilities as partisan politics favoring the local antifederalist leader, but hearing Henry in court he reportedly exclaimed without hesitation "Gracious God! He is an orator indeed!" Andrew Jackson, who happened to hear Henry in court while traveling through Virginia, conceded that "no conception I had ever formed, had given me any just idea of the man's powers of eloquence." Later claims by political opponents that Henry's abilities only impressed local, uneducated audiences simply do not hold-up to scrutiny.[18]

Henry's success owed much both to his deep understanding of the human condition and to his great empathy for the common man. To jurors and judges alike, he always seemed filled with real sympathy or anger or remorse or indignation for his clients, and he was capable of making others see things from his clients' perspective – perhaps the most important skill for a trial attorney. In a notorious murder case, Henry presented to the court and jury the well-respected parents of the accused. Explaining how stricken they would be if their son was wrongly convicted, he caused "the jury to lose sight of the murder they were trying, and weep with old Holland and his wife . . . it was impossible for the stoutest heart not to take sides with the criminal." "[H]is most irresistible charm was the vivid feeling of his cause with which he spoke. Such feeling infallibly communicates itself to the breast of the hearer." Reverend Alexander said that at one trial he appeared "lean rather than fleshy," with his clothes "something the worse for wear." But this tended to draw his audience in. As he proceeded, "there was expressed such an intensity of feeling that all my doubts were dispelled; never again did I question whether Henry felt, or only acted a feeling."[19]

As with his political and financial success, Henry's triumphs as an attorney were criticized by some. It was often said that Henry would do anything for a large fee (a common canard against lawyers). Jefferson insisted that Henry "received great fees for his services, & had the reputation of being insatiable in money." And there is no doubt that he often charged a great deal for his services (when the client could afford it). In more than one instance, Henry declined a case, either because he was too busy, he was ill, or the case was too distant, and a client offered an exorbitant fee to gain his services. Since Henry was practicing law to pay his debts and create bequests for his children, he often could not resist. He was also accused, as criminal lawyers often are, of working to free murderers and horse thieves.[20]

One prominent case provides evidence of both Henry's ability and the reasons why he was criticized: In what was among the most scandalous stories in eighteenth-century Virginia, Richard Randolph, of the wealthy and politically influential Randolph family, was accused of murdering a baby born to his unmarried sister-in-law, 16-year-old Ann Randolph, who had come to stay at the home of Richard and his wife Judith, Ann's sister, after Ann's widowed father married a young women only a few years older than her. People assumed that Richard was the father of the dead infant. Appropriately enough, the plantation where Richard and Judith lived was named Bizarre. (Ann was also a cousin and sister-in-law of Jefferson's daughter, Martha; such interlocking family connection being not uncommon in Virginia in that period.)

When Richard was indicted for murder, the wealthy Randolph family sought to hire Patrick Henry and John Marshall. After initially refusing the case, Henry was reportedly paid 500 guineas to defend Richard. (One guinea was originally a gold piece worth 1 pound sterling.) The government's case was built on circumstantial (although substantial) evidence, including Ann's sickness, screams in the night, blood, and testimony from an enslaved person who saw a dead infant (although testimony of slaves was inadmissible in court). Yet, authorities found no body, and the defense seemed to question whether Ann had even been pregnant. One witness reported peeping through a keyhole and seeing a visibly pregnant Ann Randolph. On cross-examination, Henry mocked the witness: "Which eye did you peep with?" As the jurors laughed, Henry walked away declaring, as if to himself (but loud enough so the jurors could hear), "Great God deliver us from eavesdroppers!" Randolph was eventually acquitted for lack of evidence. John Randolph, brother of the accused and future political opponent of Henry, soon to be a noted orator himself, was heard to say that Henry was "the greatest orator that ever lived"; he spoke like "Shakespeare and Garrick combined, and spake as never man spake."[21]

Was Richard Randolph guilty? Perhaps. Some doubt was cast on the government's sensational theory when Ann later claimed that she had been engaged to Richard's brother, Theodorick, who had died early in 1792, the year of the alleged murder. History will probably never know the truth of the matter.[22]

Henry, however, performed his job as defense attorney masterfully: The government must prove its case in a criminal trial beyond a reasonable doubt, and a defense attorney should take all honest means to defend his or her client, to make the government prove its case rather than winning conviction based on innuendo and assumptions. Without competent defense lawyers, the legal system could not be trusted to ensure that only the guilty are convicted (although in the eighteenth century, as today, in too many instances a guilty person goes free, and in too many instances the innocent suffer – it is an imperfect system).

Criticism of Henry's efforts as an attorney often came from those who were jealous of his legal and financial success, or who were otherwise political opponents. For example, William Loughton Smith, a Federalist leader in Congress, wrote in 1791 that Henry makes:

> . . . a great deal of money by large fees of £50 or £100 for clearing horse thieves and murderers, which has lost him much of the great reputation he enjoyed in his neighborhood; he has been left out of the Assembly at the last election; some say . . . that his conduct has given general disgust. I am told that he will travel hundreds of miles for a handsome fee to plead for criminals, and that his powers of oratory are so great he generally succeeds, insomuch, that a man in his neighborhood has been heard to say he should have no apprehension of being detected in horse stealing, for that Governor Henry, or Colonel Henry, as he is sometimes called, would for £50 clear him.

Years later, Thomas Jefferson, having declared Henry a personal and political enemy, made similar claims, insisting that "his judgment . . . in matters of law it was not worth a copper: he was avaricious & rotten hearted. his two great passions were the love of money & of fame: but when these came into competition the former predominated." Both reports must be taken with a grain of salt. Given Henry's continued popularity in Virginia (including having a second county named after him in 1790 and being again elected governor in 1796 by a Jeffersonian assembly), it appears far more reasonable to accept Henry's claim that he chose to retire from the political arena than Smith's argument that he was forced out because of his legal work. It is also worth noting that the criminal cases that Henry won were before juries, which is to say that the common man of Virginia agreed that Henry was properly casting doubt on his clients' alleged guilt. Henry was so successful because he could convince jurors to empathize with his clients, to see them as humans facing difficult situations, to see things from their perspective.[23]

In evaluating Henry's legal career and ability, some consideration might also be given to Henry's largest and most famous case during this period, the British Debts case. Not only was this an important case legally, eventually going to the Supreme Court (although reaching a final decision against his clients in *Ware v. Hylton* (1796) after Henry had retired from the case), but it was clearly important to Henry and many Virginians for broader, political reasons.

In the 1780s, the question of debts owed to British merchants from before the Revolution became a critical issue in Virginia. During the war, the Virginia legislature had acted to "confiscate" those debts, seizing them from people that were seen as "enemies." The legislators reasoned that this was no different than seizing an enemy's horse or corn, a war-time practice that was well-established. Once it seized the debts, Virginia told its citizens who owed money to British merchants that the money could now be paid to the Virginia government, and it could be paid in Virginia currency (the paper money that had been issued to finance the war and which had dropped rapidly in value). Many Virginians happily took advantage of the new law and "paid" their debts to British merchants by giving the Virginia government depreciated currency.

Unfortunately for the debtors, as part of the Treaty of Paris of 1783 settling the war, the United States guaranteed creditors the right to recover debts from before the war. Yet, for years after the treaty, there was no effective way for British creditors to collect in Virginia; a law (which Henry had supported) barred suits for British debts. Yet once the U.S. Constitution was adopted, making the Paris Treaty (and other treaties) the "supreme law of the land" and creating a federal court system that Virginia could not control, creditors brought hundreds of cases in the new federal courts in Virginia. Henry was among the team of leading attorneys, including future Chief Justice Marshall, hired to defend the debtors.

The legal intricacies of the case need not be rehearsed in detail here. The weight of the argument, though, was carried by Henry who focused on two key points: First, he argued that debts were legitimately subject to confiscation in the war, just like other enemy property. Lawyers for the British creditors made what seemed like a sound, although technical, legal argument: governments at war could seize goods and real property, but they could not seize intangible property like a debt; a debt was simply an obligation between two private parties. Henry scoffed at this argument. "Debts are too sacred to be touched?" he asked incredulously. "It is a mercantile idea that worships Mammon instead of God."[ii] To Henry, the argument that horses, crops, tools, wagons, and farms owned by "enemies" could be seized in a war, all of the wealth of the small landowner, tradesman, or farmer, but not the debt owed

---

ii Mammon is money or material wealth. Henry was referring to Matthew 6:24: "You cannot serve both God and mammon."

to the wealthy, was ludicrous. Such a law would protect only the wealthy at the expense of ordinary citizens. Certainly, Henry reasoned, the dire circumstances faced by the new state during the war justified the decision to confiscate the debts and use the proceeds to help to fund the war effort. He reminded the court of what would have happened had America lost the war: "had we been subdued, would not every right have been wrested from us? . . . Would it not be absurd to save debts, while they [the British if they had won] should burn, hang, and destroy?" Henry's argument in this respect was eventually upheld by a majority of the Supreme Court.[24]

Second, and critically, Henry argued that the British creditors could not rely on the Paris Peace Treaty because Britain was in violation of the treaty in at least two key respects: It continued to maintain forts on U.S. territory (Detroit and Niagara) and during evacuation of their troops, the British took with them stolen "property" (enslaved people). While the treaty clearly intended to require the British to leave behind slaves who had crossed into their lines seeking freedom, mercifully, British commanders refused to return previously enslaved people and evacuated thousands to Canada and other British dependencies. Henry's argument was certainly appealing to many white Virginians; the Virginia legislature, supported by Henry, had complained to the Confederation Congress about this treaty violation as early as 1784. (Of course, the British pointed to the failure of Virginia and other states to honor the debts as a justification for not evacuating the forts.)[25]

Given both the importance of the case and who was leading the defense (perhaps the last time he would speak in Richmond), when Henry began his argument at the trial in September 1791, the court had an overflowing audience. So many political and legal minds wanted to watch that the legislature could not get a quorum to do business during the trial. Henry did not disappoint; he was particularly adept at taking apart the arguments of opposing counsel. One observer noted the striking mannerisms of Henry in this regard: "If the answer which he was about to give was a short one, he would give it without removing his spectacles from his nose – but if he was ever seen to give his spectacles a cant to the top of his wig, *it was a declaration of war*, and his adversaries must stand clear." (It is believed that the famous Sully painting of Henry, with his glasses propped back upon his wig (see Document 1), was made from a sketch taken during the British Debts case.)[26]

The case proceeded for years, starting in 1791 and being reargued before the district court (with a change in judges and plaintiffs) in 1793. Henry initially won the case before the district court, but the Supreme Court reversed in *Ware v. Hylton* in 1796 (after Henry was no longer involved). The Court ruled that the treaty had to be enforced (and individuals or states could not declare a foreign country in violation of a treaty and thus avoid its terms); the British creditors had to be paid.

Several things are important about the case. First, this was not a criminal case in which Henry could effectively appeal to the emotions of jurors. This was a complex legal proceeding involving difficult questions of international, statutory, and business law argued before learned judges. Even Jefferson had to admit that Henry did an extraordinary job in preparing for the case (although Jefferson did so only grudgingly, saying that Henry's great effort was "totally foreign to his character"). Second, Henry's position in the case was wildly popular in Virginia, tending to enhance his formidable popularity. After the case, Edmund Randolph, Washington's attorney general, reported to the president that Henry's "ascendancy has risen to an immeasurable height." Henry's work in the British Debts case apparently contributed to President Washington's decision to offer him a position on the Supreme Court, a position which Henry declined (discussed below).[27]

After 1793 and the British Debts argument, Henry began to wind-down his legal work, although he continued to train sons and grandsons in the law and practiced at a much reduced rate until shortly before his death. He hoped to finish his days as a Virginia farmer. Political issues, however, continued to intervene in Henry's life.

* * * * *

After Virginia's ratification convention, and before he retired from the political arena, Patrick Henry had returned to the Virginia General Assembly and worked hard to have anti-federalists elected to the new national government, to encourage a second constitutional convention, and to ensure the passage of strong amendments to the Constitution. He was less than successful in each of those areas. While many scholars believe that anti-federalists outnumbered the federalists at the time of ratification, the federalists gained control of the national government in the first several federal elections. To some extent, having been badly out-maneuvered in the ratification process, anti-federalists were discouraged; there was also a sense among some that the federalists, having created the new government, should be given an opportunity to make it work. Having done what he could, Henry made it clear that he would be a peaceable citizen and work within the system that had been adopted, a position that he maintained after retiring from politics. In 1795, he seemed happy to be able to write to Henry Lee, then governor of Virginia, that "Since the adoption of the present constitution . . . I have never omitted to inculcate a strict adherence to the principles of it. And I have the satisfaction to think that in no part of the union have the laws been more pointedly obeyed, than in that where I have resided and spent my time."[28]

Still, Henry and his concerns had not been forgotten after Virginia's convention. For example, in 1789, as the U.S. Senate struggled with what titles should be used to address the president (and John Adams embarrassed himself by suggesting "His Highness, the President of the United States, and Protector of their Liberties"), a friend of Washington's wrote that "The Opponents to the government affect to smile at it, and consider it as a verification of their prophecies and the tendency of the government. Mr. Henry's description of it, that it squinted towards monarchy, is in every mouth, and has established him in the general opinion, as a true Prophet." In some respects, concerns with the Constitution which Henry voiced in the ratification convention became a framework by which the document and government would be judged. In time, they helped to form the basis of the rising Democratic-Republican party, which opposed the centralizing tendencies of the Federalists.[29]

During his years of retirement, Henry's political thought continued to mature; several factors had a major influence. First, as time went on, Henry became more comfortable with how the federal government was actually operating; it was not living up to (or living down to) his fears during the ratification process. Certainly he disapproved of a number of actions taken by the government, Hamilton's expansive scheme for a national bank and payment of the state and national war debt, for example. Yet, over all, the government seemed to function fairly well and public servants seemed to be acting in a responsible manner. Within months of the new government coming into being, Senator Richard Henry Lee wrote to assure Henry that the new judiciary act removed his concerns with "vexations and abuses that might have been warranted by the terms of the constitution." By late in 1790, little more than two years after ratification, Henry wrote to one correspondent that "Truth obliges me to declare that I perceive in the Federal Characters I converse with in this Country an honest & patriotic care of the general Good."[30]

Second, eruption of the French Revolution would have a major impact on politics in America and around the world, and on Henry. Most Americans, including Henry, initially embraced the French Revolution as a democratic revolution not unlike their own, throwing off monarchy and aristocracy; but over the course of the 1790s, France devolved into chaos. As time went on, Henry was increasingly disillusioned by the abusive series of governments that controlled France after its revolution, not only their persecution of religion, but also their political failings. While Henry had been an advocate for the voice of the middle and working class people (excluding African-Americans), and would continue to be so, the French Revolution demonstrated that allowing all power to be exercised by the whims of a vocal populace without checks and balances might devolve into the mob rule that conservatives had always warned against. Henry correctly anticipated that the radical democracy of the French Revolution and the chaos in France might create a backlash and an opportunity for a dictator. The risk was made much worse by the fact that the French had lived for years under a strict monarchy and had not developed strong experience with civic responsibility and virtue, selfless work for the common good. Henry warned that "the present generation in France is so debased by a long despotism, they possess so few of the virtues that constitute the life and soul of republicanism, that they are incapable of forming a correct and just estimate of *rational* liberty." When a young Napoleon began to win battle after battle on behalf of Republican France, Henry saw the danger long before most of his contemporaries and warned those who continued to support France: "Their revolution will terminate differently from what you expect – their state of anarchy will be succeeded by despotism, and I should not be surprised, if *the very man* at whose victory you now rejoice [Napoleon], should, Caesar-like, subvert the liberties of his country." It was only after Henry's death that Napoleon seized power, but developments in France led Henry to rethink his politics. While he had always supported a balanced government (with separation of powers, and checks and balances), he became more concerned with consistency and dependability. In short, the French Revolution made the aging Henry somewhat more politically conservative and supportive of stable government.[31]

A third major influence on Henry's political thinking was the growth of partisanship as U.S. political parties coalesced in the 1790s. This concern was shared by Washington, John Adams, and others who believed virtuous citizens should participate in public service for the general good rather than particular interests. To Henry, too many politicians seemed to be more concerned with promoting their own party than working for the good of the country and their fellow citizens. Henry was increasingly disillusioned by political parties that promoted an "us" versus "them" mentality. He was particularly annoyed with the Democratic-Republican party (Jefferson's and Madison's party), heir to the anti-federalist philosophy that Henry had advocated during the ratification debates. Not only did many Democratic-Republicans continue to support the French Revolution long after it became clear that it had run amok, but in the name of party politics they exaggerated problems with the Washington administration and engaged in character assassination even of the beloved Washington. "I see with concern our old commander-in-chief most abusively treated," Henry wrote in 1796. He conceded that he did not support all of Washington's actions, but he thought that political leaders in a republic should be given some benefit of the doubt and that the politically-motivated attacks were unfair. "[N]or are his long and great services remembered, as any apology for his mistakes in an office to which he was totally unaccustomed." Henry, speaking for the ages, was concerned that the "baneful effect of faction" (party politics) risked tearing the nation apart.[32]

While his political thought continued to develop, Henry remained focused on his retirement and running his plantations and legal practice. This did not prevent others from seeking Henry's political support. In fact, few if any politicians have ever been courted as seriously and offered the breadth of important political positions that were offered to Henry during his retirement, with him consistently refusing the offers.

Twice Henry declined the opportunity to be appointed a U.S. senator, first upon William Grayson's death in 1790 and again in 1794 when James Monroe resigned to become ambassador to France. In 1794, Henry wrote to Virginia's governor that he must decline the office given his "Time of life – combined with the great Distance to Philadelphia" (where the federal government was still meeting). In 1796, the Virginia General Assembly, at that point dominated by Jeffersonians, elected Henry governor for a sixth time. Henry also declined that position.[33]

Most interestingly, during his presidency, George Washington repeatedly sought to get Henry – the leading anti-federalist during the ratification debates – out of retirement and into the Federalist administration.[iii] Undoubtedly Washington was seeking both Henry's substantive input and the political goodwill that would have accompanied appointing one of the most popular men in America. Washington offered Henry positions as Ambassador to Spain to negotiate a treaty concerning the Mississippi (1794) and as secretary of state (1795). Henry was told that Washington would appoint him to the Supreme Court (1795) if he would take the position, and Washington wrote that he would have offered Henry the position of Ambassador to France in 1796, but he knew that he would not accept.

Henry, while now wishing well to the national government, consistently turned down the offers. Declining the position of secretary of state, Henry wrote to Washington to explain: "what is of decisive weight with me, my own health and strength I believe are unequal to the dutys [sic] of the station you are pleased to offer me." Henry was clear that he was not declining because of his earlier opposition to ratification. "Believe me, Sir, I have bid adieu to the distinction of federal and antifederal ever since the commencement of the present government." As Henry said at the time of ratification, he would do what he could to improve the system, and he would not seek

---

iii Political groupings during the ratification process were neither particularly organized nor continuing organizations. Thus, when speaking of ratification, it is common to use "federalist" and "anti-federalist," without capitalization. In the 1790s, formal party structures were beginning to form, and the "Federalists," including Washington, John Adams, and Alexander Hamilton can be compared to the "Democratic-Republican" party of Jefferson and Madison.

to undermine it. The former governor told Washington that he would come out of retirement only in the case of a dire necessity:

> ... if my Country is destined in my day to encounter the horrors of anarchy, every power of mind or body which I possess will be exerted in support of the government under which I live, and which has been fairly sanctioned by my countrymen. I should be unworthy the character of a republican or an honest man, if I withheld from the government my best and most zealous efforts because in its adoption I opposed it in its unamended form.[34]

It is telling that in 1795 Henry's response focused on the "horrors of anarchy," rather than the danger of tyranny which had been at the center of his political philosophy during the American Revolution and ratification debates. Perhaps he was thinking of France. Developments in his own country, though, were also clearly on his mind. He wrote to Governor Henry Lee at about this time that he did not like the "Democratic Societies," supporters of the Democratic-Republican party, that were stirring up opposition to the administration. While declining to join Washington's cabinet, Henry could not resist expressing his disdain for leaders of political parties who seemed to put party interests above those of the public and to incite political discord. "And I do most cordially execrate the conduct of those men who lose sight of the public interest from personal motives."[35]

After Washington left office, Henry continued to receive offers of positions in the federal government during John Adams' presidency. (Adams and Henry had worked together in the First Continental Congress, and they always had great mutual respect.) Many of Adams' supporters thought that Henry would be a perfect vice-presidential candidate, with an Adams–Henry ticket certainly being unbeatable. (Alexander Hamilton also thought that promoting Henry's candidacy might result in Henry being elected president rather than Adams, whom Hamilton had come to detest, a plan which Hamilton later dropped in favor of promoting Thomas Pinckney whom he thought would be more supportive of Federalist principles. Once Pinckney was the preferred alternative to Adams, Hamilton supporters made clear that they wanted to "be rid of P. H.") The possibility had received enough consideration in 1796 that Henry, concerned that he might deflect votes from serious candidates, actually took out an advertisement in the newspaper saying that he was retired and could not "discharge the duties" of vice president. He asked electors not to vote for him to avoid "embarrassment in the suffrages." Still, during Adams' term, Henry was offered the position of special ambassador to France, but again declined.[36]

While Washington and Adams and their supporters were courting Henry, political opponents sought to prevent any such alliance. What was somewhat surprising is that Henry's chief political opponents in the 1790s were from the newly forming Democratic-Republican party under Jefferson and Madison, a party that stressed states' rights and democratic principles, many of the same principles that Henry had championed during the ratification debate. The attacks took various and sometimes inconsistent forms. One way that opponents sought to undermine Henry's return to politics was to create a political and personal controversy between Washington and Henry. This vicious effort to create animosity between two heroes of the Revolution failed, although it came close to succeeding.

Henry had always had a great respect for Washington, not only his accomplishments, but for his selfless service and his role as the American Cincinnatus, being willing to step down voluntarily from power. During the British Debts case, for example, Henry was at a dinner in the home of John Syme who was becoming an enthusiastic member of the Democratic-Republican party; when Syme began the traditional dinner toasts with "The people" (an obvious reference to the party platform of the new party), an annoyed Patrick Henry chastened his older half-brother: "What, brother, not drink to General Washington as we used to do? For shame, brother!" Filling his glass Henry raised a toast to "Washington!"[37]

By the mid 1790s, however, Henry had been led to believe that Washington had insulted him, a grave concern for proud men in honor-bound eighteenth-century Virginia. In 1794, when Governor Henry Lee was trying to convince Patrick Henry to accept an appointment as a member of the Supreme Court, the former governor wrote to Lee with deeply hurt feelings: Henry had been told that Washington had referred to him in 1791 as "a factious seditious character," an insult that wounded him deeply, especially given the source. When Governor Lee asked Washington about the story, the president denied the charge somewhat angrily: "A part of the plan for creating discord, is, I perceive, to make me say things of others, and others of me, w[hi]ch have no foundation in truth," the president wrote. While Washington recognized that they had taken different sides on the question of ratification of the Constitution, he noted that "personally, I have always respected and esteemed him [Patrick Henry]; nay more, I have conceived myself under obligations to him for the friendly manner in which he transmitted to me some insidious anonymous writings that were sent to him in the close of the year 1777, with a view to embark him in the opposition that was forming against me at that time." Henry, while still unwilling to serve in the cabinet or on the Supreme Court, was very pleased to hear this and clearly reciprocated Washington's respect, as demonstrated in Henry's letter to Washington in 1795 declining appointment as secretary of state.[38]

Washington was correct; efforts to alienate Henry and him were political. Who was attempting to alienate Washington and Henry is not entirely clear, but it is telling that after both Washington and Henry had died, Jefferson told Henry's first biographer that the former governor had a "thorough contempt and hatred of Genl. Washington." This was clearly not the case. At best it speaks to Jefferson's inability to see political travelers as anything other than friends or enemies: since Henry had opposed the Constitution, he must hate Washington. (Perhaps it was more difficult for Jefferson, the intensive, introverted, easily-hurt theoretician to be so personally forgiving as the gregarious and personable Henry.) Or it may indicate how unfamiliar Jefferson was with the personal feelings of some of the leading personalities of the early republic. Arguably, it suggests that even after the deaths of Washington and Henry, Jefferson intentionally sought to estrange them in history as his supporters had attempted to do in life.[39]

Failing to alienate Henry from Washington, and Washington from Henry, it was also suggested that Henry was not competent for the positions that were offered to him and that Washington made the offers for crass political reasons only after he was convinced that Henry would not accept them. Jefferson wrote to James Monroe in 1796 that "Most assiduous court is paid to P. H. He has been offered everything which they knew he would not accept." After Henry's death, Jefferson said that Henry was only offered the position of Ambassador to Spain, a position that Washington "knew that he was entirely unqualified for," based on the knowledge that he would turn down the offer. Perhaps Jefferson was not aware of all of the facts. The offer for the position as ambassador to Spain was made in late 1794, almost a year after Jefferson had resigned from Washington's cabinet, but Jefferson was consulted on the position (offered the position himself before the offer was to be made to Henry). In any case, it is difficult to credit Jefferson's interpretation of Washington's motives. The correspondence among Washington and his supporters repeatedly seeking Henry's participation on multiple fronts suggests that Washington hoped to lure Henry into government, but the retired governor steadfastly refused.[40]

When all else failed, Jefferson sought to reconcile with Henry.

In the early days of the Revolution, Jefferson had great respect for and worked closely with the more senior Henry. While their political views diverged on a number of issues, especially Henry's effort to impose a tax to support religion, it was the decision of the General Assembly to investigate Jefferson's governorship after the British invasion in 1781 that led to their falling-out. Jefferson held Henry responsible for the investigation, and his honor insulted, Jefferson could not forgive Henry even though the investigation was dropped after victory at Yorktown. Henry tried. In 1785, while governor, Henry exchanged official correspondence with Jefferson, then U.S. ambassador in Paris. Enclosed with one of his official letters, Henry included a personal note suggesting that Jefferson and he renew their personal correspondence; Henry proposed that they might write about political developments, education, the building of the Virginia capitol (designed by Jefferson), or crops (both being devoted farmers). "If you will be so good as [to] drop me in some leisure Hour the News with you it will be highly acceptable to Dear Sir Your affte. hble. Servant." Admittedly, Henry's timing was a bit off, with his letter coming in the midst of the controversy over the general assessment to support religion that he supported and Jefferson opposed. In any case, Jefferson, still stinging from the 1781 investigation, never responded to Henry's apparent effort to mend fences.[41]

In 1795, however, when Jefferson was forming a political party and in a difficult battle for political control of the nation, and with Federalists courting Henry, Jefferson suddenly found a reason to renew their personal acquaintance. Jefferson sought to arrange a meeting and wrote to a political supporter who was still on good terms with Henry: "With respect to the gentleman we expected to see there [Bedford Court], satisfy him [Henry] if you please that there is no remain of disagreeable sentiment towards him on my part. I was once sincerely affectioned towards him and it accords with my philosophy to encourage the tranquilizing passions." Nothing came of the effort. To be clear, this was not a kindly effort on Jefferson's part to "bury the hatchet," as some historians claim. It was a crass political effort, and seeing it as such, Henry apparently decided not to respond. Jefferson and Henry never communicated directly after that time.[42]

Henry was not blameless in the quarrel – he once took a swipe at Jefferson's French cook as aristocratic, saying that he did not "approve of gentlemen abjuring their native victuals," or so Jefferson was told, but it was not the good-natured Henry who maintained the feud. Nor did Henry seek directly to disparage Jefferson's political character. Jefferson would become even more vitriolic against Henry in 1799 and in the years after Henry's death.[43]

Having avoided overtures from both parties in the mid-1790s, developments would eventually draw Henry back into politics.

To understand what finally moved Henry to re-enter public life, one needs to understand something about the politics of the 1790s. After the Constitution was adopted and the federal government began to operate, Americans tended to divide into two factions, a division that would be formalized into parties in the 1790s. The divisions represented differences in view on both domestic and foreign policy matters. The Democratic-Republicans, the party of Jefferson and Madison, generally supported a smaller federal government, democratic rights for the common man, a narrow reading of the Constitution, and greater states' rights. In many ways the party was the intellectual heir of the anti-federalists whom Patrick Henry had led during the ratification debates. On foreign policy, the Democratic-Republicans tended to favor "republican" France over monarchical Britain, maintaining that support even as the French Revolution was overwhelmed with the Reign of Terror and chaos.

The Federalists, on the other hand, led by Washington, Adams, and Hamilton, tended to support a more active federal government and interpreted the Constitution broadly. (Madison had originally favored a much stronger federal government and limiting the prerogatives of the states, but his views changed as the federal government adopted a more expansive view of the Constitution.) On foreign policy, both Washington and Adams adopted policies of official neutrality, but as a practical matter, Democratic-Republicans accused the Federalists of being pro-British, which Hamilton certainly was. (That claim was strengthened by Hamilton's efforts to copy the British model in creating an American financial system.)[44]

War broke out between Britain and Revolutionary France in 1793, a war that would be almost continuous until Napoleon's defeat at Waterloo in 1815. This put a great deal of pressure on the United States to enter the fight in support of France, its ally during the American Revolution. Believing that another war could undermine the independence won in the Revolution, Washington issued a formal proclamation of American neutrality. The neutral position became increasingly hard to maintain, however, as both Britain and France seized American ships that they believed were trading with their enemy. The conflict with France became much worse after the United States signed the Jay Treaty with Britain in 1796; although that treaty did not resolve all of the disputes between the United States and Britain, it appeared to the French that the United States was moving from a neutral position to a pro-British position. In response, France increased its attacks on U.S. ships trading with Britain.

The Jay Treaty itself became a huge political hot potato. Washington had sought a guarantee that the United States, as a neutral, could trade with either Britain or France. Since the treaty did not guarantee U.S. merchant ships the right to trade with France, Washington considered not signing it. He ultimately did sign because the treaty eased tensions with Britain and the British agreed to withdraw from the forts in the old Northwest which they had held since 1783 in violation of the Treaty of Paris. Still, the treaty was immensely unpopular; Jay, the U.S. negotiator, was burned in effigy around the country.

Even after Washington signed the treaty and it was approved by the Senate, Democratic-Republicans in the House of Representatives, led by James Madison, threatened to block the treaty by refusing to provide funds to allow it to operate. This political maneuvering angered Henry and alienated him even further from the Democratic-Republicans. During ratification, one of Henry's arguments against the Constitution was that the treaty power given to the president and the Senate was too broad. At the time, Madison defended the treaty clause. Now Madison and others who had supported the Constitution were seeking to undermine the power that they had given – and that Henry had warned about. He wrote to his daughter Betsy Aylett:

> True it is, I have condemned the conduct of our members in congress, because, in refusing to raise money for the purposes of the British treaty, they, in effect, would have surrendered our country bound, hand and foot, to the power of the British nation . . . The treaty is, in my opinion, a very bad one indeed. But what must I think of these men, whom I myself warned of the danger of giving the power of making laws by means of treaty, to the president and senate, when I see these same men denying the existence of that power, which they insisted, in our convention, ought properly to be exercised by the president and senate, and by none other? The policy of these men, both then and now, appears to me quite void of wisdom and foresight.

Eventually the Congress funded the Jay Treaty, but the political maneuvering continued.[45]

In 1797, the new president, John Adams, sent a special delegation to France trying to negotiate a treaty to maintain the peace and to improve opportunities for U.S. merchantmen. Unfortunately, the French foreign minister insisted upon a bribe before he would negotiate with the U.S. envoys, creating an international crisis. When word reached the United States of what became known as the XYZ Affair (the three French officials communicating the demand for the bribe were listed simply as "X, Y, Z" in messages made available to Congress), there was a violent U.S. reaction. America's favorite slogan became "millions for defense, but not one cent for tribute." Preparations for a war with France began. Led by "war hawks" in Adams' Federalist party, Congress dramatically increased the military budget; on the high seas, confrontations became so serious that the period is referred to as the "Quasi-war" with France. Henry was as outraged as anyone by France's demand of a bribe to negotiate with the United States, although he was not a war hawk. In 1799, he publicly supported John Marshall's candidacy for Congress in part because Marshall, one of Adams' special envoys to France, had "felt and acted as a republican, as an American" when he refused the request for a bribe.[46]

Congress, controlled by Federalists after France's insult, not only appropriated money to bulk-up America's military, but it also passed several laws which fueled the domestic political controversy: The Alien and Sedition Acts. The Alien Acts made it more difficult to become a naturalized citizen and allowed the president to deport, without trial, any alien considered "dangerous"; this was targeted at French nationals living in the United States. The Sedition Act made it a crime to criticize the government, Congress, or the president. (Significantly, the vice-president, at the time Thomas Jefferson, was left off the list of those who were protected from criticism.) It is now generally agreed that the Sedition Act violated the First Amendment's guarantees of freedom of the press and freedom of speech, but with the federal judiciary controlled by Federalist judges, it was difficult to enforce those rights. Within a few years, 25 arrests had been made, mostly newspaper editors and all Democratic-Republicans, and ten indictments went to trial resulting in convictions. Newspapers editors were being jailed for criticizing the Adams administration. (The Sedition Act provides a useful reminder that Congress, even in the very early republic, could violate the Constitution for political reasons.[47])

The Quasi-war, military preparations, and Alien and Sedition Acts created a political crisis. America was on the verge of declaring war on France, its revolutionary ally, and the federal government was actively persecuting political dissent.

The Democratic-Republicans saw the Alien and Sedition laws as a direct attack on liberty; Jefferson referred to this period as a "reign of witches," with Federalists pursuing a witch hunt against political opponents. But Jeffersonians did not stop there. They insisted that the laws threatened to bring about tyranny or even an American monarchy. In response to the Federalist over-reaching, Jefferson and Madison drafted what became known as the Kentucky and Virginia Resolutions of 1798. In essence these resolutions, passed by the Kentucky and Virginia legislatures, said that the United States was a confederation of states (a position which Madison had expressly rejected during the Philadelphia Convention) and that states could "nullify" federal laws which they believed violated the Constitution. (Madison's Virginia Resolutions were a bit more tempered but still gave the states a paramount role in challenging federal authority.) When other states were asked to join the Kentucky and Virginia Resolutions, they consistently rejected the idea, but the threat to the federal government remained. There were even rumors that Virginia's governor, Jefferson ally James Monroe, was buying arms for its militia in case there were to be a future clash with the federal government.[48]

Concerned that a war with France was not in America's best interest, and ignoring the war hawks in his own party, in 1799 President Adams sent a second delegation of special envoys to France, a delegation to which he nominated Henry. Writing Adams in April to decline the appointment because of his health, Henry stated that the administration's "ability, patriotism, and virtue, deserve the gratitude and reverence of all their fellow-citizens." The new envoys eventually reached a treaty with France, averting any talk of war. Unfortunately for Adams, word of the treaty did not reach America until after the 1800 election was decided, with Jefferson defeating Adams in a close race. Had word arrived earlier, Adams almost certainly would have won the election. Ironically, the Federalist war hawks who were unhappy with Adams' decision to negotiate further with France had delayed the departure of the special envoys so long that the ultimate resolution was also delayed, costing their party the presidency.[49]

While Henry had studiously avoided political office for years, he watched the developments of the late 1790s with increasing distress. He was concerned not only with the threatened war but, equally, with the internal division, especially the spirit of faction – party politics – which he believed contributed to the conflict and threatened the new nation. While Henry recognized that there were real differences of opinion on how best to proceed, politicians were intentionally inflaming differences. He thought that Americans needed to remember that what united the country, including fundamental principles like American liberty, was more important than what divided it. "Men might differ in ways and means, and yet not in principles," Henry told Judge John Tyler, a Democratic-Republican. (Interestingly, Jefferson would famously make a similar comment in his first inaugural address in 1801: "but every difference of opinion is not a difference of principle. We have called by different names brethren of the same principle. We are all republicans: we are all federalists." That is not to say that Jefferson was taking Henry's idea, but this point was at the center of Henry's concern over bitter partisan politics.)[50]

Also watching with increasing concern was George Washington in retirement at Mount Vernon. After Jefferson's and Madison's Kentucky and Virginia Resolutions were adopted, claiming that states could interfere with federal law, Washington decided that the constitutional structure of the nation which guaranteed the supremacy of federal law was threatened. Action was needed. On January 15, 1799, he wrote to Patrick Henry reminding him of his prior commitment to re-enter politics if his country needed him:

> ... at such a crisis as this, when every thing dear & valuable to us is assailed; when this Party [the Jeffersonian Democratic-Republicans] hang upon the Wheels of Government as a dead weight, opposing every measure that is calculated for defence & self preservation; abetting the nefarious views of another Nation [France], upon our Rights; ... When every Act of their own Government is tortured by constructions they will not bear, into attempts to infringe & trample upon the Constitution with a view to introduce Monarchy. ... When measures are systematically, and pertenaciously pursued [the Kentucky and Virginia Resolutions], which must eventually dissolve the Union or produce coertion [federal military action against a state's refusal to abide by the law].

I say, when these things have become so obvious, ought characters who are best able to rescue their Country from the pending evil to remain at home?[51]

Henry had been having similar thoughts. In his early January letter supporting John Marshall's campaign for Congress, he warned that Democratic-Republican leaders were willing to dissolve the union if necessary to take control of the government. "And I am free to own, that in my judgment most of the measures, lately pursued by the opposition party, directly and certainly lead to that end." (As Henry undoubtedly expected, this letter was reprinted in the newspapers during the ensuing political campaign.)[52]

When he received the letter from Washington, an increasingly frail Henry could not resist the call. He wrote back on February 12, 1799 saying that he would be embarrassed if his children ever heard that Washington had "asked him to throw in his Mite for the public Happiness, [and] he refused to do it." Henry was as deeply concerned as Washington. "[E]ven in the present State of Things," he wrote the former president, "it may be doubted whether a Cure can easily be found for the Mischiefs they ["Democrats"] have occasioned. God grant it may be effected without coming to Extremity – yes my dear sir, I accord with every Sentiment you express to me." Henry, like Washington, was concerned that the growing political battle might incite violence and/or undermine the Constitution. After years of refusing appointments to high office, he agreed to re-enter politics.[53]

Henry, the greatest anti-federalist, entered his final political campaign as a Federalist, opposing the radical states' rights position of the Jeffersonian Democratic-Republicans.

Washington had hoped that Henry would run for Congress. Henry, perhaps feeling the infirmity that would soon lead to his death, declined that option believing that Philadelphia was too far away. Instead, he declared for a seat in the Virginia General Assembly from Charlotte County. He told Washington that there he would seek to undo the political efforts of the radicals.

Henry traveled to Charlotte County Courthouse in March 1799 to make a speech about the election, and the report that he would be there drew a crowd from Charlotte and surrounding counties. Hampden-Sydney College, in adjacent Prince Edward County was abandoned that day as students and faculty came to hear Henry's speech, what would prove to be his last.

Henry appeared ill and frail when he rose to speak, standing with difficulty, and he started in a soft voice. A student from Hampden-Sydney College who had come to watch reported what happened:

But in a few moments a wonderful transformation of the whole man occurred, as he warmed with his theme. He stood erect, his eye beamed with a light that was almost supernatural; his features glowed with the hue and fire of youth; and his voice rang clear and melodious, with the intonations of some grand musical instrument whose notes filled the area, and fell distinctly and delightfully upon the ears of the most distant of the thousands gathered to hear him.[54]

Speaking of the Virginia Resolutions, Henry told the voters that "the late proceedings of the Virginia Assembly had filled him with apprehension and alarm; that they had planted thorns upon his pillow." Henry explained that while he had expressed fears about the possible power of the federal government during the ratification debates, he had been outvoted; the Constitution was properly adopted. Now, if the federal government seemed to be too powerful, or seemed to be assuming powers not granted in the Constitution, people should change the system in a legal manner – starting at the ballot box. The suggestion by Democratic-Republicans that Virginia or any state could ignore what it believed to be excessive federal authority struck Henry as ridiculous and dangerous, and inconsistent with what had been said during the debates over ratification. He asked "whether the county of Charlotte would have any authority to dispute an obedience to the laws of Virginia; and he pronounced Virginia to be to the Union what the county of Charlotte was to her." Henry spun a story of the likely consequences of active, extra-constitutional opposition by Virginia to federal authority: "such opposition on the part of Virginia to the acts of the General government must beget their enforcement by military power . . . civil war, foreign alliances." Virginia would face an army led by George Washington, and, Henry asked, "Who will dare to lift his hand against the father of his country, to point a weapon at the breast of a man who had often led them to battle and victory?" A drunk in the audience (there was usually at least one drunk at court days in eighteenth-century Virginia) shouted out that he would fight Washington. "[Y]ou dare not do it," Henry thundered; "in such a parricidal attempt, the steel would drop from your nerveless arm!"[55]

Henry seemed to concede that there were problems with the Alien and Sedition laws (although some would later claim that he supported the laws[iv]), but he insisted that "whatever might be their merits or demerits, it belonged to the people who held the reins over the head of Congress [the voters], and to them alone, to say whether they were acceptable or otherwise. . . ." It was "necessary to submit to the constitutional exercise of that Power" and to make changes in the constitutionally prescribed manner. The danger to the nation was real. "You can never exchange the present government but for a monarchy. If the administration have done wrong, let us all go wrong together." Echoing the sentiments of Zachariah Johnson's speech from the ratification convention that some trust must be placed in

iv Henry's position on the Alien and Sedition Acts is discussed in some detail in the Appendix.

the public officials elected by the people, Henry exhorted his listeners: "Let us trust God and our better judgment to set us right hereafter. United we stand, divided we fall. Let us not split into factions which must destroy that union upon which our existence hangs."[56]

Henry had not lost all of his passion for democratic government nor was he endorsing unlimited government power:

> If I am asked what is to be done when a people feel themselves intolerably oppressed, my answer is ready: *Overturn the government*. But do not, I beseech you, carry matters to this length without provocation. Wait at least until the infringement is made upon your rights which cannot be otherwise redressed; for if ever you recur to another change, you may bid adieu forever to representative government.[57]

Henry, whether intentionally or not, was echoing George Washington's famous Farewell Address from 1796:

> The basis of our political systems is the right of the people to make and to alter their constitutions of government. But the Constitution which at any time exists, till changed by an explicit and authentic act of the whole people, is sacredly obligatory upon all. The very idea of the power and the right of the people to establish government presupposes the duty of every individual to obey the established government.[58]

After Henry's speech, John Randolph of Roanoke, a rising star in the Democratic-Republican party who had previously idolized Henry, rose to oppose him, but he could not make a dent in Henry's arguments or continued popularity. Reportedly after Randolph's speech Henry took his hand and said "Young man, you call me father; then, my son, I have something to say unto you. *Keep justice, Keep truth* – and you will live to think differently."[59]

Henry, of course, was elected to the Virginia General Assembly from Charlotte County.

Henry was never to take his seat in Richmond. He died in June 1799, which proved to be a good thing for Jefferson. Had Henry been in Richmond in the fall of 1799, Jefferson would almost certainly never have been elected president in 1800. First, that fall, in an effort to promote Jefferson's election, Virginia switched its system of electoral college voting for the presidency to a "winner-take-all" system that would give all of Virginia's electoral votes to the winner of the popular vote (undoubtedly Jefferson) rather than splitting Virginia's electoral votes among the candidates based on the vote in various districts. (Massachusetts had earlier switched to a "winner-take-all" system to benefit Adams.) "Had Patrick Henry lived, and taken his seat in the

Assembly," John Randolph conceded, "that law would never have passed. In that case, the electoral votes of Virginia would have been divided and Mr. Jefferson lost his election!" Preventing adoption of the winner-take-all system, with no other changes, would likely have thrown several electoral votes to Adams in what proved to be a very close election, although that alone would not likely have given the election to Adams. Add to that, however, Henry's almost certain support for Adams and opposition to Jefferson's candidacy, and it would likely have been enough to change the course of history. Noting that a shift of only five electoral votes would have changed the election, Randolph added hyperbolically (as was his way) "Patrick Henry was good for five times five votes doubled in that assembly." (George Washington was also to die in December of 1799; as with Henry, had he lived, Jefferson almost certainly would not have been elected president.)[60]

Jefferson understood the implications of Henry's election, and he was outraged, almost frothing in anger. He wrote to a political supporter in May that Henry's "apostacy must be unaccountable to those who do not know all the recesses of his heart." "Apostasy" is a strong word for a political disagreement; it means renunciation of a religious faith or of a previous loyalty, but Jefferson continued to use the term to describe Henry's 1799 political campaign even after Henry's death.[61]

In fairness, Jefferson thought Henry, living happily in retirement far from the political turmoil, was ignoring the "reign of witches" that infested the federal government and resulted in imprisonment of newspaper editors who criticized Adams' administration. Still, the assault on Henry was violent, personal, and political. Renunciation of Henry became a standard doctrine for Democrat-Republicans, and they sought to tar his reputation. Loyal party newspapers published claims that Henry's "mind [was] no longer quick"; that he had entered a "*second-childhood.*" "His mind unstrung by age appears insensible to their [Federalists'] purpose." A bit more kindly, Spencer Roane, a son-in-law, but a dedicated member of the Democratic-Republican party, said that Henry's "seclusion and debility arising from the infirmity of age and disease" caused him to carry his views "to greater lengths against the measures of the Republicans than he would otherwise have gone." More than 30 years later, John Marshall explained that to question the Virginia Resolutions was still "deemed political sacrilege" in Virginia.[62]

Henry's correspondence and the speech at Charlotte Courthouse make clear that he was not suffering from senility, but Democratic-Republicans had to find some explanation for his opposition to their measures, other than the obvious one that the Kentucky and Virginia Resolutions were an affront to the constitutional structure.

The attacks continued even after Henry died in June: For example, after Henry's death, a resolution was introduced into the Virginia General

Assembly for a marble bust of Henry, the state's first governor, to be placed in the House of Delegates, but opposition by the Jeffersonians doomed this tribute to the man who led the state, and the nation, into the American Revolution. Some were embarrassed by the virulence of these attacks. John Tyler, a strong Jeffersonian, said that while Henry might have erred in his political views in 1799, "His principles were too well fixed" to justify a claim of apostasy. One newspaper wrote that "If any are disposed to censure Mr. Henry for his late political transition, if anything has been written upon that subject, let the Genius of American Independence drop a tear, and blot it out for ever!"[63]

Not only were there attacks during the campaign of 1800, but Henry's "apostasy" was used to try to undermine his memory in history. Jefferson wrote to Henry's first biographer that:

> mr Henry's apostacy, sunk him to nothing, in the estimation of his country. he lost at once all of that influence which federalism had hoped, by cajoling him, to transfer with him to itself, and a man who, through a long & active life, had been the idol of his country, beyond any one that ever lived, descended to the grave with less than it's indifference, and verified the saying of the philosopher, that no man must be called happy till he is dead.

John Taylor, who had introduced Madison's Virginia Resolutions in the House of Delegates, had to insist that Henry's actions were not based on sound principles but rather were the result of "personal enmity" to Jefferson and Madison, an effort to achieve their "destruction." After the Civil War, E.A. Pollard, an unrepentant Confederate journalist who sought to revise history by shifting blame for the Civil War away from slavery and to states' rights, was still complaining about Henry's failure to support the radical states' right position, saying that he was "the most inconsistent of politicians, and the most detestable 'turn-coat' of his day." Pollard even tried to cast doubt on Henry's abilities as an orator and his support for independence.[64]

Still today, some historians downplay Henry's 1799 campaign as a Federalist, seeing it as inconsistent with their efforts to cast Henry simply as an opponent of a powerful government and supporter of states' rights. One scholar dismisses the 1799 campaign in a footnote simply as a "puzzle." Some cast it as a personal battle, with Henry "influenced unduly by his enmity toward Republican leaders and by the pleadings of Washington to jump into the fray." Others generally ignore it, all the easier to use Henry's name to support a radical states' rights position.[65]

What the Jeffersonians seemed incapable of contemplating was that, perhaps, the Kentucky and Virginia Resolutions had gone too far. Rather than being an apostate, Henry's political campaign in 1799 was among his finest hours. He rose to defend the rule of law by the federal government against the attack of party politics even though he had led the effort to warn the people that the Constitution created a government that could be too powerful. Henry (and Washington) feared that vehement party politics, the "baneful effect of faction," threatened to destroy the nation. In 1799, Henry was concerned that the actions of the Democratic-Republicans to set the states up in direct opposition to the federal government would "directly and certainly lead to that end," disunion, and that some members of that party saw disunion as a means to gain power for themselves (in the regional confederacies that would likely result). He told Washington that he hated "the conduct of those men who lose sight of the public interest from personal motives," and that is what he believed had happened to the Democratic-Republicans.[66]

From Jefferson's perspective, there was a crisis. He would have conceded that the will of the majority controlled, and he recognized that political disputes should be resolved by the majority at the ballot box. Yet, he refused to accept that the Alien and Sedition Acts represented the will of the majority, and imprisonment of newspaper editors drew into question the efficacy of the ballot box to resolve the dispute. (Although, notably, Jefferson supported state indictments of Federalist newspaper editors for libeling him when he was president.) In such extreme circumstances, Jefferson was drawn to talk about nullification. (In later life, Madison would try to disavow the radical nature of the Kentucky and Virginia Resolutions when secessionists used them as a precedent to support dominant states' rights in the period before the Civil War.)[67]

Living in retirement at Red Hill, Henry may have underestimated the dangerous effects of the Sedition law. He may also have entertained ill will toward Jefferson after almost two decades of feuding. Still, he was not an apostate nor was he acting primarily out of personal animosity. Perhaps Henry provided one explanation for his mature political views in a letter he wrote in early January 1799. In that January 8 letter supporting Marshall's candidacy for Congress, recognizing the political turmoil of the times, Henry still expressed a sincere hope that his "countrymen should learn wisdom and virtue, and in this their day know the things that pertain to their peace." Henry believed that the nation's problems should be resolved peacefully through the electoral process and that the Kentucky and Virginia Resolutions were a serious threat to peaceful resolution of political differences.[68]

Both sides in the dispute had legitimate points. The vilification of Henry, though, was uncalled for, and has unfairly diminished his historic standing.

In a broader sense, Henry's and Washington's fight was part of a far-reaching political battle and changing political sentiments in the early republic. While such changes are never clear-cut, a shift was occurring; certainly many of the older leaders, including Henry and Washington, thought so. Historians Richard Beeman, Ralph Ketcham, and Mark Noll, while not specifically discussing the conflict of 1799, provide very useful general descriptions of the changes. The national polity originally reflected a balance between "classical, civic republican, convictions that a good society required good government, that good government required active leadership, and that active leaders required the support of public-spirited citizens" and newer liberal ideas of "'checks and balances' and . . . the Bill of Rights, all designed to restrain government and protect individual rights." The former tended to be communitarian. "In its classical form, republicanism was often a system in which the individual's liberty was confined to those things that the society at large defined as useful." Liberalism, on the other hand, focused on a very broad individual liberty, and it seemed to be the wave of the future. While most politicians (and most people) shared some views that were classically republican and some views that were liberal, there was a distinct difference in where they put their emphasis. Henry and Washington would have agreed with John Adams that "There must be a positive Passion for the public good, the public Interest . . . or there can be no Republican Government, nor any real Liberty." Jefferson and Madison would not necessarily have disagreed with that sentiment, but as time progressed, their focus was elsewhere. Liberal ideas of "capitalist enterprise, industrial revolution, diversifying interests, individualism, and democratic politics" seemed to many to be replacing "traditional ideas of community, moral purpose, political obligation, and patriot leadership." For those who tended toward classic republicanism, like Henry and Washington, "if competition for power encouraged 'factions' to promote their private interests, or if a love of luxury supplanted the exercise of public-spirited service, then corruption followed inevitably." And corruption would lead to tyranny. "[T]he incessant party disputes and sharpening of conflict that the conventional wisdom of a later age would declare to be essential to the good health of democratic politics," discouraged both Henry and Washington. They seemed to be fighting a losing battle in which American liberalism, the rights (and interests) of the individual, fought for in open political and economic warfare, would triumph over an older (more old-fashioned) notion of republican virtue. Yet, the full triumph of party politics, and of liberalism (some would say self-interest) over republicanism, was a result that neither Henry nor Washington would live to see.[69]

Henry died before he could take his seat in Richmond. Jefferson won the election of 1800.

* * * * *

Within a month of Henry's speech at the Charlotte Courthouse, a consistent health complaint became more serious. In early June, Dr. George

Cabell was sent for as Henry was living in great pain with suffering "like the gravel" (like kidney stones). He would die from his condition, what was probably a bowel obstruction. As with much of Henry's history, the particular words spoken at the time, recorded after the fact, may not be precisely what was said, but the general story of his death is important to understanding Henry.

On June 6, having decided that there was little else that he could do to relieve his patient's suffering, and knowing that the bowel blockage would kill Henry if extreme measures were not taken to clear it, Dr. Cabell offered Henry a vial of liquid mercury, explaining that "It will give you immediate relief, or—," his voice trailed off. "You mean, doctor," Henry said, "that it will give relief or will prove fatal immediately?" The doctor nodded. Henry took a moment to say a silent prayer and took the mercury. Dr. Cabell left the room in tears, returning a few minutes later to see Henry surrounded by his family and quietly watching the blood congeal under his fingernails. Henry, who had engaged Cabell in a number of arguments about Christianity, could not resist telling the doctor to observe how religion was a comfort to a dying man. Henry spoke some comforting words of farewell to his family, and he died.[70]

Within days, John Marshall wrote to Washington that "Virginia has sustained a very serious loss which all good men will long lament, in the death of Mr. Henry." Washington, hearing of Henry's death, wrote "At any time I should have received the account of this gentleman's death with sorrow. In the present crisis of our public affairs, I have heard it with deep regret." The *Virginia Gazette* (a Federalist newspaper) published a memorial:

> Mourn, Virginia, mourn! Your Henry is gone! Ye friends to liberty in every clime, drop a tear . . . Farewell, first-rate patriot, farewell! As long as our rivers flow, or mountains stand – so long will your excellence and worth be the theme of homage and endearment, and Virginia, bearing in mind her loss, will say to rising generations, imitate my Henry.[71]

Henry left his family a substantial financial legacy. His will (written on November 20, 1798) also commended to his "dear family . . . the religion of Christ"; this, he said, "will make them rich indeed." With his papers was found a sealed envelope with his version of the Stamp Act Resolves from 1765 (discussed in Chapter 2). He included with those resolves a final admonition for his fellow citizens. Noting that opposition to the Stamp Act had started the movement that led to American independence, Henry wrote:

> Whether this will prove a blessing or a curse, will depend upon the use our people make of the blessings which a gracious God hath bestowed on us. If they

are wise, they will be great and happy. If they are of a contrary character, they will be miserable. Righteousness alone can exalt them as a nation. Reader! Whoever thou art, remember this; and in thy sphere practise [sic] virtue thyself, and encourage it in others.[72]

Notes

1. Letter from Patrick Henry to Elizabeth ("Betsy") Aylett, October 30, 1791, quoted in Meade, *Patrick Henry*, II: 397.
2. Henry, *Patrick Henry*, II: 516.
3. Patrick Henry Fontaine, "New Facts in Regard to the Character and Opinions of Patrick Henry," *DeBow's Review: Agricultural, Commercial, Industrial Progress and Resources* (October 1870), 811 *et seq.*
4. Spencer Roane Memorandum to William Wirt, Morgan, *True Patrick Henry*, 438.
5. Elliot, *Debates*, III: 590. Henry's will can be found in Morgan, *True Patrick Henry*, 455 *et seq.*
6. Letter from Patrick Henry to Archibald Blair, January 8, 1799, Henry, *Patrick Henry*, II: 592. Gary B. Nash, "The American Clergy and the French Revolution," *William and Mary Quarterly*, 22: 3 (July 1965): 402. Letter from Edmund Winston to William Wirt, Henry, *Patrick Henry*, II: 490.
7. Henry, *Patrick Henry*, II: 519. Letter from Patrick Henry to Elizabeth ("Betsy") Aylett, August 20, 1796, ibid., II: 570.
8. Memorandum from Spencer Roane to William Wirt, in Morgan, *True Patrick Henry*, 451–452. See also Meade, *Patrick Henry*, II: 442. See generally Thomas S. Kidd, *Patrick Henry: First Among Patriots* (New York: Basic Books, 2011).
9. Meade, *Patrick Henry*, II: 435.
10. Memorandum from Spencer Roane to William Wirt, Morgan, *True Patrick Henry*, 438.
11. Henry, *Patrick Henry*, II: 514.
12. Letter from Patrick Henry to Edward Telfair, October 14, 1790, ibid., II: 507. Thomas P. Abernathy, *The South in the New Nation, 1789-1819* (Baton Rouge: Louisiana State University Press, 1961), 91. Letter from Patrick Henry to Robert Walker, November 20, 1790, Henry, *Patrick Henry*, II: 508–509.
13. Charles Homer Haskins, *The Yazoo Land Companies* (reprinted from the *Papers of the American Historical Association,* iv: 4 (October 1891)) (New York: Knickerbocker Press, 1891): 21 (413), 18 (410).
14. Irving Brant, "Comment on Pendleton Letter," *Maryland Historical Magazine* XLVI: 2 (June 1951): 80. Haskins, *Yazoo Land*, 21 (413). Letter from Thomas Jefferson to George Washington, April 24, 1791, *Papers of Thomas Jefferson*, 20: 252. See also Abernathy, *South in the New Nation*, 96–97; Morgan, *True Patrick Henry*, 400–402 n. The 1791 letter from Jefferson to Washington, showing that he understood that Henry was involved in the first set of Yazoo transactions, makes his later effort to involve Henry with the second, fraudulent transaction particularly troubling.
15. Memorandum from Spencer Roane to William Wirt, Morgan, *True Patrick Henry*, 447.
16. Wirt, *Patrick Henry*, 260. Henry, *Patrick Henry*, II: 484.
17. Morgan, *True Patrick Henry*, 378–379.
18. James W. Alexander, *The Life of Archibald Alexander, D.D.* (New York: Charles Scribner, 1854): 183. Henry, *Patrick Henry*, II: 475. James Parton, *Life of Andrew Jackson*, vol. 1 (New York: Mason Brothers, 1861): 165.
19. Memorandum from Spencer Roane to William Wirt, Morgan, *True Patrick Henry*, 446. Meade, *Patrick Henry*, II: 414. Henry, *Patrick Henry*, II: 489 (footnote omitted). Alexander, *Archibald Alexander*, 185.
20. Memorandum from Thomas Jefferson to William Wirt, *Papers of Thomas Jefferson* (Retirement Series), 4: 603.

21. Meade, *Patrick Henry*, II: 420. Henry, *Patrick Henry*, II: 493. David Garrick was the greatest English actor of that period. Converting the value of money in the eighteenth century into a modern equivalent is fraught with difficulty; 500 pounds sterling in 1792 would be worth from US$75,000 to more than $1 million today. See http://eh.net/howmuchisthat/.

22. See Cynthia A. Kierner, *Scandal at Bizarre: Rumor and Reputation in Jefferson's America* (Charlottesville: University of Virginia Press, 2006).

23. Meade, *Patrick Henry*, II: 321–322. Memorandum from Thomas Jefferson to William Wirt, *Papers of Thomas Jefferson* (Retirement Series), 4: 596.

24. Wirt, *Sketches*, 256, 244. See *Ware v. Hylton*, 3 U.S. 199 (1796), e.g. opinion of Justice Chase, ibid., 223–227.

25. Even in Virginia, Henry's hardline position was losing support in part because westerners were desperate to get the British out of the northwest forts. In November 1787, when George Mason introduced a resolution calling for repeal of all laws in violation of the Treaty of Paris, it was approved after adding a simple amendment that it should be suspended until other states agreed to do the same. Henry's proposed amendment, suspending the resolution until Britain complied fully with the Treaty, was rejected 42: 75. Risjord, *Chesapeake Politics*, 295.

26. Wirt, *Sketches*, 255, quoting Hardin Burnley.

27. Henry, *Patrick Henry*, II: 472. Letter from Edmund Randolph to George Washington, June 24, 1793, *Papers of George Washington* (Presidential Series) 13: 139.

28. Letter from Patrick Henry to Henry Lee, June 27, 1795, Henry, *Patrick Henry*, II: 551.

29. Letter from David Stuart to George Washington, July 14, 1789, *Papers of George Washington* (Presidential Series), 3: 199.

30. Letter from Richard Henry Lee to Patrick Henry, May 28, 1789, Henry, *Patrick Henry*, III: 388. Letter from Patrick Henry to Robert Walker, November 12, 1790, ibid., II: 510.

31. Wirt, *Sketches*, 284.

32. Letter from Patrick Henry to Elizabeth (Betsy) Aylett, August 20, 1796, Henry, *Patrick Henry*, II: 569. Letter from Patrick Henry to George Washington, October 16, 1795, ibid., II: 559.

33. Letter from Patrick Henry to Henry Lee, July 14, 1794, ibid., II: 547.

34. Letter from Patrick Henry to George Washington, October 16, 1795, ibid., II: 558–559.

35. Letter from Patrick Henry to Henry Lee, June 27, 1795, ibid., II: 551. Letter from Patrick Henry to George Washington, October 16, 1795, ibid., II: 558–559.

36. Jeffrey L. Pasley, *The First Presidential Contest: 1796 and the Founding of American Democracy* (Lawrence: University Press of Kansas, 2013): 205–206. *Gazette of the United States* (Philadelphia), November 15, 1796, Vol. X: 1306, reprinted from Richmond newspaper.

37. Henry, *Patrick Henry*, II: 538.

38. Letter from Henry Lee to George Washington, August 17, 1794, *Papers of George Washington* (Presidential Series) 16: 572. Letter from George Washington to Henry Lee, August 26, 1794, ibid., 16: 602–603.

39. Memorandum from Thomas Jefferson to William Wirt, August 4, 1805, *The Pennsylvania Magazine of History and Biography* XXXIV: 4 (1910): 395.

40. Letter from Thomas Jefferson to James Madison, July 10, 1796, *Papers of Thomas Jefferson*, 29: 147–148. Memorandum from Thomas Jefferson to William Wirt, August 4, 1805, *Pennsylvania Magazine of History and Biography*, 395.

41. Letter from Patrick Henry to Thomas Jefferson, September 10, 1785, *Papers of Thomas Jefferson*, 8: 510. An unsuccessful effort had also been made in 1791 to mend fences between Henry and James Madison. Compare Letter from William Madison to James Madison, December 3, 1791, *Papers of James Madison* (Congressional Series) 14: 137, and Letter from James Madison to William Madison, December 13, 1791, Ibid. 14: 149. Who initiated that effort is not clear. Interestingly, Henry reportedly said at one point that "he could forgive everything else in Mr. Jefferson, but his corrupting Mr. Madison." Letter from Timothy Pickering to John Marshall, December 26, 1828, *Papers of John Marshall*, 11: 193.

42. Letter from Thomas Jefferson to Archibald Stuart, April 18, 1795, *Papers of Thomas Jefferson*, 28: 331–332.

43. Henry, *Patrick Henry*, II: 549.
44. Many good books discuss the politics of the 1790s. See, e.g., Bernard A. Weisberger, *America Afire: Jefferson, Adams, and the Revolutionary Election of 1800* (New York: William Morrow, 2000).
45. Letter from Patrick Henry to Elizabeth (Betsy) Aylett, August 20, 1796, Henry, *Patrick Henry*, II: 569.
46. Letter from Patrick Henry to Archibald Blair, January 8, 1799, ibid., II: 593. John Marshall won that election by only 108 votes, almost certainly because of Henry's support. While then serving in Congress, Marshall came to the attention of John Adams and was appointed secretary of state and then chief justice of the Supreme Court.
47. See generally Frank Maloy Anderson, "The Enforcement of the Alien and Sedition Laws," *Annual Report of the American Historical Association* (1912): 115–126.
48. Letter from Thomas Jefferson to John Taylor, June 4, 1798, *Papers of Thomas Jefferson*, 30: 389. The word "nullify" only occurred in Jefferson's draft of the Kentucky Resolutions, but, while the word was removed as unnecessarily inflammatory, the concept was retained. Compare Jefferson Draft of Kentucky Resolutions, ibid., 30: 539. Arguments for "nullification" of federal laws would play a role in the coming of the Civil War.
49. Letter from Patrick Henry to John Adams, April 16, 1799, Henry, *Patrick Henry*, II: 624.
50. Lyon G. Tyler, *The Letters and Times of the Tylers*, vol. 1 (Richmond, VA: Whittet and Shipperson Co., 1884): 183. First Inaugural Address, March 4, 1801, *Papers of Thomas Jefferson*, 33: 149.
51. Letter from George Washington to Patrick Henry, January 15, 1799, *Papers of George Washington* (Retirement Series) 3: 318.
52. Letter from Patrick Henry to Archibald Blair, January 8, 1799, Henry, *Patrick Henry*, II: 591, reprinted, for example, in South Carolina *State-Gazette*, October 24, 1800, Portland (ME) *Gazette*, November, 17, 1800.
53. Letter from Patrick Henry to George Washington, February 12, 1799, *Papers of George Washington* (Retirement Series) 3: 371.
54. Henry, *Patrick Henry*, II: 607.
55. Ibid., II: 608.
56. Ibid., II: 609.
57. Ibid.
58. Washington's Farewell Address, 1796, at http://avalon.law.yale.edu/18th_century/washing.asp. Washington's Farewell Address had been reprinted broadly around the country. See, e.g., *The Virginia Gazette, and General Advertiser* (Richmond), September 28, 1796; *Virginia Gazette and Weekly Advertiser* (Richmond), October 1, 1796; *Virginia Gazette* (Staunton), October 7, 1796. See Victor Hugo Paltsits, *Washington's Farewell Address* (New York: New York Public Library, 1935).
59. Henry Adams, *John Randolph* (1882, reprint, Greenwich, CN: Fawcett Publications, Inc., 1961): 36.
60. William Cabell Bruce, *John Randolph of Roanoke: 1773–1833*, vol. 1 (New York: G.P. Putnam's Sons, 1922): 147.
61. Letter from Thomas Jefferson to Archibald Stuart, May 14, 1799, *Papers of Thomas Jefferson*, 31: 110.
62. *Aurora, General Advertiser* (Philadelphia) May 27, 1799 (republished *Vermont Gazette*, June 6, 1799). Henry, *Patrick Henry*, II: 452–453. Letter from John Marshall to Joseph Story, July 31, 1833, *Papers of John Marshall*, 12: 291.
63. Henry, *Patrick Henry*, II: 630. Memorandum from John Tyler to William Wirt, ibid., II: 622. *Centinel of Liberty* (Georgetown), June 21, 1799.
64. Memorandum of Thomas Jefferson to William Wirt, *Papers of Thomas Jefferson* (Retirement Series), 4: 604. Letter from John Taylor to James Madison, March 4, 1799, *Papers of James Madison* (Congressional Series), 17: 245. Edward A. Pollard, "Historic Doubts Concerning Patrick Henry," *The Galaxy* X: 3 (Sept. 1870), 327 *et seq.* As for Jefferson's claim that Henry's 1799 campaign resulted in his reputation being "sunk," consider eulogies to Henry: For example, *Maryland Herald and Hager's Town Weekly Advertiser* (among volunteer toasts on July 4,

1799, "The memory of Patrick Henry; the genuine republican . . ."); *Virginia Argus* (Richmond), June 25, 1799 ("Perhaps no age or country ever produced a more eloquent man . . . compare his efforts in the cause of Liberty, to those of the ardent Chatham [William Pitt], or the persuasive and resplendent Mirabeau."); *City Gazette* (Charleston), June 26, 1799 ("unshaken efforts to establish republican principles . . . call for the best tribute . . . which . . . the gratitude of freemen can bestow"); *Georgia Gazette*, June 27, 1799 ("a man whose equal, in some respects, has scarcely, perhaps, appeared in the world"); same, *Virginia Gazette*, June 11, 1799; *General Advertiser* (New York), June 20, 1799; *Connecticut Gazette*, June 26, 1799 ("one of the most able, eloquent, and steadfast affectors of American Independence").

65. Kevin R. C. Gutzman, *Virginia's American Revolution: From Dominion to Republic, 1776–1840* (Lanham, MD: Lexington Books, 2007): 112 n. 163. Beeman, *Patrick Henry*, 188–189.

66. Letter from Patrick Henry to George Washington, October 16, 1795, Henry, *Patrick Henry*, II: 559.

67. See, e.g., Brian Steele, "Thomas Jefferson, Coercion, and the Limits of Harmonious Union," *Journal of Southern History*, 74: 4 (November 2008): 823–854.

68. Letter from Patrick Henry to Archibald Blair, January 8, 1799, Henry, *Patrick Henry*, I: 591–594.

69. Beeman, "Democratic Faith," 304. Ralph Ketcham, "Executive Leadership, Citizenship and Good Government," *Presidential Studies Quarterly*, 17: 2 (Spring 1987): 278. Letter from John Adams to Mercy Otis Warren, April 16, 1776, *Papers of John Adams, The Adams Papers*, 4: 124. Ketcham, "Executive Leadership," 278, 275; Mark A. Noll, *America's God: From Jonathan Edwards to Abraham Lincoln* (New York: Oxford University Press, 2005): 57.

70. Tyler, *Patrick Henry*, 376–377.

71. Letter from John Marshall to George Washington, June 12, 1799, *Papers of John Marshall*, 4: 18. Letter from George Washington to Archibald Blair, June 24, 1799, printed in the South Carolina *State-Gazette*, October 24, 1800. *Virginia Gazette*, June 14, 1799, quoted in Henry, *Patrick Henry*, II: 627.

72. Morgan, *True Patrick Henry*, 457. Morgan includes a copy of Henry's will in an Appendix. Ibid., 455 *et seq.* Henry, *Patrick Henry*, II: 632.

CHAPTER **6**

LEGACY

Undoubtedly, Henry's most well-known legacy is his eloquence, the stirring words which he spoke to encourage his countrymen toward a revolution. In 1824, even Jefferson, by that time a bitter political enemy, conceded that in the early days of the struggle, "It was to him that we were indebted for the unanimity that prevailed among us. He would address the assemblages of people . . . in such strains of native eloquence as Homer wrote in." Henry "was far before all in maintaining the spirit of the Revolution." He was the essential voice that could speak to, and for, the people of Virginia and of America, the common farmer and tradesman. It was the faith that the people placed in Henry that made him effective, but it was his genius, and his deep empathy for the people, that produced that faith. In recognition of these efforts, Henry has often been referred to as the "trumpet" of the American Revolution (with Washington the "sword" and Jefferson the "pen"). There is a danger, though, that glib titles can hide the nature and depth of Henry's contributions, including the significance of his famous speeches.[1]

Jefferson's recognition that Henry gave "the first impulse to the ball of revolution" was not mere idle chatter. Before Henry came to the Virginia House of Burgesses in 1765, there was every reason to believe that the Stamp Act protests would fizzle. While Britain was undoubtedly imposing taxation without representation, American objections had been met with silence and contempt. Benjamin Franklin, acting as a colonial agent in London, felt that there was little else to do but acquiesce. Thomas Hutchinson, Lieutenant Governor of Massachusetts, and soon a victim of Stamp Act riots, opposed the Stamp Act, but believed it was the duty of British citizens (including Americans) to obey Parliament's laws once enacted. Other

American leaders seemed rudderless. Henry's Stamp Act resolutions and his speech indicting the king – comparing King George to the assassinated Caesar and Charles I – turned a foundering protest into a crisis.[2]

Of course, this was not Henry's act alone: Others played a role in the distribution and the drafting of Virginia's Stamp Act resolutions. "Sons of liberty" in Boston and elsewhere took the resolutions and formed a firm commitment to boycott British goods. Women across the colonies acted to support the boycotts. Mobs, stirred to action, rioted in Boston and other cities. Yet, in considering Henry's legacy, one cannot help but to ask "what if" he had not been there in May 1765, to get "the ball of revolution" rolling. And it was not just Jefferson who saw Henry's role as seminal, nor only the early Founders. When the colonial Virginia capitol building burned in 1832, Virginia's governor noted in his diary with regret that the lost "edifice is that which has been rendered so dear to the memory of all Virginians from its being the same in which Patrick Henry, the greatest orator in the world, thundered forth the irresistible floods of eloquence which produced the American Independence which made freemen of an entire continent." Henry's own assessment of his Stamp Act opposition was clear: "This brought on the war which finally separated the two countries, and gave independence to ours."[3]

Ten years later, in early 1775, as the nation quivered between resistance and revolution, Henry made his most memorable speech, ending with the declaration "give me liberty, or give me death." Again, Henry's words made an impact. Virginians were struggling with which path to take. One path included open opposition, arming to resist Britain; another path seemed to offer the prospect of reconciliation and maintaining a safe place within the British Empire. Many feared taking the path of independence, open warfare with the greatest military power of the day, what one cautious Pennsylvanian described as a "leap in the dark." Henry's speech – answering the fears of the timid, rousing the hearts of the hopeful – propelled the decision of Virginia to arm. After his death, one newspaper editor asked, "Was it not his eloquence that first confirmed the bold, convinced the doubting, decided the wavering, and inspired the timid?" Soldiers in Virginia marched to war with hunting jackets emblazoned with "Liberty or Death," as legislators plotted next steps with the same words stitched into their coats. Having committed itself to the war, a year later, with Henry's active support, Virginia directed its delegates to the Continental Congress to propose independence, the critical final step that led to adoption of the Declaration of Independence.[4]

But the influence of Henry's words did not stop with the victory at Yorktown. Dr. Benjamin Rush, a leading revolutionary, explained in 1787:

> The American war is over: but this is far from being the case with the American revolution. On the contrary, nothing but the first act of the great drama is

closed. It remains yet to establish and perfect our new forms of government; and to prepare the principles, morals, and manners of our citizens, for these forms of government, after they are established and brought to perfection.[5]

Henry's words, their ability to stir the mind and soul and encourage a commitment to values, particularly the defense of liberty, continued to play a role in the broader American revolution, the formation of a new nation and development of its principles. Thousands read and memorized his words (or what had been recorded as his words) and took them to heart; his legacy inspired generations. Henry's impact must be evaluated not simply by his own historical role, but by his role in history as it developed for more than 200 years. This is not to say that Henry's words have always been used for the good; for example, he would be deeply concerned to the extent that his speeches were used to support an expansive American empire. Yet the power of the words cannot be denied. Read the "Liberty or Death" speech (see Document 5). Henry spoke to the American people in 1775, and he has not been silenced for more than 200 years.

For many years, this is where Henry's legacy stopped. Jefferson, and an easily convinced William Wirt, created an icon who could make powerful speeches – speeches that were, at best, imperfectly remembered – and do little else. After Henry's death, Jefferson worked assiduously to promote this myth. In 1824, he told Daniel Webster, a rising young politician, that Henry "was a man of very little knowledge of any sort. He read nothing, and had no books . . . He wrote almost nothing; he *could* not write . . . in his heart he preferred low society, and sought it as often as possible" – strange words from someone who became known as the "man of the people." Many historians accepted the myth, making Henry a demagogue of the masses, a politician of the mobs, a view promoted by Henry's political opponents. But this is to mischaracterize his politics and to underestimate the man. Modern analyses of Henry's library, his letters and speeches, as well as contemporary statements by those who knew him at least as well as Jefferson tell a different story. John Marshall, by then chief justice, said that Wirt's biography, memorializing Henry as a great orator, missed a broader picture; "he was that and much more, a learned lawyer, a most accurate thinker, and a profound reasoner . . . If I were called upon to say who of all the men I have known had the greatest power to convince, I should perhaps say Mr. Madison, while Mr. Henry had without doubt the greatest power to persuade."[6]

While his oratory was very significant, there are other important legacies, perhaps less concrete, for which Henry deserves to be remembered.

Many analysts credit Henry with laying the foundation for a democratic movement – recognizing the rights of the common man – on which

Jefferson would later capitalize. It was Henry's embracing the "lesser sort," using the intentionally egalitarian language of evangelicals, that laid the groundwork for change in the political system. He was seen "as the organ of the great body of the people; as the instrument by whom the big-wigs were to be thrown down, and liberty and independence established." For Henry, this meant not just challenging the aristocracy, but empowering the people. In the early years leading-up to the Revolution, seeing how Henry challenged the establishment on behalf of the people, Jefferson said of Henry that "the exact conformity of our political opinions strengthened our friendship." But by the 1780s, Jefferson and Madison were deeply concerned that Henry went too far in embracing populist interests. "Henry's work in mobilizing an active, new constituency for liberty was crucial," Henry Mayer explains; "yet many Whig leaders, including Jefferson, felt ambivalent about introducing this radical new element into the political equation and worked hard to keep it under control." Madison's growing concerns with the possible tyranny of the majority were evident in the battle over religious freedom in 1784–1786. Henry's influence with the people, what Jefferson later refers to as "low society," was a significant factor in encouraging Madison to seek the essentially conservative reforms in the Constitution, reforms that tended to create distance between the people and government. When federalist (and Madison ally) Edmund Randolph urged during the ratification debates that the distance between the people and the federal government under the Constitution was a good thing – "I would rather depend upon the virtue and knowledge of some few men, than on ever so many" – Henry was outraged. In many respects, Henry was more of a "Man of the People" than the "Sage of Monticello," certainly so in the 1780s.[7]

Yet, as time went on, Jefferson and Madison became more "democratic" in the face of Alexander Hamilton's programs and the growth of federal power which Henry had warned against. At the same time, while Henry never lost his passion for the people, as he grew older (and more religious), and faced with the French Revolution, he did evidence greater concerns for stability. As Richard Beeman observes, it is inaccurate to characterize Henry simply as either a classical republican (supporting tradition and stability) or as the leader of an egalitarian insurgency. While Henry spoke eloquently for the common man, Henry was no leveler or promoter of mob rule. Particularly in later life, Henry emphasized stability and the rule of law. While the "lesser sort" were to share political power, they had to work within the system. There was a "noblesse oblige" in Henry's classical republicanism: the duty of virtuous, educated citizens to support the government and the responsibility of government officials to act in the community's interest rather than personal interests. Not unlike Edmund Burke, the great orator of the British Parliament, these views made Henry a prime mover of the Revolution, but also caused him to recoil in horror from the excesses of the French Revolution.

In many respects, after his death, political parties, the growth of capitalistic self-interest, and the industrial revolution overtook Henry's ideas. The rights and interests of the individual become paramount, and political parties, the anathema of classical republicans, become the primary means by which the common man could participate effectively in governance of the republic. These are developments for which Jefferson and Madison rightfully take precedence. Henry's earlier role in supporting popular interests, though, was foundational. Richard Beeman concludes that "the heritage that we celebrate . . . of a democratic nation genuinely mindful of the liberties of individuals – is the result of the integration of the legacies of Jefferson and Madison on the one hand, and Patrick Henry on the other." As with the Revolution, in key respects, Henry got the ball rolling.[8]

Beyond encouraging the rights of the people, and his influence on the growth of what became an American democracy, Henry left additional political legacies. In particular, Henry's willingness on two occasions to stand against the political establishment played an important role in the political and philosophical development of the early republic. Most notably, Henry was the leading anti-federalist in the Virginia Convention for ratification of the Constitution. He believed that the Constitution would create a government that was too powerful and demanded that amendments be made to limit its power and protect the rights of the people. He lost his fight to block the Constitution and was unsuccessful in his efforts to have amendments or a second convention dramatically limit the authority of the federal government to impose taxes and regulate commerce and the ability of the president to be elected again and again. Yet, the demand of Henry's anti-federalists for amendments, including a Bill of Rights, was a critical element in adoption of the first ten amendments to the Constitution. Of course, the battle for the Bill of Rights was historically complicated, many things are: Henry was focused on structural amendments and thought that the amendments which were adopted were too weak, and Jefferson was urging Madison to support a Bill of Rights at the same time as Henry's anti-federalists. Still, Henry's role was critical, leading many to conclude that he, not Madison, should be seen as the father of the Bill of Rights.

The significance of Henry's actions after ratification, and into the 1790s, is even more complicated, perhaps more subtle, but arguably equally important. Today, the viability of a multi-party, functioning democracy can be taken for granted. This was not the case in the late eighteenth century. Monarchies were the rule, and while history provided examples of republics (Greece, Rome, the Dutch republic, England in the seventeenth century), most had failed. As Madison and other political thinkers made clear, one of the essential problems was that different people had different interests in society and these differing interests created different factions which fought each other. When one faction gained dominance, "party" disputes could result in persecution. Madison, Henry, Jefferson, and other Founders understood that there was a serious risk that this internal conflict would bring on a slide toward tyranny, either tyranny of a powerful elite against the people or the tyranny of a majority violating the rights of a minority. Were this to happen, the American system of republican government could collapse and a monarchy result. As the Constitution was adopted, the question of how a republic could function with parties in serious disagreement was an open question. In simple terms, and ironically for these purposes, that question was resolved in the presidential election of 1800 when a peaceful change of power occurred between two opposed political parties, Adams' Federalists and Jefferson's Democratic-Republicans. Jefferson and Madison are often credited with developing the party system, recognizing that political parties, while potentially dangerous, could also be effective mechanisms to allow a broad range of people to participate effectively in a republic.

What Jefferson referred to as the Revolution of 1800, though, did not occur in a vacuum. It was important for that monumental change, and for the development and stability of the American republic, to be able to have a "loyal opposition," – that is, those who believed that a political decision was fundamentally wrong (such as adoption of the Constitution), or that a party in power was fundamentally misguided, but who would work within the system to promote reform.

By supporting the new nation even after strongly opposing the Constitution, Henry provided an important (and still relevant) example of appropriate participation in public discourse. This is not to suggest that Patrick Henry was the only person to adopt that position. Yet, in studying the Founding, it is significant that Henry did so. When Henry made it clear that if he lost the ratification debate he would live peaceably within the new system (although continue to fight within that system for major reforms), he not only quieted some anti-federalists who proposed a more active (and destructive opposition), but he also created an important example for his time and ours.

The same questions were still at play when Henry accepted Washington's call to come out of retirement in 1799, defending the constitutional and electoral system against a radical proposal from Jefferson and Madison (the Kentucky and Virginia Resolutions) which would have drawn into question the fundamental relationship of the federal and state

governments. Henry explained to his constituents that he had opposed ratification of the Constitution for fear that the federal government would be
too powerful but that since the system was legally adopted, reforms should
be made in a legal manner and through the ballot box. He demonstrated
that support of the government did not require one to agree with all of the
decisions that were made by a party in power, such as the Alien and Sedition Acts. He also rejected a facile alignment with a political party in favor
of what he saw as the good of the country. John Kennedy might have been
speaking about Henry's 1799 campaign when he declared "Let us not seek
the Republican answer or the Democratic answer but the right answer. Let
us not seek to fix the blame for the past. Let us accept our own responsibility for the future." This type of commitment, even when the government is
of a different political party, is essential to the stability of the republic and
speaks loudly today.

This important legacy of Henry's action is not only often forgotten, but
increasingly suppressed. Today, when extremists seek to rely on Henry's
compelling calls for liberty and freedom to support a radical states' rights
agenda and to attack the federal government – search the "Patrick Henry
Society" or "Patrick Henry Caucus" or patrickhenryteaparty.com or the use
of Patrick Henry by other radical groups and individuals – they misunder-
stand Henry and distort and misuse his legacy in two ways. First, they tend
to ignore Henry's repeated decisions to support the legitimate government
even when he disagreed with its actions. It was for this reason that Patrick
Henry, the greatest of anti-federalists, fought his last political campaign as
a Federalist.

Second, too often Henry's words are removed from the context of his
time. Henry's dedication to individual liberty and states' rights was from a
period when the challenge of the age came from restraints on liberty, from
monarchy, hierarchy, from a world in which most people were denied an
education, much less a right to participate in government. It is a complicated question, not easily answered, how Henry would react to the size
and power of the federal government and the questions of individual liberty and states' rights today – after a bloody Civil War fought over slavery
which sometimes attempted to hide behind a claim of states' rights, in an
interconnected world in which we cannot avoid complex interactions with
nations from around the world, in an environment where actions on private property can harm migratory species and poison watersheds, in a time
when broadcast airwaves and the internet, not to mention communicable
diseases and pollution, potentially permeate the planet and require effective
regulation. The challenge of his age was individual liberty; the challenge of
ours may be living together in an increasingly interdependent world. Henry
would likely agree: While radical elements today often like to quote Henry's

devotion to liberty, they studiously ignore his equally important devotion to community interests, the rule of law, and working within that system to promote change.

This is not to "take sides" in difficult political questions faced today, but it is to say that great care must be taken in seeking to apply the wisdom of the Founders to modern situations. This is clearly so in the case of Patrick Henry. Was he a trumpet for freedom and liberty? Absolutely. Did he speak in a principled voice about the importance of freedom and the necessity of defending it? Certainly. How does his understanding apply to us today? That is more complicated.

Further complicating Henry's legacy is the fact that, since he did not hold national office or produce extensive political writings, it is more difficult to see him as the father or advocate of an integrated political philosophy. Unlike many of the Founders, say Jefferson, or Adams, or Hamilton, Henry has not been plumbed for theories of political science. Still, if one does seek to distill a political philosophy from Henry's speeches and actions, it would certainly include his devotion to the rights of the common man against aristocracy and support of the right of the people to participate in their own governance. During the ratification debates, Henry declared that "I consider myself as the servant of the people of this commonwealth, as a sentinel over their rights, liberty, and happiness." While some mocked this claim, he clearly embraced it long before formation of Jefferson's Democratic-Republican party. Edmund Randolph, sometimes a political ally, sometimes an opponent, said fairly, "His ability as a writer cannot be insisted on, nor was he fond of a length of details; but for grand impressions in the defense of liberty, the Western world has not yet been able to exhibit a rival."[9]

Of course, there have been attacks on his legacy. While opponents accused Henry of being a demagogue, his voluntary retirement from politics and repeated refusal to accept national offices demonstrate that Henry was not simply trying to promote himself. In the midst of his refusal to accept high office, he wrote to one daughter that "I have long learned the little value which is to be placed on popularity, acquired by any other way than virtue." Henry's life and decades of public service were monuments to his support of the public good, and his decision to decline high offices as he grew older, as well as the decision of an ailing man to come out of retirement to address what Washington and he saw as a serious threat of disunion, demonstrate the depth of that commitment.[10]

Beyond the political battles that he fought and won (and sometimes lost), Patrick Henry's personal legacy is also worth consideration, although in many respects it has been compromised since the day he died. With his death in the midst of a political campaign to slow the Jeffersonian

Democratic-Republican political tidal wave, Henry was personally attacked almost immediately after his final illness and for years thereafter, often unfairly. His greatest fame, the product of his eloquent words, was also compromised because his most famous and stirring speeches had not been recorded when given, a fact that an early biography set to work to try to remedy in the years after his death. Still, his life seems to loom large to those who look.

In terms of a personal legacy, it is not inappropriate to note first that Henry, who had 17 children and 77 grandchildren, today has thousands of living descendants. He certainly would view that legacy with pride. This is not to trivialize his legacy; thousands of Americans have sought to emulate the dedication and service of their famous ancestor. Guided by the memory of Henry, many descendants have played an important role in preserving the history of the Revolution, encouraging civic engagement, and supporting various charitable organizations. For example, Patrick Henry Family Services and Patrick Henry Boys and Girls Home, supported by Henry descendants, have helped hundreds of families and children in need, honoring Henry's commitment to family.

Henry also provides the student of history a fitting example of a life well lived. It is always interesting to look back at those whose lives have affected their times and nation and to see if they provide appropriate models to emulate, and in many respects Henry meets that test. Henry certainly overcame many trials, particularly as a young man, and served his nation well. He persevered through challenges, failures, and tragedy. He warned friends and family that "the characteristic of the good or the great man is not that he has been exempted from the evils of life, but that he has surmounted them." He tried to teach his own children a sense of humility and principle: "to be true & just in all my dealings. To bear no malice nor hatred in my heart . . . Not to covet other mens [sic] goods; but to learn & labor truly to get my own living, & to do my duty in that state of life into which it shall please God to call me." Henry was also among the most effective of orators, a skill understood at the time to be important for a people who were to govern themselves. He also was an unmatched attorney.[11]

Still, care must be taken in placing historic figures, including American Founders, on a pedestal. They were human, and suffered from human faults and frailties, Henry no less than others. Henry's participation in the vile institution of slavery, his failure to take action to end the institution generally or to free his own slaves, is an obvious example; he was no saint. Beyond that, in assessing Henry, Jefferson's attacks have to be confronted. While Jefferson conceded that no one was more eloquent than Henry and that Henry was instrumental in lighting the fuse of the Revolution, Jefferson thought he was a demagogue and an incompetent and greedy lawyer;

Jefferson insisted that he was poorly-read and generally uneducated; most significantly, Jefferson saw Henry as an "apostate" to the revolutionary cause because he tried to stand in the way of Jefferson's attacks on Federalists' abuse of power.

As has been noted throughout, Jefferson was often simply wrong about his claims concerning Henry, for example how he received his law license, his education, his considerable library and learning, his relationship with Washington, and the sincere offers of high political office in the federal government that Henry consistently declined. More generally, Jefferson's objections were often misplaced. Many of Jefferson's claims seem to be born in anger or jealousy: anger especially at Henry's support for the 1781 investigation of Jefferson's governorship, jealousy of Henry's ability as a speaker and success as an attorney and planter. Perhaps Jefferson reacted so strongly to his growing differences with Henry because he had idolized Henry when a young man, he had been proud to associate with him in the early, heady days of resistance to British tyranny – the feud speaking to a lost time of youth and relative innocence. Still, Henry did earn very large fees as a criminal defense attorney, and no doubt relished the opportunity to do so. He undoubtedly enjoyed, perhaps a bit too much, the adulation of his fellow citizens.

And the apostasy claim remains. Jefferson, were he here, might explain that Henry had re-entered politics after years of absence while living comfortably in a backwater, and in 1799 he was interfering in a crucial national political battle without understanding what was at stake. Dozens of Democratic-Republican newspaper editors had been arrested and many jailed under the Sedition Act which made a mockery of the First Amendment by making it a crime even to criticize the government. The Federalists were undermining the very fabric of the nation for which the Revolution had been fought. Saying that such disputes should be addressed at the ballot box was easy for Henry, living in retirement, but how could there be fair and free elections when the press was gagged? Henry would likely reply that he was well-aware of the extensive power of the federal government. He had fought against it during the ratification debates, fighting many of Jefferson's supporters, including Madison, who, at the time, had been federalists. But he had lost. The Constitution clearly mandated federal supremacy; if the government was acting beyond its powers, the answer lay at the polls or in the courts. This was not like the Revolution when the people had no representation in Parliament and faced military attacks by Redcoats. It was essential for Henry that any changes in that system of government be made legally, without interfering with the constitutional regime that had been properly adopted. Extra-constitutional attacks on that regime – which the Kentucky and

Virginia Resolutions were seen to be – threatened disunion and could bring about a tyrannical government. One of Henry's great grandsons insisted that Henry had not changed; "[t]he change was in his opponents who, having forced upon him the system of Government, after being warned of its powers, and confessing them, afterwards denied the very powers they had first admitted."[12]

Who was right? History offers no simple answer, and students of history must decide for themselves, but certainly Jefferson's personal attacks on Henry were largely unfounded and inappropriate.

Perhaps in this respect, Henry unintentionally provides us with another legacy: an appreciation for how complex and contested history can be. The simple stories that have been told about Henry for 200 years, both good (his stirring speeches) and bad (Jefferson's effort to portray him as ignorant, greedy, and incompetent), may often reflect as much about the person telling the story as about the real history. Sources should be analyzed carefully.[13]

Similarly, we do history an injustice if we do not recognize that what we know as Henry's speeches were often only recorded many years after the fact and, inevitably, imperfectly. For reasons discussed in the Appendix, those speeches may be good and fair representations of Henry's eloquence and the content of his dramatic oratorical interventions. Even Jefferson, who was present for the Stamp Act and Liberty or Death speeches, and who was more than willing to criticize Henry, never suggested that Wirt's efforts to reconstruct those speeches were inaccurate or too kind. In fact, others suggest that the recorded words cannot hope to capture the power of his speech. Still, in praising Henry's eloquence and the impact of his speeches, one has to concede that what is available to us are not his precise words, and one cannot accept them without at least engaging in a careful analysis of their content and sources.

The skills of a historian are invaluable if one hopes to understand Henry.

* * * * *

Patrick Henry entered life as the son of a loyal member of the middling gentry in the King's old dominion of Virginia. He struggled with what he was to become. He failed at various professions. With perseverance and talent, he became an extraordinarily successful attorney, amassing land and wealth for a large flock of children. He also helped to lead a fight that changed the world. The Virginia that he left in 1799 was very different from the colony in which he was born, and Henry had been intimately involved in the changes. He was not the only revolutionary leader, certainly. Not even the most successful. During the Revolution, though, none were more loved by the people that they led than Henry.

Shortly after his death, at a July 4 celebration in 1799 in neighboring Maryland, volunteers raised a toast to Henry that might well serve as an epitaph: "The memory of Patrick Henry; the genuine republican."[14]

NOTES

1. Letter from Thomas Jefferson to Leavitt Harris, October 11, 1824, quoted in Couvillon, *Demosthenes*, 53. Notes of Daniel Webster, Curtis, *Life of Daniel Webster*, 1: 584–585.
2. Memorandum from Thomas Jefferson to William Wirt, August 4, 1805, *Pennsylvania Magazine*, 327. See, e.g., Bernard Bailyn, *The Ordeal of Thomas Hutchinson* (Cambridge, MA: Belknap Press, 1974): 36–37.
3. Diary of John Floyd, April 11, 1832, quoted in Couvillon, *Demosthenes*, 42. Wirt, *Sketches*, 50.
4. John Ferling, *A Leap in the Dark: The Struggle to Create the American Republic* (New York: Oxford University Press, 2003): xiii. *Virginia Gazette and General Advertiser* (Richmond), May 20, 1800, quoted in Patrick Daily, *Patrick Henry: The Last Years, 1789–99* (Bedford, VA: Patrick Henry Memorial Foundation, 1987): 207.
5. Benjamin Rush, "Address to the People of the United States," January 1787, in *Annual Report of the Board of Regents of the Smithsonian Institution*, Part 2 (Washington, DC: Government Printing Office, 1901).
6. Curtis, *Life of Webster*, I: 585. Henry, *Patrick Henry*, II: 376.
7. Spencer Roane Memorandum to William Wirt, Morgan, *True Patrick Henry*, 442. Thomas Jefferson Memorandum to William Wirt, April 12, 1812, *Papers of Thomas Jefferson* (Retirement Series), 4: 600. Mayer, "Patrick Henry and Thomas Jefferson," 5. See also Beeman, "Democratic Faith," 308–311. Elliot, *Debates*, III: 141.
8. Beeman, "Democratic Faith," 316.
9. Elliot, *Debates*, III: 21. Randolph, *History of Virginia*, 181.
10. Letter from Patrick Henry to Elizabeth (Betsy) Aylett, August 20, 1796, Henry, *Patrick Henry*, II: 570.
11. "Patrick Henry," *Southern Literary Magazine*, XIX: 5 (May 1853): 317 (emphasis omitted). Fontaine, *Patrick Henry: Corrections*, 4 (emphasis omitted).
12. Henry, "Patrick Henry: A Vindication," (December 1873), 353.
13. Jefferson's enormous contribution to the republic is better known than Henry's. He played a critical role in the birth of the nation and in drafting a political vision that has been rightly termed America's mission statement. Still, when confronted by a political enemy, particularly when he felt betrayed, Jefferson could be a brutal political opponent.
14. *Maryland Herald and Elizabeth-town Advertiser*, July 11, 1799.

ARE PATRICK HENRY'S SPEECHES
ACCURATELY REPORTED?

It is striking that Patrick Henry is known primarily for his rousing speeches, but his most famous speeches – the Parsons' Cause, the Stamp Act speech, the Liberty or Death speech, and the speech at Charlotte Courthouse – were not recorded when Henry made them and in some cases were not written down until long after his death and decades after the speeches were given. Most of these orations first appeared in print in William Wirt's biography of Patrick Henry in 1817, and while those speeches have been passed down through the years and for two centuries memorized by thousands of school children, many historians question their accuracy. The words are more Wirt's than Henry's is a common conclusion, although Wirt expressly declined just to write Henry's speeches himself (a practice that was not unheard of in the period). Others declare simply that the speeches attributed to Henry are myth.[1]

Sources for the speeches are limited. Henry did not work from a text; he spoke extemporaneously. Even notes for his speeches have never come to light, lost or likely destroyed by Henry if they ever existed. There were stenographers present for Henry's speeches at the ratification convention and during the British Debts case, and their recorded words certainly demonstrate his great skill as a speaker and belie the claim that his speeches only charmed the uneducated and the backward. Yet, the general view has been that the stenographers were unable to keep up with Henry's true eloquence, "either the captivating flights of Mr. Henry's fancy, or those unexpected and overwhelming assaults which he made upon the hearts of his judges." The stenographer at the convention "confesse[d] his inability to follow" Henry. "Wirt's correspondents confirmed" that the transcriptions were "far inferior to anything which Henry ever delivered."[2]

It is known that, almost without exception, those who heard Henry were overwhelmed by the power of his oratory. A year before the Liberty or Death speech, George Mason reported that "Mr. Henry is by far the most powerful speaker I have ever heard." Still, while one might acknowledge that Henry was known far and wide as a remarkable orator, it must be recognized that the available texts of many of Henry's key speeches are simply reconstructions, calling for serious consideration of how the texts were developed and how they should be evaluated by historians.[3]

When Wirt decided to prepare a biography of a man who many believed was the greatest speaker who ever lived, the lack of transcripts of his most famous speeches was a major problem. Wirt expressed an author's lament: He could not simply say over and over again that Henry had given a powerful speech. Seeking some detail by which he could reflect Henry's genius, he sent requests to a bevy of people who had heard Henry speak and asked them for their recollections. What he received in return was a mix of sometimes inconsistent general recollections and specific details. His treatment of three speeches will be considered here.[4]

Among the famous declarations that have been attributed to Henry, the Brutus speech in support of his Stamp Act resolutions has received some particularly telling modern treatment. The "story," as given by Wirt, apparently provided by Judge John Tyler more than 40 years after the fact, is that as Henry declaimed against the tyranny of Parliament and king for taxation without representation:

> . . . he exclaimed in a voice of thunder, and with the look of a god: "Caesar had his Brutus – Charles the First, his Cromwell – and George the Third" – ("Treason," cried the speaker. "Treason, treason!" echoed from every part of the house. It was one of those trying moments which is decisive of character. Henry faltered not for an instant; but rising to a loftier attitude, and fixing on the speaker an eye of the most determined fire, he finished his sentence with the firmest emphasis) – *"may profit by their example. If this be treason, make the most of it."*

In publishing this account, Wirt noted that he had been told somewhat different versions of this speech and its conclusion, leaving him concerned for its accuracy. (A very similar account had been published by John Burk in his 1805 *History of Virginia*, but Burk was not always the most dependable source.) As a result, Wirt confirmed the version he printed with Thomas Jefferson, who, as a student at William & Mary, stood listening to the Stamp Act debate in the House of Burgesses. Jefferson insisted that he remembered well "the cry of treason, the pause of Henry at the name of George III, and the presence of mind with which he closed his sentence, and baffled the charge [of treason] vociferated."[5]

And so the story would have laid, another example of Henry's commanding oratory and brilliance, even if his exact words may have differed somewhat from what was written, until fortuitously, more than 150 years after the fact, a contemporaneous account of the debate was found in Paris in the archives of the Service Hydrographique de la Marine. In 1921, a version of the speech recorded at the time by a French traveler who happened to be in Williamsburg that day in May 1765 (perhaps a French spy) was published. The traveler reported in a different tone:

> Shortly after I Came in one of the members stood up and said that he had read in former times that tarquin and Julus had his Brutus, Charles had his Cromwell, and he Did not Doubt but some good american would stand up, in favour of his Country, but (says he) in a more moderate manner, and was going to Continue, when the speaker of the house rose and Said, he, the last that stood up had spoke traison, and was sorey to see that not one of the members of the house was loyal Enough to stop him, before he had gone so far. upon which the Same member stood up again (his name is henery) and said that if he had afronted the speaker, or the house, he was ready to ask pardon, and he would shew his loyalty to his majesty King G. the third, at the Expence of the last Drop of his blood, but what he had said must be atributed to the Interest of his Countrys Dying liberty which he had at heart, and the heat of passion might have lead him to have said something more than he intended, but, again, if he said anything wrong, he beged the speaker and the houses pardon.

Many have taken the publication of this account entirely to undermine the "mythical" story that had been told for well more than a century.[6]

The French traveler's account, though, is thin gruel on which to reject Tyler's conventional story confirmed by Jefferson and others. The key discrepancy seems to be the observation that Henry apologized, but Henry, a seasoned trial lawyer, would well know the trick of making an inflammatory statement and, when challenged, withdrawing it with an appropriate apology – the listeners (juries or members of the House of Burgesses) have heard what the speaker wanted to say and they get the point. An obsequious apology would have been consistent with the times (and perhaps evidenced Henry's lack of sincerity to those who were more familiar with the characters and directly involved in the proceedings). Henry was certainly capable of such theatrics. St. George Tucker reported that when forced to answer an objection in court, Henry "had a half sort of smile, in which the *want of conviction* was, perhaps, more strongly expressed than that cynical or satirical emotion which probably prompted it." The French traveler may not have noticed such subtlety.[7]

Given the results, adoption of five of Henry's resolves against the Stamp Act over strong opposition, any apology must be understood in context not to have undermined the fundamental argument and impact of the speech. Certainly what was reported at the time in London did not sound apologetic. Henry "blazed out at the assembly," claimed a Virginia correspondent, apparently Commissary William Robinson, "where he compared ****** to a Tarquin, a Caesar, a Charles the First, threatening him with a Brutus, or an Oliver Cromwell; yet Mr. H— was not sent to the Tower; but having prevailed in getting some ridiculously violent resolves passed, rode off in triumph."[8]

Nor is the French traveler's account necessarily inconsistent with the claim that others joined in the cry of "treason." The speaker's declaration that he was sorry that no one had stopped Henry does not mean that no one joined him when he called "treason."

The question of the final phrase in the traditional account – "If *this* be treason, make the most of it" – is more complicated. Might Henry have made that point *sotto voce* so that the French traveler, listening from a public space, did not hear it? Or perhaps the traveler did not fully understand its significance. Perhaps Henry, or someone else, added the comment a few moments later. After all, Jefferson and others, who had every incentive to challenge Wirt's version of Henry's speech, did not do so. The truth likely cannot be known, but all accounts seem to confirm the "Caesar had his Brutus" element and the implicit threat to King George, as well as the exclamation of "treason" by the speaker of the house.

Ironically, the greatest question about the accuracy of the texts of Henry's speeches concerns his most famous speech, the "Liberty or Death" speech. Wirt notes that the text that he used for this speech (see Document 5) came "almost entirely" from Judge St. George Tucker who would have been 22 years old when the speech was given and who recorded his thoughts at least 30 years later, saying that the "scene can never be effaced from my mind."[9] Edmund Randolph, who had also been present, confirmed only a phrase. Unfortunately, Tucker's letter to Wirt is lost, but several people who did see the letter have provided detailed information. (For example, Tucker's great grandson, who had the letter for some time, notes that Tucker also told Wirt that he had a personal grievance against Henry dating from the Revolution, certainly suggesting that he was not embellishing to promote Henry's reputation.)[10]

Some of those who call Henry's speech a "myth," a creation of Wirt, insist that only several paragraphs, less than "one fifth," came from Tucker. This, though, is to misread the sources. Moses Coit Tyler, who wrote a biography of Henry published in 1887, apparently had access to the Tucker letter when writing and repeated the first part of the speech as reported by Wirt and then digresses to quote from Tucker's letter some of his recollections not included in Wirt's book about how the speech affected people;

Tyler continues, "Then follows, in Tucker's narrative, the passage given in the last two paragraphs of the speech as given above." This has been interpreted by some to mean that Tucker's letter only provided "the last two paragraphs of the speech." Tyler, though, did not say that Tucker was not also responsible for the prior text; he merely notes where Tucker broke his narrative to talk about the power and impact of the speech followed by several paragraphs taken from Tucker. William Wirt Henry, who also had the letter, makes much the same point when he states that "Judge Tucker's letter giving the passages included in the last two paragraphs" was "prefaced" by a statement which does not appear in Wirt and must have come from the original Tucker letter. That passage reads:

> It was on that occasion that I first felt a full impression of Mr. Henry's powers. In vain should I attempt to give you any idea of his speech. He was calm and collected – touched upon the origin and progress of the dispute between Great Britain, and the colonies – the various conciliatory measures adopted by the latter, and the uniformly increasing tone of violence and arrogance on the part of the former.

William Wirt Henry continues: "He [Tucker] follows the passage by the following description of the scene," including Tucker's further description of the scene which is included in a footnote in Wirt's book. This can certainly be confusing, but Tyler concludes that from Tucker's recollections "the substance of the speech is given, besides one entire passage in almost the exact language of the version by Wirt." The "one entire passage" comment must refer to the two paragraphs which is all that critics are willing to attribute to Tucker, but Tyler makes clear that the substance of the rest of the text also comes from Tucker, as did Wirt. Although, apparently, given Tyler's comment about "the substance of the speech," Wirt had modified the other segments somewhat.[11]

Other sources also tend to confirm the substance of Tucker's account. Jefferson, who was present for the speech, does not question the account in Wirt. (Nor has evidence been produced that those alive when Wirt's book was published who had heard the speech questioned the accuracy of the reporting.) John Roane who was present for the speech as a young boy of nine confirmed the accuracy of Wirt's version when in his sixties. Similarly, Henry St. George Tucker, who said that he read the original version of the Tucker letter repeatedly, did not question Wirt's account. Without more, it is unfair to say, as George Morrow, a modern, popular author, does, that Wirt's version is "mostly fictitious" and that Wirt had to "gild the oratorical lily" in writing the speech. Undoubtedly the particular phraseology used by Tucker as edited by Wirt was not precisely Henry's, although some of the more memorable lines undoubtedly were. Still, recognizing that the content was controversial and not a verbatim report, William Wirt Henry quotes with approval Moses Coit Tyler's conclusion that "Wirt's version certainly gives the substance of the speech as actually made by Patrick Henry; and for the form of it . . . it is probably far more accurate and authentic than most of the famous speeches attributed to public characters before reporters' galleries were opened, and before the art of reporting was brought to his present perfection."[12]

John Roane's account further demonstrates the problems that historians face in trying to source the "Liberty or Death" speech. Edward Fontaine, one of Henry's great grandsons, reports that in 1834 John Roane, a well-known Virginia politician, discussed the closing of the speech in detail with Fontaine and "verified the correctness of the speech as it was written by Judge Tyler for Mr. Wirt." (In fact, Edward Fontaine was repeating, almost verbatim, a story told him by his father, Patrick Henry's oldest grandson, Patrick Henry Fontaine.) Fontaine also states, incorrectly, that the 68-year-old Roane was in his nineties when he provided his observations, and this error has been repeated by those seeking to discredit the text.[13]

Roane's comment set-off a scramble to find what Judge Tyler told Wirt and apparently accounts for William Wirt Henry's comment that Wirt's version was provided principally by Judges Tucker and Tyler, even though Wirt said that he took the account "almost entirely" from Tucker. Complicating matters further, in 1859, William Winston Fontaine (another one of Henry's great grandsons) gave a detailed account in his diary of Judge John Tyler's recollections of the "Liberty or Death" speech as told to him by former President Tyler (John Tyler's son), but, while Judge Tyler's account was consistent with Wirt's account, it was not published until 1908, and Fontaine's diary could not have been the source for Wirt's *Sketches* or Roane's comments. No written recollections from Tyler have been located which might have informed Wirt's work (and historians have rejected an illegible letter from Judge Tyler found among William Wirt's papers as the source). Of course, it is possible that Tyler related his recollections to Wirt orally or in a letter that has been lost.[14]

Based upon the evidence, Stephen Olsen dismisses Roane's recollection by arguing that he was over 90 (which was not true) and may have been confusing the "Liberty or Death" speech with the Stamp Act speech, which he witnessed in the House of Burgesses (which *was* provided by Tyler in Wirt's biography). This though, is clearly wrong: Roane uses the words from Henry's "Liberty or Death" speech. Moreover, Roane was not born until 1766, the year after the Stamp Act speech.[15]

Two points should be made: First, whatever Wirt's source, Roane confirms the general text used by Wirt (as does Judge Tyler through his son). Second, while no evidence of Judge Tyler having provided Wirt with text from the speech has been found, it is equally likely that Roane misspoke, or Fontaine misrecorded, and what was recorded as "Judge Tyler" was meant to be "Judge Tucker."

In an effort to answer the question of authorship, linguists have looked beyond the sources of the historical documents to compare the text of the "Liberty or Death" speech as reported by Wirt to other documents and speeches of Henry, Wirt, and St. George Tucker. Such linguistic analysis tends to rule out Wirt as a source for the speech, but confirms the notion that the wording is heavily influenced by Tucker, although it also shares many characteristics with other Henry performances. Olsen concludes that Tucker likely wrote in Patrick Henry's style "as he remembered it." Another analyst, in an effort to emphasize Tucker's likely contribution, notes that "this reconstructed text is rhetorically superior to that of any other of Henry's reported speeches. It has a sustained literary quality that the others do not possess." This may be unfair: Would one analyzing Martin Luther King's "I Have a Dream" speech conclude that it has, to use Louis Mallory's words, "a polish" that did not exist in other speeches?[16]

The fact remains that the words recorded by Wirt cannot be attributed simply to Patrick Henry, nor do we necessarily have all that Henry said, but that does not make the speech a "myth." Mallory concludes that "it appears that although Wirt's version of this famous speech is not apocryphal, as has been sometimes asserted, it should be regarded as incomplete. He has taken the high points of the speech, those soaring moments when language, action, and emotion perfectly complement each other, moments that would naturally be fixed in the memory of the listener." In any case, whatever the particular words, one should not lose sight of the clear impact that Henry had on listeners. Richard Beeman, noted historian at the University of Pennsylvania, writes that while he is an agnostic on the particular wording of the text, "I am now more impressed than ever" in the style, content, and impact of the speech. As Spencer Roane said of Henry, "his ideas were remarkably bold, strong, and striking."[17]

Students of history can begin to see why the content of the speech is controversial.

Other objections have also been raised. For example, Ray Raphael, another popular modern writer, claims that a contemporaneous account in a letter written by a Tory merchant from Norfolk to a friend in England is "seriously out of sync with Wirt's later rendition." The entire content of the letter relating to Henry's speech relied upon by Raphael is worth quoting:

> You never heard anything more infamously insolent than P. Henry's speech: he called the K – a Tyrant, a fool, a puppet, and a tool to the ministry. Said there

was no Englishmen, no Scots, no Britons, but a set of wretches sunk in Luxury, that they had lost their native courage and (were) unable to look the brave Americans in the face. Creature is so infatuated, that he goes about I am told, praying and preaching amongst the common people.

Yet, the Tory account, which one must recognize is hostile (and from the American perspective treasonous), does not disprove the Tucker account. It does tend to confirm what Mallory and others have concluded, that the speech as related by Tucker and reported by Wirt is probably not the complete speech as given by Henry. Given the pattern of eighteenth-century speeches, it would be no surprise if Henry speech was much longer than that related by Wirt. The fact that the Tory did not report everything that Henry said, including some of his more stirring calls for liberty, is also hardly a surprise.[18]

Some of the other attacks on Wirt's version are clearly political and clearly misplaced. As noted previously, for example, Edward Pollard, an unrepentant Confederate, journalist, and ideologue, who vilified Henry for his final political campaign against radical states' rights, claims that Wirt created the speech from whole cloth, that "there is reason to believe that he [Henry] never did utter said oft-quoted invocation," "give me liberty or give me death."[i] Pollard is wrong; the evidence indicates that the text comes primarily from Tucker and multiple sources support the general tone and certainly the most memorable lines. More importantly, Pollard's additional argument that there is no substantial evidence of Henry's abilities as a great orator, he was merely a backwoods demagogue according to Pollard, is clearly belied by testimony from all those who heard Henry (which did not include Pollard), including many of the leading political figures of the day, many of whom were political enemies (including Jefferson), not to mention the transcriptions which are available of the ratification convention and British Debts case. Henry Cabot Lodge, somewhat more kindly but equally erroneously concluded that "Henry's reputation as an orator is based wholly on tradition."[19]

Of course, modern historians love to try to knock famous Founders off of their pedestal, and this tendency is evident in some of the criticisms of the "Liberty or Death" speech. For example, part of Raphael's argument against the authenticity of the speeches as reported by Wirt is that Henry's

---

i   Pollard was the author of *The Lost Cause: A New Southern History of the War of the Confederates* (1866), which attempted to rewrite history by shifting the cause of the Civil War from the southern defense of slavery, which is the primary issue in the states' declarations of secession as well as the Confederate constitutional convention debates, to states' rights. His revisionist history continues to speak to many today who wish to minimize the role of slavery in the secession of the Confederacy and the Civil War.

speeches having been "whitewashed" because none of those remembered after the fact preserve any defense of or argument based upon slavery, even though Henry was a slave-owner and the topic was often at the center of eighteenth-century politics. "It is even more implausible that Henry never played the 'slave card' – his ace in the hole – in politicking. Yet nowhere in any of his speeches, as rendered by later writers, do we see even a hint of pandering to instincts less noble than the lover of liberty." Of course, as Raphael has to concede, Henry did, unfortunately, use a fear of slave emancipation in his recorded speech near the end of the Virginia ratifying convention, but this hardly provides evidence that the other speeches as recorded were wrong or that the topic would have entered every Henry speech. After all, the point was made only late in the ratification convention, after days of Henry speeches which did not mention slavery. In fact, it is hardly surprising that the topic would not feature in Henry's revolutionary speeches. Given the hypocrisy of slavery among the patriots, it was rarely mentioned in revolutionary speeches (other than to insist that George III was seeking to enslave the patriots). Raphael is grasping at straws (in an effort to show that Wirt was grasping at straws); at most, this point could suggest that parts of the speeches were omitted from the recorded recollections years later, a point which is almost certainly true whether or not slavery featured in the speeches.[20]

Raphael also attacks the conventional dramatization of Henry throwing off the "chains [of] slavery" as he declares "Forbid it, Almighty God!" and enacting his own death at the conclusion of the speech with an ivory letter opener serving as a dagger. Raphael argues that the only source for that account was from a 90-year-old man 59 years after the fact. He is apparently referring to the account that John Roane, then 68 (not 90), gave to Henry's grandson, Patrick Henry Fontaine, in 1834. The bigger concern with that account might have been that Roane was only nine years old when he heard the speech. Be that as it may, Henry's dramatization is not only consistent with eighteenth-century oratorical style, particularly as learned from evangelical preachers, as Henry's was, but Roane's account is confirmed by the account that Judge John Tyler gave to his son, President John Tyler.[21]

Some of the earliest reported concerns about the reported "Liberty or Death" speech came in 1855 from gentleman, amateur historian Hugh Blair Grigsby who, in a particularly confusing passage, wrote "Although it may be doubted that much of the speech published by Wirt is apocryphal, some of its expressions and the outlines of the argument are believed to be authentic." Moses Coit Tyler's more generous deduction about the "substance" of the speech, joined by William Wirt Henry, seems fair. Biographer Robert Douthat Meade, analyzing the various sources and arguments, provides a very useful summary: Wirt "had ample proof for certain burning phrases especially in the last part of Henry's speech, and for its general substance."[22]

The reported version of Henry's final speech at Charlotte County Courthouse has far stronger indications of its authenticity. There are multiple sources for the general outline and key phrases, including John Randolph of Roanoke who opposed Henry during that election, students who came from Hampden-Sydney College to listen, and others. Wirt's primary source had written his recollections down shortly after the speech and noted that "I am conscious of having given a correct transcript of his opinions, and in many instances, his very expression." Generally, the sources agree as to the broad content, arguments, key phrases, and tone.[23]

One point, though, continues to be contested: While Henry clearly called upon his listeners to take their political concerns to the ballot box, rather than pushing a direct challenge to federal authority by the states, what did Henry say about the detested Alien and Sedition Acts that stood as examples of the tyranny that the Jeffersonian Democratic-Republicans were fighting? The version of the Charlotte Courthouse speech printed by Wirt, apparently written by a political opponent, reports that Henry said that "His private opinion was, that they [the Alien and Sedition Acts] were *good* and *proper*." Henry's children and grandchildren vehemently denied that Henry had ever supported those Acts. His eldest grandchild wrote that "My father has often told me that he [Henry] never made any such assertion; and in conversing about the matter he generally lost his patience, and said most emphatically that the statement was false; on the contrary he said in his speech that they were *odious and tyrannical laws*; and that they ought to be repealed." But Henry insisted that the people needed to "try every peaceable remedy to secure repeal . . . before resorting to a dissolution of the Union, at the risk of plunging the country into all the unspeakable calamities of civil war." Other sources, including a Hampden-Sydney student who recorded his memories many years after the speech, also strongly deny the charge that Henry endorsed those laws, as do a series of recollections gathered in the 1830s that were compiled by a grandson, William Spotswood Fontaine, in an effort to rebut this assertion. Most telling, John Randolph, who was at Charlotte Courthouse and stood immediately after Henry to oppose his position and seek election as a Democratic-Republican member of Congress, relates that Henry only indicated that the laws were passed by Congress, a "wise body," but that they were "too deep for him."[24]

While the precise wording used by Henry is likely lost to history, it seems most likely that he opposed the Alien and Sedition Acts, as his family contended, but that the force of the speech at Charlotte Courthouse was obviously his denunciation of the Kentucky and Virginia Resolutions. Whatever he said about the Sedition law, he certainly was emphatic that if the laws were to be changed, they needed to be changed in a legal manner.

So, where do all of these conflicting and contested facts and arguments leave the student and historian?

First, it should certainly be recognized that what Wirt and others reported as Henry's speeches are undoubtedly not word-for-word what Henry said. Still, there are good reasons to believe that the main points and the most memorable lines were Henry's. After all, while many of the speeches were recorded years after the fact, Virginia at the end of the eighteenth century had a culture which relied heavily on oral communication and memorization of speeches and texts, not to mention that Henry was an extraordinary speaker. In providing their recollections of Henry's speeches, a number of observers noted that they remembered the scenes vividly. As one observer of the Charlotte Courthouse speech in 1799 told Henry Howe years later, "many of its passages were indelibly impressed upon his memory." One is reminded of the tradition that Henry as a boy reportedly memorized long passages of Samuel Davies' sermons and repeated them to his mother while returning from church.[25]

It is also likely that much more was said by Henry than was later recorded. This is obviously the case with Henry's Stamp Act speech, for which only one short passage is recorded, and also highly likely with the other speeches. Still, there is strong reason to believe that what Wirt reported provides the general outline of Henry's speeches, his main arguments, the appropriate tone, and some of his more memorable phrases (which were apparently plentiful). It is unlikely that historians will ever be able to say much more. Given the centrality of his oratory to the impact that Henry had upon his times, the student of history has little option but to work with the texts of the speeches as they have come down to us while, at the same time, recognizing the serious limitations inherent in those texts.

In any case, whatever the particular text of the speeches and the versions passed-on through history, there was universal contemporaneous agreement on the extraordinary power of the speeches to enchant and move. John Randolph of Roanoke, who had become a strong political opponent of Henry and a noted orator in his own account, conceded that Henry "was the greatest orator who ever lived . . . he was Shakespeare and Garrick [a great British actor] combined, and spake as never man spake." Jefferson's comment that Henry "appeared to me to speak as Homer wrote" is to the same effect.[26]

Finally, it is worth noting for the student of history that this debate over the content of Henry's speeches evidences part of the task of the professional historian: To review all available evidence, to search the archives for additional scraps of information, and then to synthesize the information, recognizing both the limitations of the information available and the background provided by the context of the period, and try to reach conclusions that inform our understanding.

NOTES

1. Letter from William Wirt to Dabney Carr, August 20, 1815, John P. Kennedy, *Memoirs of the Life of William Wirt*, vol. 1 (Philadelphia: Lea and Blanchard, 1850): 345. See generally Stephen T. Olsen, "Patrick Henry's 'Liberty or Death' Speech: A Study in Disputed Authorship," in *American Rhetoric: Context and Criticism*, ed. by Thomas W. Benson (Cardondale, IL: Southern Illinois University Press, 1989): 19–65.
2. Wirt, *Sketches*, 221. Henry, "Patrick Henry: A Vindication," 272 *et seq*. Judy Hample, "The Textual and Cultural Authenticity of Patrick Henry's 'Liberty or Death' Speech," *Quarterly Journal of Speech*, 63 (October 1977): 299 (footnote omitted).
3. See, e.g., Couvillon, *Demosthenes*. "Letter from George Mason to Martin Cockburn," May 26, 1774, *Virginia Historical Register*, 3: 1 (January 1850): 28.
4. See Kennedy, *Memoirs of the Life of William Wirt*, I: 345. Recollections of Henry's speech in the Parson's Cause were recorded within days of the speech being delivered, and it is not discussed in detail here.
5. Wirt, *Sketches*, 55.
6. "Journal of the French Traveller in the Colonies, 1765," *The American Historical Review* 26: 4 (July 1921): 745. E.g. Ray Raphael, *Founding Myths: Stories That Hide Our Patriotic Past* (New York: The New Press, 2004): 154.
7. Memorandum from St. George Tucker to William Wirt, 1805, Henry, *Patrick Henry*, I: 126.
8. *Public Ledger* (London), August 13, 1765.
9. A number of authors, including Tyler, have turned the report from Tucker that Wirt published into a direct transcription, removing Tucker's commentary, as if Wirt was publishing what was recorded. Thus, for example, while Wirt published "'Mr. President,' said he, 'it is natural to man to indulge in the illusions of hope,'" Tyler wrote: "Mr. President, it is natural to man to indulge in the illusions of hope," tending to obscure the fact that Wirt made clear: he was merely reporting another's recollections. Compare Wirt, *Sketches*, 92; Tyler, *Patrick Henry*, 124. This can add to the confusion concerning this speech.
10. Henry St. George Tucker, "Patrick Henry and St. George Tucker," *University of Pennsylvania Law Review and American Law Register* 67: 1 (January 1919): 69–74, 71–72. Judy Hample points out that it is possible that Wirt had access to other reports of Henry's "Liberty or Death" speech that he does not cite. "Textual and Cultural Authenticity," 300.
11. See Raphael, *Founding Myths*, 147, 149; also Ray Raphael, "Patrick Henry's 'Liberty or Death' – Grandaddy of Revolution Mythologies," *Journal of the American Revolution* (July 13, 2015). Tyler, *Patrick Henry* (1887), 132. Henry, *Patrick Henry*, I: 264. Tyler, *Patrick Henry*, 133.
12. Fontaine, *Corrections*, 25–27. George T. Morrow, II, *"We Must Fight:" The Private War between Patrick Henry and Lord Dunmore* (Williamsburg, VA: Telford Publications, 2012): 36. Henry, *Patrick Henry*, I: 266.
13. Fontaine, *Corrections*, 25–26. Compare Fontaine, "New Facts."
14. William Winston Fontaine, "Diary of Col. William Winston Fontaine," *William & Mary Quarterly*, 16: 3 (January 1908): 157–159.
15. Compare Olsen, "Patrick Henry's," 37 and William G. and Mary Newton Stanard, *The Colonial Virginia Register* (Albany, NY: Joel Munsell's Sons, 1902).
16. Olsen, "Patrick Henry's," 57. Louis A. Mallory, "Patrick Henry," in *A History and Criticism of American Public Address*, ed. by William Norwood Brigance, vol. II (New York: McGraw-Hill Book Co., Inc., 1974): 590.

17. Mallory, "Patrick Henry," II: 591. Beeman, "Democratic Faith," 302 n. 3. Spencer Roane Memorandum to William Wirt, Morgan, *True Patrick Henry*, 447.

18. Raphael, *Founding Myths*, 150. Letter from James Parker to Charles Stewart, April 6, 1775, "Letters from Virginia," *Magazine of History* (March 1906), 158, quoted in Raphael, *Founding Myths*, 150.

19. Pollard, "Historical Doubts," 328. Henry Cabot Lodge, *Daniel Webster* (New York: Houghton Mifflin, 1883), 200. Compare Couvillon, *Demosthenes*.

20. *Founding Myths*, 154. The nature of Raphael's effort to knock the Founders off of their pedestal is obvious when he argues "a man who played upon fears of slaves and Indians would not be honored" today, ignoring Jefferson, Washington, and most of the other Founders, including certainly all of the signers of the Declaration of Independence (which plays on precisely those fears).

21. Ibid., 313, note 24. See Couvillon, *Demosthenes*, 121. Roane's account appears in Fontaine, *Corrections*, 25–27. Hample also wrongly refers to Roane as "ninety years old." "Textual and Cultural," 302.

22. Hugh Blair Grigsby, *Virginia Convention of 1776* (Richmond, VA: J.W. Randolph, 1855), 150 n. Meade, *Patrick Henry*, II: 39.

23. Wirt, *Sketches*, 275.

24. Wirt, *Sketches*, 275. Fontaine, "New Facts," *DeBow's Review*, 811 *et seq*. *Petersburg Index*, August 21, 1867. Randolph in Henry, *Patrick Henry*, II: 607–610. See also Tyler, *Patrick Henry*, 374; Henry, "Patrick Henry: A Vindication of his Character" (December 1873).

25 Henry, *Patrick Henry*, I: 15. Quoted in Couvillon, *Demosthenes*, 80. On the oral culture in this period and the reliance on memorization generally, see Carolyn Eastman, *A Nation of Speechifiers: Making an American Public after the Revolution* (Chicago: University of Chicago Press, 2009): Chapter 1.

26. Henry, *Patrick Henry*, II: 493, I: 83.

PART **II**

DOCUMENTS

PORTRAITS OF HENRY AND PLACES ASSOCIATED WITH HENRY (PHOTOGRAPHS)

Figure 1 Hanover County Courthouse

It was at Hanover Courthouse that Patrick Henry first came to fame as an attorney. Here, in the Parsons' Cause, Henry attacked both the King and the Anglican clergy for acting against the interests of the people. The original 1735 building still stands.

Photograph by author. Special thanks to Hanover County, Virginia.

Figure 2 House of Burgesses

Patrick Henry's Stamp Act resolutions were introduced into the Virginia House of Burgesses on May 29, 1765. It was then that Henry made his "Caesar-Brutus" speech. The present building was reconstructed on the original site of the 1705 house and rededicated in 1934.

Photograph by author with permission of the Colonial Williamsburg Foundation.

Figure 3 Scotchtown

Built in 1719, Scotchtown was a fine colonial mansion, although not nearly as fancy as many Virginia plantation homes. Henry bought the plantation in 1771 and moved there with his family. Sadly, his beloved wife, Sarah, died in the basement of Scotchtown from complications related to her mental illness in early 1775. Henry, bereaved by his loss, sold the home in 1777.

Photograph by author. Special thanks to Preservation Virginia.

Figure 4 St. John's Church

Patrick Henry's "Liberty or Death" speech was delivered to the Second Virginia Convention on March 23, 1775 at St. John's Church in Richmond, Virginia. Henry spoke in support of his resolution for the colony to prepare itself militarily for a likely conflict with Britain.

Photograph by author. Special thanks to St. John's Church Foundation.

Figure 5 Governor's Palace

When Henry became the first governor of the Commonwealth of Virginia in 1776, he moved his family into what had been the royal governor's palace in Williamsburg. Finished in 1722, this was certainly the finest home in which Henry ever lived. The present building was reconstructed on the original site and opened in 1934. The original building burned to the ground in 1781 while being used as a hospital for wounded soldiers from the battle of Yorktown.

Photograph by the author with permission of the Colonial Williamsburg Foundation.

Figure 6 Red Hill Law Office

Henry moved to Red Hill in 1794 and maintained this law office there. It was used primarily for training young lawyers, including sons and grandsons, for whom Henry was a mentor.

Photograph by author. Special thanks to the Red Hill Patrick Henry National Memorial.

Figure 7 Patrick Henry

This portrait by Thomas Sully is the most famous image of Patrick Henry; unfortunately, it was not painted from life. It was completed in 1815 apparently from a small image of Patrick Henry which had been painted by Sully's brother, Lawrence, in 1795 and a painting of Captain James Cook, who was said to bear a striking resemblance to Henry. Charles Henry Hart, *Portraits of Patrick Henry* (1913, reprint). Family members reported, however, that the painting was a very good likeness.

Special thanks to the Colonial Williamsburg Foundation.

PATRICK HENRY'S FAMILY

Patrick Henry, born 29 May 1736 at Studley, died at "Red Hill" in Charlotte Co., Virginia on June 6, 1799, age 63.
Married: Sarah Shelton 1754, died at "Scotchtown" in Hanover Co., Virginia, in 1775.
Children

1. Martha (Patsey) born 1755 at "Pine Slash" in Hanover County, Virginia, died 1818, age 63 at "Leatherwood" in Henry Co., Virginia; married Oct. 2, 1773 to John Fontaine born 1750 at Beaverdam, Virginia, died at "Leatherwood" in 1792.
   - Patrick Henry, b. 1775, d. 1852
   - Edward Winston, b. 1776, d. 1792
   - Charles de LaBoulay, b. 1779, d. 1818
   - Martha, b. 1781, d. 1845
   - William Winston, b. 1786, d. 1816
   - John James, b. 1787, d. 1852
   - Dorothea Spotswood, b. 1791, d. 1793

2. John born 1757 at "Pine Slash," died ca. 1791, age 34 at "Leatherwood"; married to Susannah Walker.
   - Edmund, b. 1791, d. 1835

3. William born 1763 Hanover Co., Virginia, died 1798, age 35 at New Bern, North Carolina; married Aug. 21, 1787 to widow Elizabeth Graves Cooke.

4. Anne (Annie) born July 19, 1767 at "Roundabout" in Louisa Co., Virginia, died May 22, 1799, at age 31 at "Montvale" in King William Co., Virginia, married Sept. 7, 1786 to Spencer Roane.
   - William Henry, b. 1787, d. 1845
   - Patrick, b. 1789, d. 1791

- Fayette, b. 1792, d. 1819
- Patrick Henry, b. 1793, d. 1814
- Julia, b. 1796,
- Anne, b. 1797,
- Elizabeth, b. 1798, d. 1799

5. Elizabeth (Betsey) born Hanover Co., Virginia, April 23, 1769, died Sept. 14, 1842, age 73 at "Fontainbleau," King William Co., Virginia; married Oct. 12, 1786 to Philip Aylett.
   - William, b. 1788, d. 1798
   - Patrick Henry, b. 1789, d. 1799
   - Philip, Jr., b. 1791, d. 1848
   - Mary Macon, b.1793, d. 1836
   - John, b. 1795, d. 1796
   - Elizabeth Henry, b. 1798, d. 1818
   - Anne Henry, b. 1799, d. 1800
   - Martha Dandridge, b. 1801, d. 1833
   - Anne Henry, b. 1803, d. 1828
   - Louisa Fontaine, b. 1805, d. 1822
   - William Aylett, b. 1806, d. 1829
   - Patrick Henry, b. 1808, d. 1829
   - Sarah Shelton, b. 1811, d. 1876

6. Edward (Neddy) born 1771 "Scotchtown," Hanover Co., Virginia, died Oct. 28, 1794, age 23 at "Winton," New Glasgow, Amherst Co., Virginia.

Married: Dorothea Dandridge, Oct. 25, 1777, born Sept. 25, 1755 (or 1757), died Feb. 14, 1831 at age 73 at "Seven Islands," Halifax Co., Virginia.
Children

1. Dorothea Spotswood (Dolly) born Oct. 20, 1778 at Governor's Mansion, Williamsburg, Virginia, died June 17, 1854 at age 75 in Memphis, Tennessee; married June 18, 1795 at "Red Hill" to George Dabney Winston.
   - William, b. 1797, d. 1815
   - Edmund Dabney, b. 1799, d. 1875
   - Patrick Henry, b. 1802, d. 1868
   - George Dabney, b. ca. 1805
   - Sarah Butler, b. 1807, d. 1834
   - Edward Henry, b. 1811, d. 1852
   - Fayette Henry, b. 1813, d. 1839
   - James, b. ca. 1815, d. 1853
   - Elvira Virginia, b. 1817, d. 1854

2. Sarah (Sallie) Butler born Jan. 4, 1780 at "Leatherwood," Henry Co., Virginia, died Dec. 10, 1856, age 76 at "Seven Islands," Halifax Co., Virginia; married Aug. 31, 1799 to Robert Campbell who died Sept. 1808, married to Alexander Scott Aug. 18, 1813.
   - Patrick Henry, b. 1815, d. 1865
   - Henrietta Dandridge, b. 1817, d. 1895
   - Catherine Henry, b. 1819, d. 1845

3. Martha Catharina (Kitty), born Nov. 3, 1781 at "Leatherwood," Henry Co., Virginia, died May 22, 1801, age 19 at Fleets Bay, Virginia; married July 17, 1797 to Edward Hugh Henry.
   - Dorothea Dandridge, b. 1800, d. 1813

4. Patrick, Jr. born Aug. 15, 1783 at "Leatherwood," Henry Co., Virginia, died Sept. 22, 1804, age 21 at Union Hill, Nelson Co., Virginia; married Feb. 9, 1804 to Elvira Cabell.
   - Elvira Ann Patrick, b. 1804, d. 1870

5. Fayette born Oct. 9, 1785 in Richmond, Virginia, died March 16, 1813, age 27 near Richmond; married March 26, 1807 to Anne Elcan.
   - Fayette, b. 1808, d. 1808

6. Alexander Spotswood, born June 2, 1788 at "Pleasant Grove," Prince Edward Co., Virginia, died Jan. 6, 1854, age 65 at Aspenwall, Charlotte Co., Virginia; married Paulina Cabell Feb. 10, 1814.
   - George Lafayette, b. 1814, d. 1884
   - Laura Sade, b. 1817, d. 1831
   - Patrick, b. 1818, d. 1891
   - Alexander Spotswood Jr., b. 1820, d. 1828
   - Sarah Winston, b. 1822, d. 1906
   - John Robert Lewis, b. 1823, d. 1903
   - Paulina, b. 1824, d. 1884
   - Marion Fontaine Cabell, b. 1826, d. 1912
   - Alexander Spotswood III, b. 1828, d. 1830
   - William Lewis Cabell, b. 1830, d. 1855
   - Alice Winston, b. 1831
   - Marie Antionette, b. 1832, d. 1900

7. Nathaniel West, born April 7, 1790 at "Pleasant Grove," Prince Edward Co., Virginia, died Sept. 6, 1851, age 61 Jacksonville, Virginia; married Virginia Woodson 1812.
   - Martha Catherine, b. 1813, d. 1900
   - Capt. Patrick Miller, b. 1815, d. 1873
   - Mary, b. 1816

- Lucy Ann, b. 1817, d. 1888
- William Robertson, b. 1821, d. 1862
- Dorothea Virginia, b. 1823, d. 1905

8. Richard, born March 27, 1792 at "Pleasant Grove," in Prince Edward Co., Virginia, died Aug. 24, 1793, age 17 months, at "Long Island," Campbell Co., Virginia.
9. Edward Winston (Winston), born Jan. 21, 1794 "Long Island," Campbell Co., VA, died Oct. 12, 1872, age 78 at "Winston-on-the-Staunton," Charlotte Co., Virginia; married Jane Yuille Oct. 19, 1817.
   - Maria Rosalie, b. 1818, d. 1898
   - Thomas Yuille (twin), b. 1821, d. 1869
   - Patrick LaFayette (twin), b. 1821, d. 1852
   - Lucy Dorothea, b. 1823, d. 1898
   - Sarah Jane, b. 1825, d. 1899
   - Celine, b. 1827, d. 1874
   - Ella, b. 1831, d. 1831
   - Ada Byron, b. 1835
   - Edward Winston, Jr., b. 1840, d. 1904
10. John born Feb. 16, 1796 at "Red Hill," Charlotte Co., VA, died Jan. 7, 1868 at "Red Hill," age 71; married Elvira McClelland Jan. 19, 1826.
    - Margaret Ann, b. 1827, d. 1881
    - Elvira McClelland, b. 1829, d. 1874
    - William Wirt, b. 1831, d. 1900
    - Thomas Stanhope McClelland, b. 1833, d. 1912
    - Laura Helen, b. 1836, d. 1856
    - Emma Cabell, b. 1838, d. 1905
    - John, died at birth ca. 1840, d. ca. 1840

11. Jane Robertson, born Jan. 15, 1798 at "Red Hill," died Jan. 19, 1798 "Red Hill," 4 days old.

Source

Modified from version authored by Edith C. Poindexter, with thanks to the Patrick Henry Memorial Foundation.

PATRICK HENRY PARSONS' CAUSE SPEECH

For, I cannot recollect, that the Court expressed either surprise or dislike that a more proper jury had not been summoned. Nay, though I objected against them, yet, as Patrick Henry (one of the Defendant's lawyers) insisted they were honest men, and, therefore, unexceptionable, they were immediately called to the book and sworn. Three of them, as I was afterwards told, nay, some say four, were Dissenters of that denomination called New Lights, which the Sheriff, as they were all his acquaintance, must have known . . .

Mr. Henry . . . rose and harangued the jury for near an hour. This harangue turned upon points as much out of his own depths, and that of the jury, as they were foreign from the purpose; which it would be impertinent to mention here. However, after he had discussed those points, he labored to prove 'that the act of 1758 had every characteristic of a good law; that it was a law of general utility, and could not, consistently with what he called the original compact between King and people, stipulating protection on the one hand and obedience on the other be annulled.' Hence, he inferred, 'that a King, by disallowing Acts of this salutary nature, from being the father of his people, degenerates into a Tyrant and forfeits all right to his subjects' obedience.' He further argued, 'that the only use of an Established Church and Clergy in society, is to enforce obedience to civil sanctions, and the observance of those which are called duties of imperfect obligation; that, when a Clergy ceases to answer these ends, the community have no further need of their ministry, and may justly strip them of their appointments; that the Clergy of Virginia, in this particular instance of their refusing to acquiesce in the law in question, had been so far from answering, that they had most notoriously counteracted, those great ends of their institutions; that, therefore, instead of useful members of the state, they ought to be considered as enemies of the community; and that, in the case now before them [the jury], Mr. Maury, instead of countenance, and protection and damages, very justly deserved to be punished with signal severity.' And then he perorates to the following purpose, 'that excepting they (the jury) were disposed to rivet the chains of bondage on their own necks, he hoped they would not let slip the opportunity which now offered, of making such an example of him as might, hereafter, be a warning to himself and his brethren, not to have the temerity, for the future, to dispute the validity of such laws, authenticated by the only authority, which, in his conception, could give force to laws for the government of this Colony, the authority of a legal representative of a Council, and of a kind and benevolent and patriot Governor.' You'll observe I do not pretend to remember his words, but take this to have been the sum and substance of this [part] of his labored oration. When he came to that part of it where he undertook to assert, 'that a King, by annulling or disallowing acts of so salutary a nature, from being the Father of his people degenerated into a Tyrant, and forfeits all right to his subjects' obedience;' the more sober part of the audience were struck with horror. M[r.] Lyons called out aloud, and with an honest warmth, to the Bench, 'That the gentleman had spoken treason,' and expressed his astonishment 'that their worship[s] could hear it without emotion, or any mark of dissatisfaction.' At the same instant, too, amongst some gentlemen in the crowd behind me, was a confused murmur of Treason, Treason! Yet Mr Henry went on in the same treasonable and licentious strain, without interruption from the Bench, even without receiving the least exterior notice of their disapprobation . . .

After the Court was adjourned, he [Henry] apologized to me for what he had said, alleging that his sole view in engaging in the cause, and in saying what he had, was to render himself popular.

SOURCE

Letter from the Reverend James Maury, who had brought suit against the vestry whom Henry represented in the Parsons' Cause, to the Reverend John Camm, December 12, 1763 in Kennedy, ed., *Journals of the House of Burgesses of Virginia*, 1761–1765, li–liii.

* * * * *

We have heard a great deal about the benevolence and holy zeal of our reverend clergy, but how is this manifested? Do they manifest their zeal in the cause of religion and humanity by practicing the mild and benevolent precepts of the Gospel of Jesus? Do they feed the hungry and clothe the naked? Oh, no, gentlemen! Instead of feeding the hungry and clothing the naked, these rapacious harpies would, were their powers equal to their will, snatch from the hearth of their honest parishioner his last hoe-cake, from the widow and her orphan child their last milch cow! the last bed, nay, the last blanket from the lying-in woman!

SOURCE

Recollections of Thomas Trevilian, a member of the audience, Henry, *Patrick Henry*, I: 41.

STAMP ACT RESOLUTIONS

Resolved, That the first adventurers and settlers of this his Majesty's colony and dominion brought with them, and transmitted to their posterity, and all other his Majesty's subjects since inhabiting in this his Majesty's said colony, all the privileges, franchises, and immunities that have at any time been held, enjoyed, and possessed by the people of Great Britain.

Resolved, That by two royal charters, granted by King James the First, the colonists aforesaid are declared entitled to all the privileges, liberties, and immunities of denizens and natural-born subjects, to all intents and purposes as if they had been abiding and born within the realm of England.

Resolved, That the taxation of the people by themselves, or by persons chosen by themselves to represent them, who can only know what taxes the people are able to bear, and the easiest mode of raising them, and are equally affected by such taxes themselves, is the distinguishing characteristick [sic] of British freedom, and without which the ancient Constitution cannot subsist.

Resolved, That his Majesty's liege people of this most ancient colony have uninterruptedly enjoyed the right of being thus governed by their own Assembly in the article of their taxes and internal police, and that the same hath never been forfeited or any other way given up, but hath been constantly recognized by the kings and people of Great Britain.

Resolved, therefore, That the General Assembly of this colony have the only and sole exclusive right and power to lay taxes and impositions upon the inhabitants of this colony, and that every attempt to vest such power in any person or persons whatsoever, other than the General Assembly aforesaid, has a manifest tendency to destroy British as well as American freedom.

SOURCE

Copy found upon Henry's death with his papers, Henry, *Patrick Henry*, I: 80–81. With this paper was the following:

* * * * *

The within resolutions passed the House of Burgesses in May, 1765. They formed the first opposition to the Stamp Act and the scheme of taxing America by the British Parliament. All the colonies, either through fear, or want of opportunity to form an opposition, or from influence of some kind or other, had remained silent. I had been for the first time elected a Burgess a few days before, was young, inexperienced, unacquainted with the forms of the House, and the members that composed it. Finding the men of weight averse to opposition, and the commencement of the tax at hand, and that no person was likely to step forth, I determined to venture, and alone, unadvised, and unassisted, on a blank leaf of an old law-book, wrote the within. Upon offering them to the House violent debates ensued. Many threats were uttered, and much abuse cast on me by the party for submission. After a long and warm contest the resolutions passed by a very small majority, perhaps of one or two only. The alarm spread throughout America with astonishing quickness, and the Ministerial party were overwhelmed. The great point of resistance to British taxation was universally established in the colonies. This brought on the war which finally separated the two countries and gave independence to ours. Whether this will prove a blessing or a curse, will depend upon the use our people make of the blessings which a gracious God hath bestowed on us. If they are wise, they will be great and happy. If they are of a contrary character, they will be miserable. Righteousness alone can exalt them as a nation. Reader! whoever thou art, remember this; and in thy sphere practise [sic] virtue thyself, and encourage it in others. P. Henry.

SOURCE

Ibid., I: 81–82.

* * * * *

RESOLVES OF THE HOUSE OF BURGESSES IN VIRGINIA, JUNE 1765

"That the first Adventurers and Settlers of this his Majesty's Colony and Dominion of Virginia, brought with them, and transmitted to their Posterity, and all other his Majesty's Subjects since inhabiting in this his Majesty's

Colony, all the Liberties, Privileges, Franchises, and Immunities, that at any time have been held, enjoyed, and possessed, by the People of *Great Britain*.

That by Two Royal Charters, granted by King *James* the First, the Colonies aforesaid are Declared Entitled, to all Liberties, Privileges and Immunities, of Denizens and Natural Subjects (to all Intents and Purposes) as if they had been Abiding and Born within the realm of *England*.

That the Taxation of the People by Themselves, or by Persons Chosen by Themselves to Represent them, who can only know what Taxes the People are able to bear, or the easiest Method of Raising them, and must themselves be affected by every Tax laid upon the People, is the only Security against a Burthensome Taxation; and the Distinguishing Characteristic of *British* Freedom; and, without which, the ancient Constitution cannot exist.

That his Majesty's Liege People of this his most Ancient and Loyal Colony, have, without Interruption, the inestimable Right of being Governed by such Laws, respecting their internal Polity and Taxation, as are derived from their own Consent, with the Approbation of their Sovereign, or his Substitute; which Right hath never been Forfeited, or Yielded up; but has been constantly recognized by the Kings and People of *Great Britain*.

Resolved therefore, That the General Assembly of this Colony, with the Consent of his Majesty, or his Substitute, HAVE the Sole Right and Authority to lay Taxes and Impositions upon It's [sic] Inhabitants: And, That every Attempt to vest such Authority in any other Person or Persons whatsoever, has a Manifest Tendency to destroy AMERICAN FREEDOM.

That his Majesty's Liege People, Inhabitants of this Colony, are not bound to yield Obedience to any Law or Ordinance whatsoever, designed to impose any Taxation upon them, other than the Laws or Ordinances of the General Assembly as aforesaid.

That any Person who shall, by Speaking, or Writing, assert or maintain, That any Person or Persons, other than the General Assembly of this Colony, with such Consent as aforesaid, have any Right or Authority to lay or impose any Tax whatever on the Inhabitants thereof, shall be deemed, an Enemy to this his Majesty's Colony."

SOURCE

Maryland Gazette (Annapolis), July 4, 1765.

GIVE ME LIBERTY SPEECH

"No man," he said, "thought more highly of the patriotism, as well as the abilities, of the very worthy gentlemen who had just addressed the house. But different men often saw the same subject in different lights; and, therefore, he hoped it would not be thought disrespectful to those gentlemen, if, entertaining as he did, opinions of a character very opposite to theirs he should speak forth *his* sentiments freely, and without reserve.

"This," he said, "was no time for ceremony. The question before the house was one of awful moment to the country. For his own part, he considered it as nothing less than a question of freedom or slavery. And in proportion to the magnitude of the subject, ought to be the freedom of the debate. It was only in this way that they could hope to arrive at truth, and fulfill the great responsibility which they held to God and their country. Should he keep back his opinions at such a time, through fear of giving offence, he should consider himself as guilty of treason toward his country, and an act of disloyalty toward the Majesty of heaven, which he revered above all earthly kings.

"Mr. President," said he, "it is natural to man to indulge in the illusions of hope. We are apt to shut our eyes against a painful truth – and listen to the song of that siren, till she transforms us into beasts. Is this," he asked, "the part of wise men, engaged in a great and arduous struggle for liberty? Were we disposed to be of the number of those, who having eyes, see not, and having ears, hear not, the things which so nearly concern their temporal salvation? For his part, whatever anguish of spirit it might cost, *he* was willing to know the whole truth; to know the worst, and provide for it.

"He had," he said, "but one lamp by which his feet were guided; and that was the lamp of experience. He knew of no way of judging of the future but by the past. And judging by the past, he wished to know what there had been in the conduct of the British ministry for the past ten years, to justify those hopes with which gentlemen had been pleased to solace themselves and the house? Is it that insidious smile with which our petitions have been lately received? Trust it not, sir; it will prove a snare to your feet. Suffer not yourselves to be betrayed with a kiss.

"Ask yourselves how this gracious reception of our petition comports with those warlike preparations which darken our waters and cover our land. Are fleets and armies necessary to a work of love and reconciliation? Have we shown ourselves so unwilling to be reconciled, that force must be called in to win back our love? Let us not deceive ourselves, sir. These are the implements of war and subjugation – the last arguments to which kings resort.

"I ask gentlemen, sir, what means this martial array, if its purpose be not to force us to submission? Can gentlemen assign any other possible motive for it? Has Great Britain any enemy in this quarter of the world, to call for all this accumulation of navies and armies? No, sir, she has none. They are meant for us; they can be meant for no other. They are sent over to bind and rivet upon us those chains which the British ministry has been so long forging. And what have we to oppose them? Shall we try argument? Sir, we have been trying that for the last ten years. Have we anything new to offer upon the subject? Nothing. We have held the subject up in every light of which it is capable; but it has been all in vain. Shall we resort to entreaty and humble supplication? What terms shall we find, which have not been already exhausted?

"Let us not, I beseech you, sir, deceive ourselves longer. Sir, we have done everything that could be done, to avert the storm which is now coming on. We have petitioned—we have remonstrated – we have supplicated – we have prostrated ourselves before the throne, and have implored its interposition to arrest the tyrannical hands of the ministry and parliament. Our petitions have been slighted; our remonstrances have produced additional violence and insult; our supplications have been disregarded; and we have been spurned, with contempt, from the foot of the throne.

"In vain, after these things, may we indulge the fond hope of peace and reconciliation. *There is no longer any room for hope.* If we wish to be free— if we mean to preserve inviolate those inestimable privileges for which we have been so long contending—if we mean not basely to abandon the noble struggle in which we have been so long engaged, and which we have pledged ourselves never to abandon, until the glorious object of our contest shall be obtained – we must fight! – I repeat it, sir, we must fight!!! An appeal to arms and to the God of hosts, is all that is left us!

"They tell us, sir," continued Mr. Henry, "that we are weak – unable to cope with so formidable an adversary. But when shall we be stronger? Will it be the next week or the next year? Will it be when we are totally disarmed, and when a British guard shall be stationed in every house? Shall we gather strength by irresolution and inaction? Shall we acquire the means of effectual resistance, by lying supinely on our backs, and hugging the delusive phantom of hope, until our enemies shall have bound us hand and foot? Sir, we are not weak, if we make a proper use of those means which the God of nature hath placed in our power.

"Three millions of people armed in the holy cause of liberty, and in such a country as that which we possess, are invincible by any force which our enemy can send against us. Besides, sir, we shall not fight our battles alone. There is a just God who presides over the destinies of nations, and who will raise up friends to fight our battles for us. The battle, sir, is not to the strong alone; it is to the vigilant, the active, the brave. Besides, sir, we have no election. If we were base enough to desire it, it is now too late to retire from the contest. There is no retreat but in submission and slavery! Our chains are forged. Their clanking may be heard on the plains of Boston! The war is inevitable – and let it come!! I repeat it, sir; let it come!!!

"It is in vain, sir, to extenuate the matter. Gentlemen may cry, peace, peace – but there is no peace. The war is actually begun! The next gale that sweeps from the north will bring to our ears the clash of resounding arms! Our brethren are already in the field! Why stand we here idle? What is it that gentlemen wish? What would they have? Is life so dear; or peace so sweet, as to be purchased at the price of chains, and slavery? Forbid it, Almighty God! – I know not what course others may take; but as for me," cried he, with both his arms extended aloft, his brows knit, every feature marked with the resolute purpose of his soul, and his voice swelled to its boldest note of exclamation – "give me liberty, or give me death!"

SOURCE

Wirt, *Sketches*, 92–95.

EMPIRE SPEECH AND THUNDER SPEECH
DURING RATIFICATION DEBATES

EMPIRE SPEECH: JUNE 5, 1788

Mr. Henry.— . . . The fate of this question and America may depend on this: Have they said, we the States? Have they made a proposal of a compact between States? If they had, this would be a confederation: It is otherwise most clearly a consolidated government. The question turns, Sir, on that poor little thing – the expression, We, the people, instead of the States of America. I need not take much pains to shew, that the principles of this system, are extremely pernicious, impolitic, and dangerous. Is this a Monarchy, like England—a compact between Prince and people; ⟨⟩ ⟨with⟩ checks on the former, to secure the liberty of the latter? Is this a Confederacy, like Holland – an association of a number of independent States, each of which retain⟨s⟩ its individual sovereignty? . . . Here is a revolution as radical as that which separated us from Great Britain . . . The rights of conscience, trial by jury, liberty of the press, all your immunities and franchises, all pretensions to human rights and privileges, are rendered insecure, if not lost, by this change so loudly talked of by some, and inconsiderately by others . . .

You are not to inquire how your trade may be increased, nor how you are to become a great and powerful people, but how your liberties can be secured; for liberty ought to be the direct end of your Government . . . Liberty the greatest of all earthly blessings – give us that precious jewel, and you may take every thing else: But I am fearful I have lived long enough to become an old fashioned fellow: Perhaps an invincible attachment to the dearest rights of man, may, in these refined enlightened days, be deemed old fashioned: If so, I am contented to be so....

Guard with jealous attention the public liberty. Suspect every one who approaches that jewel ...

The Confederation; this same despised Government, merits, in my opinion, the highest encomium: It carried us through a long and dangerous war: It rendered us victorious in that bloody conflict with a powerful nation: It has secured us a territory greater than any European Monarch possesses: And shall a Government which has been thus strong and vigorous, be accused of imbecility and abandoned for want of energy? Consider what you are about to do before you part with this Government. Take longer time in reckoning things: revolutions like this have happened in almost every country in Europe: Similar examples are to be found in ancient Greece and ancient Rome: Instances of the people losing their liberty by their own carelessness and the ambition of a few ...

But we are told that we need not fear, because those in power being our Representatives, will not abuse the powers we put in their hands: I am not well versed in history, but I will submit to your recollection, whether liberty has been destroyed most often by the licentiousness of the people, or by the tyranny of rulers? ... Happy will you be if you miss the fate of those nations, who, omitting to resist their oppressors, or negligently suffering their liberty to be wrested from them, have groaned under intolerable despotism. Most of the human race are now in this deplorable condition: and those nations who have gone in search of grandeur, power and splendor, have also fallen a sacrifice, and been the victims of their own folly: While they acquired those visionary blessings, they lost their freedom ... The Honorable Gentleman said, that great danger would ensue if the Convention rose without adopting this system: I ask, where is that danger? I see none: ... Is there a disposition in the people of this country to revolt against the dominion of laws? Has there been a single tumult in Virginia? Whither is the spirit of America gone? Whither is the genius of America fled? It was but yesterday, when our enemies marched in triumph through our country: Yet the people of this country could not be appalled by their pompous armaments: They stopped their career, and victoriously captured them: Where is the peril now compared to that? ...

The way to amendment, is, in my conception, shut ... Two-thirds of the Congress, or, of the State Legislatures, are necessary even to propose amendments: If one-third of these be unworthy men, they may prevent the application for amendments; but what is destructive and mischievous is, that three-fourths of the State Legislatures, or of State Conventions, must concur in the amendments when proposed . . . For four of the smallest States, that do not collectively contain one-tenth part of the population of the United States, may obstruct the most salutary and necessary amendments: Nay, in these four States, six tenths of the people may reject these amendments; and suppose, that amendments shall be opposed to amendments (which is highly probable) Is it possible, that three-fourths can ever agree to the same amendments? A bare majority in these four small States may hinder the adoption of amendments; so that we may fairly and justly conclude, that one-twentieth part of the American people, may prevent the removal of the most grievous inconveniencies and oppression, by refusing to accede to amendments . . . Is this the spirit of republicanism? . . .

A standing army we shall have also, to execute the execrable commands of tyranny: And how are you to punish them? Will you order them to be punished? Who shall obey these orders? . . . The clause before you gives a power of direct taxation, unbounded and unlimited . . . Let me here call your attention to that part which gives the Congress power, 'To provide for organizing, arming, and disciplining the militia, and for governing such part of them as may be employed in the service of the United States, reserving to the States respectively, the appointment of the officers, and the authority of training the militia, according to the discipline prescribed by Congress.' By this, Sir, you see that their controul over our last and best defence, is unlimited . . .

The Honorable Gentleman then went on to the figure we make with foreign nations; the contemptible one we make in France and Holland; which, according to the substance of my notes, he attributes to the present feeble Government. An opinion has gone forth, we find, that we are a contemptible people: The time has been when we were thought otherwise: Under this same despised Government, we commanded the respect of all Europe: Wherefore are we now reckoned otherwise? . . . Shall we imitate the example of those nations who have gone from a simple to a splendid Government⟨?⟩ Are those nations more worthy of our imitation? What can make an adequate satisfaction to them for the loss they suffered in attaining such a Government for the loss of their liberty? If we admit this Consolidated Government it will be because we like a great splendid one. Some way or other we must be a great and mighty empire; we must have an army, and a navy, and a number of things: When the American spirit was in its youth, the language of America was different: Liberty, Sir, was then the primary object. We are descended from a people whose Government was founded on liberty . . . But now, Sir, the American spirit, assisted by the ropes and chains of consolidation, is about to convert this country ⟨in⟩to a powerful and mighty empire . . .

There will be no checks, no real balances, in this Government: What can avail your specious imaginary balances, your rope-dancing, chain-rattling, ridiculous ideal checks and contrivances? But, Sir, we are not feared by foreigners; we do not make nations tremble: Would this, Sir, constitute happiness, or secure liberty? I trust, Sir, our political hemisphere will ever direct their operations to the security of those objects. Consider our situation, Sir: Go to the poor man, ask him what he does; he will inform you, that he enjoys the fruits of his labour, under his own fig-tree, with his wife and children around him, in peace and security. Go to every other member of the society, you will find the same tranquil ease and content; you will find no alarms or disturbances⟨!⟩ Why then tell us of dangers to terrify us into an adoption of this new ⟨form of⟩ Government? and yet who knows the dangers that this new system may produce; they are out of the sight of the common people: They cannot foresee latent consequences: I dread the operation of it on the middling and lower class of people: It is for them I fear the adoption of this system . . .

Will the great rights of the people be secured by this Government? Suppose it should prove oppressive, how can it be altered? Our Bill of Rights declares, 'That a majority of the community hath an undubitable, unalienable, and indefeasible right to reform, alter, or abolish it, in such manner as shall be judged most conducive to the public weal.' I have just proved that one tenth, or less, of the people of America, a most despicable minority may prevent this reform or alteration. . . . The founders of your own [Virginia] Constitution made your Government changeable: But the power of changing it is gone from you! . . .

The next clause of the Bill of Rights tells you, 'That all power of suspending law, or the execution of laws, by any authority without the consent of the Representatives of the people, is injurious to their rights, and ought not to be exercised.' This tells us that there can be no suspension of Government, or laws without our own consent: Yet this Constitution can counteract and suspend any of our laws, that contravene its oppressive operation . . . and it is declared paramount to the laws and constitutions of the States . . .

Besides the expences of maintaining the Senate and other House in as much splendor as they please, there is to be a great and mighty President, with very extensive powers; the powers of a King: He is to be supported in extravagant magnificence . . . For I never will give up the power of direct taxation, but for a scourge: I am willing to give it conditionally; that is, after noncompliance with requisitions: I will do more, Sir, and what I hope will convince the most sceptical man, that I am a lover of the American Union, that in case Virginia shall not make punctual payment, the controul of our custom houses, and the whole regulation of trade, shall be given to Congress, and that Virginia shall depend on Congress even for passports, till Virginia shall have paid the last farthing; and furnished the last soldier: Nay, Sir, there is another alternative to which I would consent: Even that they should strike us out of the Union, and take away from us all federal privileges till we comply with federal requisitions; but let it depend upon our own pleasure to pay our money in the most easy manner for our people. Were all the States, more terrible than the mother country, to join against us, I hope Virginia could defend herself; but, Sir, the dissolution of the Union is most abhorent to my mind: The first thing I have at heart is American liberty; the second thing is American Union; and I hope the people of Virginia will endeavor to preserve that Union . . .

The Honorable Gentleman [Edmund Pendleton] has told us these powers given to Congress, are accompanied by a Judiciary which will correct all: On examination you will find this very Judiciary oppressively constructed; your jury trial destroyed, and the Judges dependent on Congress . . .

This Constitution is said to have beautiful features; but when I come to examine these features, Sir, they appear to me ⟨⟩ ⟨horribly⟩ frightful: Among other deformities, it has an awful squinting; it squints towards monarchy: And does not this raise indignation in the breast of every ⟨true⟩ American? Your President may easily become King: Your Senate is so imperfectly constructed that your dearest rights may be sacrificed by what may be a small minority; and a very small minority may continue forever unchangeably this Government, although horridly defective: Where are your checks in this Government? . . . And, Sir, would not all the world, from the Eastern to the Western hemisphere, blame our distracted folly in resting our rights upon the contingency of our rulers being good or bad. Shew me that age and country where the rights and liberties of the people were placed on the sole chance of their rulers being good men, without a consequent loss of liberty? . . . If your American chief, be a man of ambition, and abilities, how easy is it for him to render himself absolute⟨!⟩ The army is in his hands, and, if he be a man of address, it will be attached to him; and it will be the subject of long meditation with him to seize the first auspicious moment to accomplish his design; and, Sir, will the American spirit solely relieve you when this happens? . . . But the President, in the field, at the head of his army, can prescribe the terms on which he shall reign master, so far that it will puzzle any American ever to get his neck from under the galling yoke. I cannot with patience, think of this idea. If ever he violates the laws, one of two things will happen: He shall come at the head of his army to carry every thing before him; or, he will give bail, or do what Mr. Chief Justice will order him. If he be guilty, will not the recollection of his crimes teach him to make one bold push for the American throne? Will not the immense difference between being master of every thing, and being ignominiously tried and punished, powerfully excite him to make this bold push? But, Sir, where is the existing force to punish him? Can he not at the head of his army beat down every opposition? Away with your President, we shall have a King: The army will salute him Monarch; your militia will leave you and assist in making him King, and fight against you: And what have you to oppose this force? What will then become of you and your rights? Will not absolute despotism ensue? . . .

The Senate, by making treaties may destroy your liberty and laws for want of responsibility. Two-thirds of those that shall happen to be present, can, with the President, make treaties, that shall be the supreme law of the land: They may make the most ruinous treaties; and yet there is no punishment for them . . .

Nine States are sufficient to establish this Government over those nine: Imagine that nine have come into it. Virginia has certain scruples. Suppose she will consequently, refuse to join with those States: – May not they still continue in friendship and union with her? If she sends her annual requisitions in dollars, do you think their stomachs will be so squeamish that they will refuse her dollars? Will they not accept her regiments? They would intimidate you into an inconsiderate adoption, and frighten you with ideal evils, and that the Union shall be dissolved. 'Tis a bugbear, Sir: – The fact is, Sir, that the eight adopting States can hardly stand on their own legs . . . The history of Switzerland clearly proves, ⟨that⟩ we might be in amicable alliance with those States without adopting this Constitution. Switzerland is a Confederacy, consisting of dissimilar Governments. This is an example which proves that Governments of dissimilar structures may be Confederated; that Confederate Republic has stood upwards of 400 years; and although several of the individual republics are democratic, and the rest aristocratic, no evil has resulted from this dissimilarity, for they have braved all the power of France and Germany during that long period . . . Shew me the reason why the American Union is to be dissolved. Who are those eight adopting States? Arc they averse to give us a little time to consider, before we conclude? . . . We have a right to have time to consider – We shall therefore insist upon it. Unless the government be amended, we can never accept it . . . The other States have no reason to think, from the antecedent conduct of Virginia, that she has any intention of seceding from the Union, or of being less active to support the general welfare. Would they not therefore acquiesce in our taking time to deliberate? . . .

Permit me, Sir, to say, that a great majority of the people even in the adopting States, are averse to this government. I believe I would be right to say, that they have been egregiously misled. Pennsylvania has perhaps been tricked into it. If the other States who have adopted it, have not been tricked, still they were too much hurried into its adoption. There were very respectable minorities in several of them; and if reports be true, a clear majority of the people are averse to it. If we also accede, and it should prove grievous, the peace and prosperity of our country, which we all love, will be destroyed. This government has not the affection of the people, at present. Should it be oppressive, their affection will be totally estranged from it – and, Sir, you know that a Government without their affections can neither be durable nor happy. I speak as one poor individual – but when I speak, I speak the language of thousands. But, Sir, I mean not to breath⟨e⟩ the spirit nor utter the language of secession . . .

Before you abandon the present system, I hope you will consider not only its defects, most maturely, but likewise those of that which you are to substitute to it. May you be fully apprised of the dangers of the latter, not by fatal experience, but by some abler advocate than me.

SOURCE

Kaminski, ed., *Documentary History of the Ratification*, XI: 951– 968 (footnotes omitted).

* * * * *

THUNDER SPEECH: JUNE 24, 1788

Mr. Henry,—Mr. Chairman.—The Honorable Gentleman who was up some time ago, exhorts us not to fall into a repetition of the defects of the Confederation. He said we ought not to declare that each State retains every power, jurisdiction and right, which is not expressly delegated, because experience has proved the insertion of such a restriction to be destructive . . . he says that I am unfair and uncandid in my deduction, that they can emancipate our slaves, though the word emancipation be not mentioned in it. They can exercise power by implication in one instance, as well as in another . . .

We were then told that the power of treaties and commerce, was the sine qua non of the Union. – That the little States would not Confederate otherwise – There is a thing not present to human view. – We have seen great concessions from the large States to the little States. But little concessions from the little States to the great States, will be refused . . .

I will ask if foreign gold be likely to operate, where will it be? In the seat of Government, or in those little channels in which the State authority will flow? It will be at the fountain of power, where bribery will not be detected. He speaks of war and bloodshed. Whence do this war and bloodshed come? I fear it, but not from the source he speaks of. I fear it, Sir, from the operation and friends of the Federal Government . . . But whoever will advert to the use made repeatedly in England, of the prerogative of the King, and the frequent attacks on the privileges of the people, notwithstanding many Legislative acts to secure them, will see the necessity of excluding implication. Nations who have trusted to logical deduction have lost their liberty . . .

I appeal therefore to the candour of the Honorable Gentleman [James Madison], and this Committee, whether amendments be not absolutely unattainable if we adopt. For he has told us, that if the other States will do like this they cannot be previously obtained. . . . The worthy Member who proposed to ratify [George Wythe], has also proposed that what amendments may be deemed necessary, should be recommended to Congress, and that a Committee should be appointed to consider what amendments were necessary. But what does it all come to at last? – That it is a vain project, and that it is indecent and improper. I will not argue unfairly, but I will ask if amendments are not unattainable? Will Gentlemen then lay their hands on their hearts, and say that they can adopt it in this shape? When we demand this security of our privileges, the language of Virginia is not that of respect. – Give me leave to deny it. She only asks amendments previous to her adoption of the Constitution . . .

He tells you of important blessings which he imagines will result to us and mankind in general, from the adoption of this system – I see the awful immensity of the dangers with which it is pregnant. – I see it – I feel it. – I see beings of a higher order, anxious concerning our decision. When I see beyond the horrison that binds human eyes, and look at the final consummation of all human things, and see those intelligent beings which inhabit the ætherial mansions, reviewing the political decisions and revolutions which in the progress of time will happen in America, and the consequent happiness or misery of mankind – I am led to believe that much of the account on one side or the other, will depend on what we now decide. Our own happiness alone is not affected by the event – All nations are interested in the determination. We have it in our power to secure the happiness of one half of the human race. Its adoption may involve the misery of the other hemispheres. – Here a violent storm arose, which put the House in such disorder, that Mr. Henry was obliged to conclude.

Source

Kaminski, ed., *Documentary History of the Ratification*, IX: 1504–1506 (footnote omitted).

SPEECH AT CHARLOTTE COURTHOUSE, MARCH 4, 1799

"He told the people that the late proceedings of the Virginia Assembly had filled him with apprehension and alarm; that they had planted thorns upon his pillow; that they had drawn him from that happy retirement which it had pleased a bountiful Providence to bestow, and in which he had hoped to pass, in quiet, the remainder of his days; that the State had quitted the sphere in which she had been placed by the Constitution; and in daring to pronounce upon the validity of Federal law, had gone out of her jurisdiction in a manner not warranted by any authority, and in the highest degree alarming to every considerate man; that such opposition on the part of Virginia to the acts of the General government must beget their enforcement by military power; that this would probably produce civil war; civil war, foreign alliances; and that foreign alliances must necessarily end in subjugation to the powers called in.

"He conjured the people to pause and consider well before they rushed into such a desperate condition, from which there could be no retreat. He painted to their imaginations Washington, at the head of a numerous and well-appointed army, inflicting upon them military execution. 'And where (he asked) are our resources to meet such a conflict? Where is the citizen of America who will dare to lift his hand against the father of his country, to point a weapon at the breast of the man who had so often led them to battle and victory?' A drunken man in the crowd, John Harvey by name, threw up his arm and exclaimed, that 'he dared do it.' 'No,' answered Mr. Henry, rising aloft in all his majesty, and in a voice most solemn and penetrating; *'you dare not do it; in such a parricidal attempt, the steel would drop from your nerveless arm!'* ' The look and gesture at this moment,' said Dr. John H.

Rice, who related the incident, gave to these words an energy on my mind unequalled by anything that I have ever witnessed.'

"Mr. Henry, proceeding in this address, asked, 'whether the county of Charlotte would have any authority to dispute an obedience to the laws of Virginia; and he pronounced Virginia to be to the Union what the county of Charlotte was to her. Having denied the right of a State to decide upon the constitutionality of Federal laws, he added that perhaps it might be necessary to say something of the merits of the alien and sedition laws, which had given occasion to the action of the Assembly. He would say of them, that they were passed by Congress and Congress is a wise body. That these laws were too deep for him, they might be right and they might be wrong. But whatever might be their merits or demerits, it belonged to the people who held the reins over the head of Congress, and to them alone, to say whether they were acceptable or otherwise to Virginians; and that this must be done by way of petition. That Congress were as much our representatives as the Assembly, and had as good a right to our confidence.

"He had seen with regret the unlimited power over the purse and sword consigned to the General government, but that he had been overruled, and it was now necessary to submit to the constitutional exercise of that Power. 'If,' said he, 'I am asked what is to be done when a people feel themselves intolerably oppressed, my answer is ready: *Overturn the government*. But do not, I beseech you, carry matters to this length without provocation. Wait at least until some infringement is made upon your rights which cannot be otherwise redressed; for if ever you recur to another change, you may bid adieu forever to representative government. You can never exchange the present government but for a monarchy. If the administration has done wrong, let us all go wrong together.' Here he clasped his hands and waved his body to the right and left, his auditory unconsciously waving with him. 'Let us,' said he, 'trust God and our better judgment to set us right hereafter. United we stand, divided we fall. Let us not split into factions which must destroy that union upon which our existence hangs. Let us preserve our strength for the French, the English, the Germans, or whoever else shall dare invade our territory, and not exhaust it in civil commotions and intestine wars.' He concluded by declaring his design to exert himself in the endeavor to allay the heart-burnings and jealousies which had been fomented in the State legislature; and he fervently prayed, if he was deemed unworthy to effect it, that it might be reserved to some other and abler hand to extend this blessing over the community."

SOURCE

Henry, *Patrick Henry*, II: 607–610, John Randolph's account, recorded shortly after the speech, is "nearly all of the foregoing." Ibid., II: 610.

BIBLIOGRAPHY

PRIMARY SOURCES

Aurora, General Advertiser (Philadelphia) May 27, 1799.

Burnett, Edmund C., ed. *Letters of Members of the Continental Congress*. 8 vols. 1921, reprint, Gloucester, MA: Peter Smith, 1963.

Centinel of Liberty (Georgetown), June 21, 1799.

Crackel, Theodore J., ed. *The Papers of George Washington* (Digital Edition). Charlottesville: University of Virginia Press, 2008.

Dexter, Franklin Bowditch, ed. *The Literary Diary of Ezra Stiles, D.D., LL.D.* 2 vols. New York: Charles Scriber's Sons, 1901.

Elliot, Jonathan. ed. *The Debates in the Several State Conventions on the Adoption of the Federal Constitution*. 5 vols. Philadelphia, PA: J. B. Lippincott & Co., 1861.

Fontaine, William Winston. "Diary of Col. William Winston Fontaine." *William & Mary Quarterly*, 16: 3 (January 1908): 157–161.

Gazette of the United States (Philadelphia), November 15, 1796, Vol. X: 1306.

Goochland County Order Book No. 8 (1757–1761), April 1760.

Henry, Patrick. *The Secret Orders & . . . Letters of Patrick Henry and George Rogers Clark*. 3 vols. Indianapolis: Indiana Historical Society, 1974.

Henry, William Wirt. *Patrick Henry: Life, Correspondence and Speeches*. 3 vols. New York: Charles Scribner's Sons, 1891.

Hobson, Charles, ed. *The Papers of John Marshall* (Digital Edition). Charlottesville: University of Virginia Press, Rotunda, 2014.

"Jefferson's Recollections of Patrick Henry." *The Pennsylvania Magazine of History and Biography* 34: 4 (1910): 385–418.

"Journal of the French Traveller in the Colonies, 1765." *The American Historical Review* 26: 4 (July 1921): 726–747.

Journals of the Continental Congress. 34 vols. (February 21, 1787).

Kaminski, John P. ed., *The Documentary History of the Ratification of the Constitution*. Madison: State Historical Society of Wisconsin, 1993.

Kennedy, John Pendleton, ed. *Journal of the House of Burgesses of Virginia, 1761–1765*. Richmond, VA: The Colonial Press, E. Waddey Co, 1907.

"Letter from George Mason to Martin Cockburn, May 26, 1774." *Virginia Historical Register*, 3: 1 (January 1850): 28.

"Letter from Patrick Henry to William Grayson, March 31, 1789." *Virginia Magazine of History and Biography* 14: 2 (October 1906): 203.

The Life of John Tyler, President of the United States. New York: Harper & Brothers, 1843.

Maryland Gazette (Annapolis), July 4, 1765.

Maryland Herald and Elizabeth-town Advertiser, July 11, 1799.

"Memorandum from Thomas Jefferson to William Wirt, August 4, 1805." *The Pennsylvania Magazine of History and Biography* XXXIV: 4 (1910): 385–418.

Oberg, Barbara B., and Looney, J. Jefferson (eds.), *The Papers of Thomas Jefferson* (Digital Edition). Charlottesville: University of Virginia Press, Rotunda, 2008–2015.

"Patrick Henry." *Southern Literary Magazine*, XIX: 5 (May 1853): 317.

Petersburg Index, August 21, 1867.

Public Ledger (London), August 13, 1765.

Randolph, Edmund. *History of Virginia*. Ed. by Arthur H. Shaffer. Charlottesville: University of Virginia Press, 1970.

———. *Richmond Enquirer*, September 2, 1815.

Rush, Benjamin. "Address to the People of the United States," January 1787. *Annual Report of the Board of Regents of the Smithsonian Institution*, Part 2. Washington, DC: Government Printing Office, 1901.

South Carolina Gazette, August 24, 1865.

Stagg, J. C. A., ed. *The Papers of James Madison* (Digital Edition). Charlottesville: University of Virginia Press, 2010.

Stanard, William G. and Mary Newton. *The Colonial Virginia Register*. Albany, NY: Joel Munsell's Sons, 1902.

Taylor, C. James, ed. *The Adams Papers* (Digital Edition). Charlottesville: University of Virginia Press, 2008–2015.

Tyler, Lyon G. *The Letters and Times of the Tylers*. 2 vols. Richmond, VA: Whittet and Shipperson Co., 1884.

Virginia Gazette and General Advertiser (Richmond), November 2, 1803.

Virginia Register and Literary Note Book, January 1850.

Ware v. Hylton, 3 U.S. 199 (1796).

Secondary Sources

Abernathy, Thomas P. *The South in the New Nation, 1789–1819*. Baton Rouge: Louisiana State University Press, 1961.

Adams, Henry. *John Randolph*. 1882, reprint, Greenwich, CN: Fawcett Publications, Inc., 1961.

Alexander, James W. *The Life of Archibald Alexander, D.D.* New York: Charles Scribner, 1854.

Bailyn, Bernard. *The Ordeal of Thomas Hutchinson*. Cambridge, MA: Belknap Press, 1974.

Beeman, Richard R. *Patrick Henry: A Biography*. New York: McGraw-Hill Book Co., 1974.

———. "The Democratic Faith of Patrick Henry." *The Virginia Magazine of History and Biography*, 95: 3 (July 1987): 301–316.

———. *Plain, Honest Men: The Making of the American Constitution*. New York: Random House, 2009.

Brant, Irving. "Comment on Pendleton Letter." *Maryland Historical Magazine*, XLVI: 2 (June 1951): 77–81.

Breen, T. H. "Ideology and Nationalism on the Eve of the American Revolution: Revisions Once More in Need of Revising." *The Journal of American History*, 84: 1 (June 1997): 13–39.

Bruce, William Cabell. *John Randolph of Roanoke: 1773–1833*. 2 vols. New York: G.P. Putnam's Sons, 1922.

Campbell, Charles. *History of the Colony and Ancient Dominion of Virginia*. Philadelphia: J. B. Lippincott & Co., 1860.

Cohen, Edward L. "Adoption and Reform of the Gregorian Calendar." *Math Horizons* 7: 3 (February 2000): 5–11.

Couvillon, Mark. *Patrick Henry's Virginia*. Red Hill, VA: Patrick Henry Memorial Foundation, 2001.

——. *The Demosthenes of his Age: Accounts of Patrick Henry's Oratory by his Contemporaries*. Red Hill, VA: Patrick Henry Memorial Foundation, 2013.

Curtis, George Ticknor. *Life of Daniel Webster*. 2 vols. New York: D. Appleton and Co., 1889.

Daily, Patrick. *Patrick Henry: The Last Years, 1789-99*. Bedford, VA: Patrick Henry Memorial Foundation, 1987.

Eastman, Carolyn. *A Nation of Speechifiers: Making an American Public after the Revolution*. Chicago: University of Chicago Press, 2009.

Ferling, John. *A Leap in the Dark: The Struggle to Create the American Republic*. New York: Oxford University Press, 2003.

Finkelman, Paul. "Antifederalists: The Loyal Opposition and the American Constitution." Review, "The Complete Anti-Federalist." Ed. by Herbert J. Storing (Chicago: University of Chicago Press, 1981). 7 vols. *Cornell Law Review*, 70 (1984-1985): 182-207.

——. "Slavery and the Constitutional Convention: Making a Covenant with Death." In *Beyond Confederation: Origins of the Constitution and American National Identity*. Ed. by Richard Beeman, Stephen Botein, and Edward Carter III. Chapel Hill: University of North Carolina Press, 1987.

——. *Slavery and the Founders: Race and Liberty in the Age of Jefferson*. Armonk, NY: M.E. Sharpe, 1996.

Fontaine, Edward. *Patrick Henry: Corrections of Biographical Mistakes, and Popular Errors in Regard to His Character*. Ed. by Mark Couvillon. 2nd ed. Patrick Henry Memorial Foundation, 2011.

Fontaine, Patrick Henry. "New Facts in Regard to the Character and Opinions of Patrick Henry." *DeBow's Review: Agricultural, Commercial, Industrial Progress and Resources* (October 1870), 811 *et seq.*

Foote, William Henry. *Sketches of Virginia Historical and Biographical*. 1850, reprint, Richmond, VA: John Knox Press, 1966.

Greene, Jack P. *The Constitutional Origins of the American Revolution*. New York: Cambridge University Press, 2011.

Grigsby, Hugh Blair. *Virginia Convention of 1776*. Richmond, VA: J.W. Randolph, 1855.

Gutzman, Kevin R.C. *Virginia's American Revolution: From Dominion to Republic, 1776-1840*. Lanham, MD: Lexington Books, 2007.

Hample, Judy. "The Textual and Cultural Authenticity of Patrick Henry's 'Liberty or Death' Speech." *Quarterly Journal of Speech*, 63 (October 1977): 298-310.

Hart, Charles Henry. *Portraits of Patrick Henry, Remarks before the Numismatic and Antiquarian Society of Philadelphia, April 17th, 1911*. Philadelphia, 1913, reprint.

Haskins, Charles Homer. *The Yazoo Land Companies*. New York: Knickerbocker Press, 1891, reprint from the *Papers of the American Historical Association*, iv: 4.

Hayes, Kevin J. *The Mind of a Patriot: Patrick Henry and the World of Ideas*. Charlottesville: University of Virginia Press, 2008.

Henry, William Wirt. "Patrick Henry: A Vindication of his Character, as an Orator and as a Man." *The Historical Magazine* (December 1873): 346 *et seq.*

——. "Patrick Henry: A Vindication of his Character, as an Orator and as a Man." *The Historical Magazine* (November 1873): 272 *et seq.*

Holton, Woody. *Unruly Americans and the Origins of the Constitution*. New York: Hill & Wang, 2008.

Howe, Henry. *Historical Collections of Virginia*. Charleston, SC: Babcock & Co., 1845.

Kennedy, John P. *Memoirs of the Life of William Wirt*. 2 vols. Philadelphia, PA: Lea and Blanchard, 1850.

Ketcham, Ralph. "Executive Leadership, Citizenship and Good Government." *Presidential Studies Quarterly*, 17: 2 (Spring 1987): 267-279.

Kidd, Thomas S. *Patrick Henry: First among Patriots*. New York: Basic Books, 2011.

Kierner, Cynthia A. *Scandal at Bizarre: Rumor and Reputation in Jefferson's America*. Charlottesville: University of Virginia Press, 2006.

Lindert, Peter H., and Williamson, Jeffrey G. "American Incomes Before and After the Revolution." *Journal Economic History*, 73: 3 (September 2013): 725–765.

Lodge, Henry Cabot. *Daniel Webster*. New York: Houghton Mifflin, 1883.

Maier, Pauline. *American Scripture: Making the Declaration of Independence*. New York: Alfred A. Knopf, 1997.

Maier, Pauline. *Ratification: The People Debate the Constitution, 1787–1788*. New York: Simon & Schuster, 2010.

Mallory, Louis A. "Patrick Henry." In *A History and Criticism of American Public Address*. Ed. by William Norwood Brigance. 2 vols. New York: McGraw-Hill Book Co., Inc., 1974: 580–602.

"Manuscripts of David Meade Randolph." *Southern Literary Messenger*, I: 7 (March, 1835): 332.

Mayer, Henry. *A Son of Thunder: Patrick Henry and the American Republic*. New York: Franklin Watts, 1986.

———. "Patrick Henry and Thomas Jefferson." *Patrick Henry and Thomas Jefferson*. Ed. by James M. Elson. Brookneal, VA: Patrick Henry Memorial Foundation, 1997.

McCusker, John J., and Menard, Russell R. *The Economy of British America, 1607–1789*. Chapel Hill: University of North Carolina Press, 1985.

Meade, Bishop William. *Old Churches, Ministers and Families of Virginia*. 2 vol. 1857, reprint, Baltimore, MD: Geneological Publishing Co., Inc., 1978.

Meade, Robert Douthat. *Patrick Henry: Patriot in the Making*. Vol. 1. Philadelphia: J.B. Lippincott Co., 1957.

———. *Patrick Henry: Practical Revolutionary*, Vol. 2 Philadelphia: J.B. Lippincott Co., 1969.

Morgan, Edmund S., ed. "Edmund Pendleton on the Virginia Resolves." *Maryland Historical Magazine*, XLVI: 2 (June 1951): 71–77.

———. "Slavery and Freedom: The American Paradox." *The Journal of American History*, 59: 1 (Jun., 1972): 5–29.

Morgan, Edmund S., and Morgan, Helen M. *The Stamp Act Crisis: Prologue to Revolution*. Chapel Hill: University of North Carolina Press, 1953.

Morgan, George. *The True Patrick Henry*. Philadelphia, PA: J.B. Lippincott Co., 1907.

Morrow, II, George T. *"We Must Fight:" The Private War between Patrick Henry and Lord Dunmore*. Williamsburg, VA: Telford Publications, 2012.

Nash, Gary B. "The American Clergy and the French Revolution." *William and Mary Quarterly*, 22: 3 (July 1965): 392–412.

Noll, Mark A. *America's God: From Jonathan Edwards to Abraham Lincoln*. New York: Oxford University Press, 2005.

Olsen, Stephen T. "Patrick Henry's 'Liberty or Death' Speech: A Study in Disputed Authorship." In *American Rhetoric: Context and Criticism*. Ed. by Thomas W. Benson. Cardondale, IL: Southern Illinois University Press, 1989: 19–65.

Paltsits, Victor Hugo. *Washington's Farewell Address*. New York: New York Public Library, 1935.

Parton, James. *Life of Andrew Jackson*. 2 vols. New York: Mason Brothers, 1861.

Pasley, Jeffrey L. *The First Presidential Contest: 1796 and the Founding of American Democracy*. Lawrence, KS: University Press of Kansas, 2013.

Pollard, Edward A. "Historic Doubts Concerning Patrick Henry." *The Galaxy* X: 3 (Sept. 1870), 327 *et seq.*

Ragosta, John A. *Wellspring of Liberty: How Virginia's Religious Dissenters Helped to Win the American Revolution & Secured Religious Liberty*. New York: Oxford University Press, 2010.

Ragosta, John. *Religious Freedom: Jefferson's Legacy, America's Creed*. Charlottesville: University of Virginia Press, 2013.

Raphael, Ray. *Founding Myths: Stories That Hide Our Patriotic Past*. New York: The New Press, 2004.

————. "Patrick Henry's 'Liberty or Death' – Grandaddy of Revolution Mythologies." *Journal of the American Revolution* (July 13, 2015).

Richards, Leonard L. *Shays's Rebellion: The American Revolution's Final Battle.* Philadelphia: University of Pennsylvania Press, 2002.

Risjord, Norman K. *Chesapeake Politics, 1781–1800.* New York: Columbia University Press, 1978.

Rives, William C. *History of the Life and Times of James Madison.* 3 vols. Boston: Little, Brown and Co., 1859.

Steele, Brian. "Thomas Jefferson, Coercion, and the Limits of Harmonious Union." *Journal of Southern History*, 74: 4 (November 2008): 823–854.

Trent, W. P. "The Case of Josiah Philips." *The American Historical Review*, I: 3 (April 1896): 444–54.

Tucker, Henry St. George. "Patrick Henry and St. George Tucker." *University of Pennsylvania Law Review and American Law Register* 67: 1 (January 1919): 69–74.

Tyler, Moses Coit. *Patrick Henry.* Boston: Houghton, Mifflin and Co., 1888.

Weisberger, Bernard A. *America Afire: Jefferson, Adams, and the Revolutionary Election of 1800.* New York: William Morrow, 2000.

Wirt, William. *Sketches of the Life and Character of Patrick Henry.* Revised ed. Ithaca, NY: Andrus, Gauntlett, & Co., 1850.

INDEX

Made in the USA
Middletown, DE
03 April 2022

63564228R00126